Light in the Wilderness

Explorations in the Spiritual Life

M. Catherine Thomas

DIGITAL
LEGEND

2010

Original printing by Amalfi Publishing, 2008

Reprint by Digital Legend Press, 2010. See us at www.digitalegend.com/catalog

ISBN 978-1-934537-74-9

Printed in the United States of America

Edited by Linda Hunter Adams and Gary Gillum
Indexed by Gary Gillum

Cover design by Chad Nelson
Designed and typeset by Benjamin Crowder

TABLE OF CONTENTS

INTRODUCTION

Have faith that there is more than you know; repent of all your present shallowness and silliness; wash off everything of this world in the waters of baptism, and be reborn ... to a course of action requiring perpetual, progressive repentance ... until you are full of grace and truth, which is nowhere in the foreseeable future.... Then "ye shall receive the gift of the Holy Ghost" and get the guidance you need (Acts 2:37–38).

Hugh Nibley[1]

ৎ১

He who gives that law is perfect, and reduces it to the capacity of finite beings in order that they may understand it and then receive more: thus the infinite being gives line upon line, reveals principle after principle, as the mind of the finite being expands, and when he has learned all his life he will then begin to see, that he has not yet entered upon the threshold of eternal things.

Brigham Young[2]

---

1. *Approaching Zion*, vol 9. of *The Collected Works of Hugh Nibley*, ed. Don Norton (Salt Lake City: Deseret Book, 1989), 283.

2. *Times and Seasons* 6:954.

There are three grand secrets lying in this chapter (2 Peter 1) which no man can dig out, unless by the light of revelation ... which unlocks the whole chapter—as the things that are written are only hints of things which existed in the prophet's mind.

Joseph Smith[3]

&

This book is written in an exploratory spirit for fellow seekers who sense that there is always more to a gospel concept than meets the eye. My intent is to travel with you for a while along your way and to encourage you in your exploration of gospel themes. It will be perhaps as much our stirring around together in fertile ideas as the fruits of these explorations that will inspire us.

We have to keep exploring because in our church experience the rich concepts and principles can pale as we necessarily reduce the infinite concepts to our finite language and then take the finite form for the whole. As a result, what was once compelling becomes more familiar, commonplace, even cliché ridden. However, considering the epigraphs above, we can have faith that there is more than we know to the gospel, lying beyond all our possible "shallowness and silliness," yes, even *"mysteries and peaceable things—that which bringeth joy, that which bringeth life eternal"* (D&C 42:61). We can be reassured that the finite mind can expand and begin to cross a threshold in its searches after the glory and wonder of the Unseen World, which glory language symbols can never fully reveal. We can know that the words of scripture do not define, but only point to the tips of truths that beckon us into the treasure house.

Language is two edged—it reveals and conceals. For all its usefulness in putting thought into communicable form, we have experienced that gospel language can with much

---

3. *TPJS*, 304.

use and reuse tend toward thinness. Even at best it can never fully express a concept, especially one that originates in Unseen Realms. Words are pointers only, always shadows only, of the thing they represent. They can through familiarity actually reduce our awareness of that which lies beyond our senses. But if we approach the sacred concepts with reverence and acknowledge that the fullness of the gospel won't ever be captured in words or in a book, we can begin to explore other avenues for gaining knowledge. The words can stimulate inquiry to which the Holy Ghost can then respond with an expanding vision that transcends language. And without the Holy Ghost in the pursuit and sharing of gospel truth, we have nothing—hollow concepts only.

The antidote to the problems of language, then, is personal spiritual experience, because without that, spiritual teachings remain theories and hearsay, lending themselves to distortion and misunderstanding. That is, whatever we think we know likely has some degree of distortion in it until we actually "gaze into Heaven," whatever form that experience may take. The prophet Joseph Smith made a similar and compelling observation:

> Reading the experience of others, or the revelation given to *them*, can never give *us* a comprehensive view of our condition and true relation to God. Knowledge of these things can only be obtained by experience through the ordinances of God set forth for that purpose. Could you gaze into heaven five minutes, you would know more than you would by reading all that ever was written on the subject.... I assure the Saints that truth, in reference to these matters, can and may be known through the revelations of God in the way of His ordinances, and in answer to prayer.[4]

---

4. *Ibid.*, 324–25.

And he said, "God hath not revealed anything to Joseph, but what He will make known unto the Twelve, and even the least Saint may know all things as fast as he is able to bear them."[5] And yet the human tendency is to relegate religion to the realm of untested theory and to do the very thing that precludes spiritual experience; that is, to make the gospel experience less labor intensive, to routinize it, to reduce it to formulas, all in order to make the living of and the presentation of principles seemingly more manageable; but in the process, these sacred and infinite concepts can be sapped of their revelatory life. Our only hope for a life in Christ is to keep searching diligently in the Light of Christ, integrating more and more of it, so as to be able to bear yet more.

But a book can help.

A book can help, because what I have learned and relearned is that the mind needs to be engaged spiritually in order to stay with spiritual development. The eternal spirit has an appetite for spiritual things. To flourish, it has to be fed with catalytic ideas which stimulate the faith that one can indeed continually interact with the miraculous. Because, when awareness of the miraculous fades with its sense of the *immediacy* of gospel powers, we languish in the ordinary world with its ordinary thoughts. The mind must be fixed on God and nourished from the hidden springs.

The inexperienced boy Joseph learned early on that he had to fix his mind on God if he was going to survive spiritually. As he knelt in the dirt over the stone box, his mind entertaining mixed motives for the use of its sacred contents, he cried out with frustration at not being able to take out the objects. Moroni, already on the scene, rebuked him and taught him the principle that the mind of man is easily turned if it is not held by the power of God through prayer. Oliver Cowdery writes

---

5. *Ibid.*, 149.

part of the angel's words on this occasion, and Joseph's mother gives the angel's additional teaching:

> Forget not to pray, that thy mind may become strong, that when he [Satan] shall manifest unto thee, thou mayest have power to escape the evil, and obtain these precious things.[6]

> Now I will show you the distance between light and darkness, and the operation of a good spirit and an evil one. An evil spirit will try to crowd your mind with every evil and wicked thing to keep every good thought and feeling out of your mind, but you must keep your mind always staid upon God, that no evil may come into your heart.[7]

And so the mind must not only be fed but filled with the things of God in order to withstand the crowding tactics of the Adversary, not to mention the general spiritual entropy of earth life. The mind is the frontier and the tool, and fixing the mind in spiritual awareness and practice is the key to continuing spiritual experience.

As to his spiritual awareness, Man lives in the midst of forces he does not perceive because he suffers from what has been called "paradigm blindness"; that is, he does not perceive things that exist outside his currently accepted set of beliefs and experience. But the scriptures teach that he is designed to go through a paradigm shift, a perception change—that is, to expand his mental and spiritual context, to get outside the confining mental structure that telestial language, thinking, and experience have created, and to receive new knowledge and new experiences and greater consciousness.

---

6. From an interview of the prophet Joseph Smith by Oliver Cowdery, *Times and Seasons* 2:13, May 1, 1843, Letter VIII.

7. Scot Proctor, *History of the Prophet Joseph Smith by His Mother,* Revised and Enhanced (Salt Lake City: Bookcraft, 1996), 109.

It is a paradigm shift we're asking for when we pray for the Mighty Change, which brings with it a new set of perceptions. Abraham expressed the desire for a paradigm shift when he sought greater happiness, peace, rest, blessings, righteousness, and knowledge (see Abraham 1:2)—he wanted things he had not experienced before. And Moses in the Lord's presence came to a knowledge that he had not before perceived or suspected: *"Now, for this cause I know that man is nothing, which thing I never had supposed"* (Moses 1:10). And in the case of Adam and Eve, we may wonder whether they and their posterity, confined in their telestial paradigm, only *perceived* that they were separated from Heaven. Because when the ancient knowledge and powers began to be restored to them, their eyes were opened, and they learned about keys of access to God and the possibility of a transcendent joy in this life (see Moses 5:10–11).

Of course one always carries his spiritual eyes with him, but they are not necessarily activated if he has not believed the Lord's revealed paradigm. Unbelief acts as a veil, and the Lord speaks of the mind darkened by unbelief (e.g., D&C 84:54). But giving oneself wholly to the revelations in the assurance that each of them represents things-as-they-really-are will produce that condition where believing becomes seeing. We learn that many spiritual realities remain hidden from Man's awareness until it is activated through belief and faith.

We will consider several awarenesses in this book: of ourselves, of each other, of the Enemy, and of Divine Forces and Beings. We will explore awareness of Natural and Spiritual, since so many blessings are predicated on making that distinction; for, as the Lord promises, *"The veil shall be rent and you shall see me and know that I am—not with the carnal neither natural mind, but with the spiritual"* (D&C 67:10).

I have included wisdom and experience from some non-Church sources. When it comes to searching for greater light and knowledge, we realize that Truth exists in our atmosphere like radio signals and that a spiritually sensitive person, or for that matter, anyone searching diligently in the Light of Christ, will begin to pick up on those signals. The Church, even as the true Church, does not claim a monopoly on Truth; indeed, *"If there is anything virtuous, lovely, or of good report or praiseworthy, we seek after these things"* (Article of Faith 13). The prophet Joseph advocated gathering in truth wherever it might be found: "One of the grand fundamental principles of Mormonism is to receive truth—let it come from where it may."[8] The Lord Himself says,

> *I bring forth my word unto the children of men, yea, even upon all the nations of the earth.... For I command all men, both in the east and in the west, and in the north, and in the south, and in the islands of the sea, that they shall write the words which I speak unto them.* (2 Nephi 29:7, 11)

Since we do not have scriptures in our canon from "all the nations of the earth," we learn here that the Lord has spoken His word to many men and women who, though they have not been authorized to call them scripture, nevertheless felt the mandate to write down what they learned from the Heavenly Spirit, whether in prose or poetry. And though perhaps incomplete by the fuller light of the Restoration, many of these works provide insights which illuminate the things of the spirit. Looking deeply into these "best books," we can enlarge our understanding of the restored gospel: *"Teach one another words of wisdom; yea, seek ye out of the best books words of wisdom"* (D&C 88:118). *"Study and learn, and become acquainted with all good books, and with languages, tongues, and people"* (D&C 90:15), and *"all this for the salvation of Zion"* (D&C 93:53). The Lord has distributed Truth in many places across time and space.

---

8. *WJS*, 229.

At the same time, we take seriously the Lord's words: *"Cursed is he that putteth his trust in man ... or shall hearken unto the precepts of men, save their precepts shall be given by the power of the Holy Ghost"* (2 Nephi 28:31). So we follow the admonition of Paul in proving all things and holding fast to the good (see 1 Thessalonians 5:21). But Latter-day Saints don't need to be afraid of Truth they may find in unexpected places. The practice of looking into Truth wherever it may be found can enrich a study of gospel themes and serve the Spiritual Seeker well.

The model for Man here is that there are more resources in him than he has discovered or developed and that he really does not fully know himself. The Holy Ghost is sent to reveal Man to himself and urge him to *"neglect not the gift that is in thee"* (1 Timothy 4:14) and to exercise his divine gifts (as in D&C 6:11, *"Thou shalt exercise thy gift, that thou mayest find out mysteries, that thou mayest bring many to the knowledge of the truth"*). These gifts often lie latent in Man, awaiting only their stirring up.

The most important part of our model here is that Man by his creation is supremely good. Brigham Young describes Man's essential nature as light-loving but also teaches that not only must he have divine help in order to discern and restrain the dark forces as he develops, he must also obtain the Lord's grace, that divine enabling power, to liberate the goodness in him:

> The spirit which inhabits these tabernacles naturally loves truth, it naturally loves light and intelligence, it naturally loves virtue, God and godliness; but [the spirit] being so closely united with the flesh their sympathies are blended, and their union being necessary to the possession of a fullness of joy to both, the spirit is indeed subject to be influenced by the sin that is in the mortal body, and to be overcome by it and by the power of the devil, unless it is constantly enlightened by that

spirit which enlighteneth every man that cometh into the world, and by the power of the Holy Ghost which is imparted through the Gospel.[9]

So Man cannot move forward without God's participating with him. We are indeed powerless without Christ, being made by and through and of Him (see D&C 88:41). The revelation that we are made "of him" is arresting. He is an intimate part of us, and we of Him (as in D&C 88:49–50). We learn also that in this sphere we are incapable even of doing good without Him, and that any good we manage to do is through yielding to the power and gifts of God (see Moroni 10:25). Our Father is the great liberator and developer of the power and divinity in Man.

And so it seems that the Lord says to each of us, "My Spirit is in you, urging you to move to your full potential. Now if you'll start working with your resources through governing your mind and body, through unlocking the love in your soul, I'll open things up for you and give you more light, so that in time, you will know and do everything I know and do. You don't have to depend on me to initiate and augment the powers; the power is already in *you*. Yes, there is already a good deal of Me in you that you've not yet scratched the surface of." That leads us to wonder where the division is between where I end and He begins. Maybe there is no division, nor throughout eternity was there meant to be. We cannot seem fully to penetrate our intimate relationship to Him and His to us. Perhaps the most important thing to know is that each of us is enmeshed in Him, and He in each of us.

In any event, Dear Reader, as Hamlet says to Horatio, there are more things in heaven and earth than are dreamt of in our philosophy, and humility becomes us as we go about seeking to draw back the curtains.

---

9. *JD* 11:237–38.

ε⁄ɔ

I wrote a good chunk of this book sitting at my laptop on the fifth floor of an apartment building on the island of Tenerife in the Canary Islands, just as my husband and I were beginning our fourth mission together. After our arrival, there were a couple of weeks of unavoidable delays in our getting to work, so we used the time to get settled, to explore the city of Santa Cruz de Tenerife, and to spend time on what seemed to us important personal projects, like this book.

I had begun the book in Provo but initially decided that I wouldn't have time to finish it before we left for Spain. Our visas for Spain had been approved for May 11. But when they actually arrived, they had been stamped for June 11. At first we were tempted to be frustrated and annoyed, but very quickly it was apparent that there was a reason. Within minutes of receiving word of the delay, I sat down at my computer and began to write in earnest. It was amazingly quiet in our home since we'd been released from everything, and everyone thought we must be gone by now. The phone hardly rang. I wrote from early to late, day after day—the quiet, uninterrupted time seemed a miracle. Before I left Provo, I had gotten eight chapters to my wonderful publisher and signed a contract for publication.

In Tenerife, as I mentioned before, there was yet another delay pending the arrival in Spain of our new mission president, and it became apparent that we might have as many as two weeks without an assignment. Though we were eager to function as missionaries, we had learned to look at events as orchestrated, so I knew what the delay was for. I got up early and wrote late, the process of writing always going slower than I wanted it to. There were long stretches when I was absolutely stalled and couldn't move forward, even though I could feel time's winged chariot and knew that soon our lives would change dramatically.

I have noticed that time is always God's. And in all phases of my life I have learned that the Spirit makes itself known in interesting and subtle ways. Here is one that happened a couple of days ago: in our new apartment we were not able to get internet for several days, but my laptop kept trying to connect to a very weak signal that must have belonged to someone in or near the apartment building. My computer kept sending me a little sign that said, "You are not connected," or "Connection could not be established." For a while I treated it like a sort of pesky mosquito and kept swatting the little "x" in the corner of the pop-up.

Then, during a stretch of time in which I felt stymied, just sitting at my computer, I realized how much I felt like my laptop, trying to connect to an elusive signal. The pop-up was a visual representation of what was going on in my spirit as I was trying to write. There would be moments when I would feel truly connected and then moments when I couldn't find the "signal." As many spiritual analogies operate in life, I came to accept the pop-up as a present-moment message from the eternal world; I stopped to tune and retune, trying to capture the delicate signal. There I was, writing about the power of the Lord and feeling this subtle energy, this Light in my mind that seemed to know where to go next, however imperfectly I may have interpreted it.

My experiences teach me that the Light in our Wilderness is literal and that it manifests itself as it continually seeks access to our awareness. This book is about that Light.

℘

Postscript: To avoid the complexities of trying to make the book apply to both sexes, I have chosen to write it nearly entirely using the masculine pronouns and capitalizing "Man," meaning Mankind, intending both genders. My intent is to include both male and female at every point, except when the discussions on Priesthood refer specifically to the male role.

Chapter One

Light in the Wilderness

And I will also be your light in the wilderness; and I will prepare the way before you, if it so be that ye shall keep my commandments; wherefore, inasmuch as ye shall keep my commandments ye shall be led towards the promised land; and ye shall know that it is by me that ye are led.

1 Nephi 17:13

&

What will ye that I should do that ye may have light in your vessels?... What will ye that I should prepare for you that ye may have light when ye are swallowed up in the depths of the sea?

Ether 2:23, 25

&

Our scene opens in the premortal world as the waiting spirits face the sobering prospect before them: the descent into the darkened world; the journey in the wilderness of mortality; the embarking upon the great waters of the telestial world in untried "vessels." This venture would take courage and faith.

And pondering the journey, we must have asked something like, *"Behold, O Lord, wilt thou suffer that we shall cross this great water in darkness?"* (Ether 2:22). And we must have heard in reply, *"Ye cannot cross this great deep save I prepare you against the waves of the sea, and the winds which have gone forth"* (Ether 2:25). We undertook extensive preparations. Covenants were entered into, light and knowledge promised, and the vessels fitted with light receptors for the journey.

Instructions came to us about the nature of the world we would descend to and the way in which the Lord would be with us. We learned that He would be in the sun and the light of the sun, in the moonlight, and in the starlight. Nevertheless, as we looked upon the furious winds, the turbulent depths of the sea with its mountain waves, and saw ourselves buried in the deep, we said, "But, the winds and the waters...." We were reassured, *"I will bring you up again out of the depths of the sea; for the winds have gone forth out of my mouth, and also the rains and floods have I sent forth"* (Ether 2:24). He would be embedded in every part of our natural world, in the seen and the unseen, His reality always nearer than we would know at first.

All would be under His sole control, and He would be our vigilant Ally in our journey through the fallen world. He told us, *"I know the end from the beginning; therefore my hand shall be over thee"* (Abraham 2:8). *"Thou shalt abide in me, and I in you; therefore walk with me"* (Moses 6:34). We would learn to cry unto Him and to walk with Him.

However, the perils in the journey were not imaginary. There would have to be waves, winds, rains, tempests, and darkness, as well as whales and monsters of the deep. Nevertheless, trusting in the promises, we left our premortal glories and set *"forth into the sea, commending [ourselves] unto the Lord [our] God"* (Ether 6:4).

And now, the great temporal adventure undertaken, we commence our search for the promised Light in the Wilderness and the Heavenly Forces upon the Great Waters.

The Book of Mormon is the manual provided for their unveiling, with its types and shadows of our own personal journey. The Jaredite mariners, for example, sailed before a great wind that drove them toward their destination: *"The Lord God caused that there should be a furious wind blow upon the face of the waters, towards the promised land; and thus they were tossed upon the waves of the sea before the wind"* (Ether 6:5). The Nephites also *"put forth into the sea and were driven forth before the wind towards the promised land"* (1 Nephi 18:8).

What is the nature of this Wind upon the Great Waters? The scriptural use of *wind* reveals the meaning. In the biblical text, the word for *wind* (Hebrew *ruach* and Greek *pneuma*) can also mean "spirit" or "breath"[1] and often refers to the presence and activity of the Spirit. We read, for example, of the "rushing mighty wind" of the Lord's spirit and glory filling places of worship (D&C 109:37; Acts 2:2). As the Jaredites felt the force of their great wind, they knew it came forth by the power of the Heavenly Spirit pressing them toward their divine destination.

When that force became more than they could handle alone, they remembered to enlist help from the One who drives the winds: *"They were many times buried in the depths of the sea, because of the mountain waves which broke upon them, and also the great and terrible tempests which were caused by the fierceness of the wind"* (Ether 6:6). But the Lord fulfilled His promise to

---

1. As in John 3:8, where the Savior plays on the words *wind* and *spirit.* It's the translator's task to determine the sense of the text and, therefore, which appropriate English word to use: *wind, breath,* or *spirit.* Some translations of John 3:8 do not use *wind* at all, but translate the word *pneuma* only as *spirit,* losing in that particular example a fuller sense of the passage. We infer from the scriptural use of *wind,* as in Ether 6, that any heavenly wind refers to the power of the Holy Spirit.

them, for *"when they were encompassed about by many waters they did cry unto the Lord, and he did bring them forth again upon the top of the waters"* (Ether 6:7).

This Wind, these Waves, and all that they stand for, can be fearsome as the Mighty Being ceaselessly tends to His eternal work: *"And it came to pass that the wind did never cease to blow towards the promised land while they were upon the waters; and thus they were driven forth before the wind"* (Ether 6:8). Tempestuous forces, rolling upon us by day and by night, drive us toward our high destiny and do not relent in their commission to deliver us back into the divine presence.

However, their force is neither lesser nor greater than it must be to accomplish the Work. Elder Richard G. Scott explains:

> Just when all seems to be going right, challenges often come in multiple doses simultaneously. When those trials are not consequences of your disobedience, they are evidence that the Lord feels you are prepared to grow more (see Proverbs 3:11–12). He therefore gives you experiences that stimulate growth, understanding, and compassion which polish you for your everlasting benefit. To get you from where you are to where He wants you to be requires a lot of stretching, and that generally entails discomfort and pain.... Your Father in Heaven and His Beloved Son love you perfectly. They would not require you to experience a moment more of difficulty than is absolutely needed for your personal benefit or for that of those you love.[2]

Even those trials that we create with our disobedience, whatever the consequences the Lord may permit to come upon us, have a benevolent purpose behind them and with repentance can be turned to our eternal benefit.

---

2. "Trust in the Lord," *Ensign*, November 1995, 16.

As to the necessity of the ordeals of winds and tempests during the mortal probation, we learn from Brigham Young:

> All intelligent beings who are crowned with crowns of glory, immortality, and eternal lives must pass through every ordeal appointed for intelligent beings to pass through, to gain their glory and exaltation.... Every trial and experience you have passed through is necessary for your salvation.[3]

> If man could have been made perfect, in his double capacity of body and spirit, without passing through the ordeals of mortality, there would have been no necessity of our coming into this state of trial and suffering. Could the Lord have glorified his children in spirit, without a body like his own, He...would have done so.... He will not exalt a spirit to thrones, to immortality, and eternal lives, unless that spirit is first clothed in mortal flesh, and with it, passes through a mortal probation, and overcomes the world, the flesh, and the devil through the atonement made by Jesus Christ and the power of the Gospel. The spirit must be clothed as He is, or it never can be glorified with him. He must of necessity subject his children to the same, through a strict observance of the ordinances and rules of salvation.[4]

It appears that every tempest, and even every monster, is necessary, but also that every ordinance and rule of salvation will keep the travelers on course, while the Heavenly Wind (whether fierce or gentle), never ceases "blowing" them across the waters.

Understanding the nature of the journey makes all the difference in our experience in the wilderness world. Realization of the purposes and forces behind the journey opens our

---

3. *JD* 8:150.

4. *Ibid.*, 11:43–44.

spiritual sight to see beyond the apparent forms. The terrors of the deep subside. It was for the very reason that the Jaredite seafarers understood the origin of the winds, even tossed as they were upon the waves, that they were able to *"sing praises unto the Lord; yea, the brother of Jared did sing praises unto the Lord, and he did thank and praise the Lord all the day long; and when the night came, they did not cease to praise the Lord"* (Ether 6:9).

Their insight and gratitude produced a continual revelation of Light: *"And they did have light continually, whether it was above the water or under the water"* (Ether 6:10). Nephi also *"did look unto my God, and I did praise him all the day long; and I did not murmur against the Lord because of mine afflictions"* (1 Nephi 18:16). In further reflection on his own journey through the Wilderness, Nephi says, *"I know in whom I have trusted. My God hath been my support; he hath led me through mine afflictions in the wilderness; and he hath preserved me upon the waters of the great deep. He hath filled me with his love, even unto the consuming of my flesh"* (2 Nephi 4:19–21). How instructive these seers are! What light they cast on the manner in which the true Seeker of Christ pursues his own journey through his appointed afflictions in the Wilderness, led by the consuming, albeit fearsome, love of the Lord. It was, in fact, their trust and gratitude that made it possible for Him to keep sending them Light as they sped along before the wind.

We notice that the Lord could have delivered them miraculously to their destination in many fewer than three hundred and forty-four days on the water. But Man's travels in the mortal probation, whether in the Wilderness or on the Waters, are designed to provide the purifying preparation for greater things.

Through their devotion, the Jaredites sensed that all Creation is permeated by the conscious, benevolent, spiritual presence of the Lord Jesus Christ (see D&C 88:41) and that, although His grace is abundantly shed forth on all His children, the greater portion of Light comes to those who comprehend Him and His purposes in the mortal probation. In fact, He is able to help them transcend the sorrows and bondages of this life to the degree that they are able to put their trust in Him:

And now ... I would that ye should remember, that as much as ye shall put your trust in God even so much ye shall be delivered out of your trials, and your troubles, and your afflictions, and ye shall be lifted up at the last day. (Alma 38:5)

The unaided sight of the Natural Man will not perceive all this embedded divinity. There is a perceptible world of Light beyond this one, but something must happen to our way of seeing; our perception must be born again, in order that the spiritual blindness we're subject to can give way to a comforting new dimension of reality. Alma shares his experience: *"Now, my son, I would not that ye should think that I know these things of myself, but it is the Spirit of God which is in me which maketh these things known unto me; for if I had not been born of God I should not have known these things"* (Alma 38:6). Many passages of scripture reassure us that our eyes can be opened to see and feel beyond the present physical world with its seemingly inexplicable sorrows. The power to "see" is already in us, but may be blocked by our spiritual inexperience and meager trust. The following passages describe the adjustments that make greater sight possible:

And if your eye be single to my glory, your whole bodies shall be filled with light, and there shall be no darkness in you; and that body which is filled with light comprehendeth all things.

Therefore, sanctify yourselves that your minds become single to God, and the days will come that you shall see him; for he will unveil his face unto you, and it shall be in his own time, and in his own way, and according to his own will. (D&C 88:67–68)

That which is of God is light; and he that receiveth light, and continueth in God, receiveth more light; and that light groweth brighter and brighter until the perfect day. (D&C 50:24)

Light for the Journey

Many arrangements were put in place premortally to ensure our success in a dangerous world. Among these, a revelatory system was engendered in each child. Through this means the Great Creator could be with His children individually as a mentor, a revelator, and an empowerer: *"And thus the Lord caused stones to shine in the darkness, to give light unto men, women, and children, that they might not cross the great waters in darkness"* (Ether 6:3).

He promised that He would arrange life situations, would intervene in earthly circumstances, and would provide means to help us accomplish the plans and covenants we entered into in the premortal stages of our existence:

> *And if it so be that the children of men keep the commandments of God he doth nourish them, and strengthen them, and provide means whereby they can accomplish the thing which he has commanded them; wherefore, he did provide means for us while we did sojourn in the wilderness.* (1 Nephi 17:3)

He promised to prepare the way ahead:

> *And I will also be your light in the wilderness; and I will prepare the way before you, if it so be that ye shall keep my commandments; wherefore, inasmuch as ye shall keep my commandments ye shall be led towards the promised land; and ye shall know that it is by me that ye are led.* (1 Nephi 17:13)

8

We do not always sense the Light; we do not always perceive that *"it is by me that ye are led."* Lehi represents all of us at one time or another when he says: *"I beheld myself that I was in a dark and dreary waste"* (1 Nephi 8:7)—just before he saw the Tree. We resonate with those in the prison who were overshadowed with a cloud of darkness and an awful, solemn fear—just before they learned that if they would *"repent, and cry unto the voice, even until ye shall have faith in Christ ... the cloud of darkness shall be removed from overshadowing you"* (Helaman 5:41–42); as they learned to cry to the Lord, the darkness was dispersed and they saw that they were encircled about as by fire.

Every day we step into the unknown on our journey. From moment to moment we do not know where it will take us. Mosiah, for example, warned by the Lord to leave the land of Nephi with as many as *"would hearken unto the voice of the Lord"* (Omni 1:13), departed into an unknown wilderness. But they were led by continual admonishments through the word of God, by many preachings and prophesyings, and by the power of the Lord's arm, until they came to the place the Lord intended them to be, temporally and spiritually. This is the refining nature of the Wilderness we travel in and the Light and Power by which we are led. We learn to cry to the Lord and to cultivate the power to hear the Voice.

So we see that if all a person knows is what he gathers from his own limited senses, his reasoning, and the distorted perceptions and traditions of fellow travelers in this earthly Wilderness, he will conclude that Man prospers only by his own genius and strength (see Alma 30:17), to prey and be preyed upon in a risky, tooth-for-tooth world. He will think that all causes begin in this world. He will miss that it is our Father who plants, nourishes, prunes, and tends the vineyard we live in (see Jacob 5); that it is He who prepares the "fruit and also wild honey" (1 Nephi 17:5); that it is He who empowers the Gazelems with stones *"which shall shine forth in darkness unto light"* (Alma 37:23), provides with Urim and Thummim, with Liahonas, with clouds and pillars of fire, and all the other manifestations and symbols of spiritual realities; that it is He who [goes] before us, leading us by day and giving light by night and doing all things for us which are *"expedient for man to receive"* (1 Nephi 17:30). And that it is He who in our afflictions is afflicted; and that it is He who, in His love and in His pity, redeems us and bears us and carries us all our days (see D&C 133:53).

And all this Light, all these temporal and spiritual gifts—what is their meaning? The chasing of food, clothes, shelter, possessions, and busyness, even spiritual wonders, so often become ends in themselves. We notice that when the Lord Himself comes among men to fulfill the ends of His ministry with them, He first takes care of physical distractions and temporal needs: He heals them (see 3 Nephi 17:7), provides bread and wine (see 3 Nephi 18:1), and baptizes them. But it becomes obvious that all these things are preliminaries only, not ends in themselves. Once the physical needs and the spiritual preparations are attended to, as Hugh Nibley says,

> That is where the gospel begins; that is where other activities end. Once we have taken care of that part of it, once the people are all fed and clothed and healed of any afflictions and cleaned up, the work is done. "What do we do now, sit around and be bored?" No—then the teaching begins. All this in preparation for real teachings and manifestations that follow. The gift of the mysteries is far beyond the imagination.[5]

We have embarked on this journey to obtain the treasure of the mysteries of godliness secured in the Lord Jesus Christ

---

5. *Approaching Zion,* ed. Don Norton (Salt Lake City: Deseret Book), 107; italics in original.

Himself. Gradually we learn to pay less heed to this or that siren song that might distract us from our spiritual purposes. We came here "in earthen vessels" to collect on the promises of Light, Knowledge, and Presence, and we cannot be satisfied with less.

> *For God, who commanded the light to shine out of darkness, hath shined in our hearts, to give the light of the knowledge of the glory of God in the face of Jesus Christ. But we have this treasure in earthen vessels, that the excellency of the power may be of God, and not of us.* (2 Corinthians 4:6–7)

This book is about journeying through the illusory physical world while participating with that Light that shines into our Wilderness, so that at the end, our thanks and praise will pour out of us to God for the easing of our burdens, for the pure knowledge that greatly enlarged our soul, and for the deliverances out of many bondages, *"for [we] were in bondage, and none could deliver [us] except it were the Lord [our] God"* (Mosiah 24:21–22).

But the journey yet lies before us; therefore, let us now commence our explorations of the Light in the Wilderness.

CHAPTER TWO

INTO THE WILDERNESS:
THE PARADISE WITHIN

I beheld myself that I was in a dark and dreary waste. And after I had traveled for the space of many hours in darkness, I began to pray unto the Lord that he would have mercy on me, according to the multitude of his tender mercies.... And it came to pass that I beheld a tree.

1 Nephi 8:7–8, 10

Through the world's great Architect, their Father, they discovered a plan fraught with intelligence and wisdom, reaching from eternity to eternity, pointing out a means whereby, through obedience to celestial laws, they might obtain the same power that he had. And if, in fallen humanity, they might have to suffer for a while, they saw a way back to God, to eternal exaltations, and to the multiplied, and eternally increasing happiness of innumerable millions of beings. And if, as Jesus, they had to descend below all things, it was that they might be raised above all things, and take their position as sons of God, in the eternal world.

John Taylor [1]

---

1. *The Government of God* (Orem, Utah: Grandin Book Company, 1992), 79.

Tyger, Tyger, burning bright,
In the forests of the night:
What immortal hand or eye,
Could frame thy fearful symmetry?

...

Did he smile his work to see?
Did he who made the Lamb make thee?

William Blake[2]

❧

At the end of John Milton's inspired epic poem, *Paradise Lost,*[3] Adam and Eve, under immediate dismissal from the blissful paradise of God, try to linger at the exit of the Garden, each holding a hand of the hastening Archangel:

> They, looking back, all the eastern side beheld
> Of Paradise, so late their happy seat,
> Waved over by that flaming brand....
> Some natural tears they dropped, but wiped them soon:
> The world was all before them, where to choose

---

2. *Songs of Experience.* William Blake (1757–1827), a British poet, visionary, and painter, deals in this passage with a question to which many have given deep consideration: How can the God who made the gentle lamb (the symbol in fact of His beloved Son) and all the other lovely things of the earth be the same God who made the tiger and many of the terrors of the earthly existence?

3. *Paradise Lost* appeared in 1667. The setting of the poem was the Garden of Eden. John Milton (1608–1674) knew a great deal about the dynamics of the events that transpired in the Garden and their meaning for humankind. The following quote describes one reception of the poem in Milton's day: "One day in the autumn of 1667, according to a member of Parliament, Sir John Denham entered the House of Commons excitedly waving a sheet of *Paradise Lost* still 'wet from the Press,' and pronounced it 'Part of the Noblest Poem that was Wrote in any Language or any Age.'" (From the Introduction to *John Milton Paradise Lost,* ed. David Scott Kastan [Indianapolis: Hackett Publishing Company, 2005], xi.)

Their place of rest, and providence their guide;
They hand in hand, with wandering steps and slow,
Through Eden took their solitary way.[4]

Into the telestial wilderness they descended, the Light receding and their bliss a fading memory. Thorns and weeds, sickness and pain, hatred, and death would obscure their earlier joys. Confusion and chaos would seem to govern the earth.

Milton's angel had described to Adam the nature of the world they would enter, with its persecution of righteousness and its empty religions. And so it would go, the earth groaning under her own weight, until the day of a Savior's appearance, Who would raise from the flaming mass of a perverted world a new heaven and a new earth: "Founded in righteousness and peace and love / To bring forth fruits, joy, and eternal bliss."[5] Eden would be restored to the earth. Adam, cheered and "greatly instructed" by the Angel's prophecy, replied that he could then depart the Garden in peace; that he would seek knowledge and would obey, "And love with fear the only God, to walk / As in his presence ... and on him sole depend."[6] The angel replied, foreshadowing another paradise:

This having learned, thou hast attained the sum of wisdom....
Then wilt thou not be loath
To leave this Paradise, but shalt possess
A paradise within thee, happier far.
Let us descend now ... for the hour precise
Exacts our parting hence.[7]

---

4. *Ibid.*, 12:641–49.

5. *Ibid.*, 12:550–51.

6. *Ibid.*, 12:557–64.

7. *Ibid.*, 12:575–76, 585–87.

So now, even with the distant hope of a restored Eden and the mysterious promise of an inner Paradise, Adam and Eve began what must have been a lengthy period of sorrow in their fallen world. Spiritual death was new to them. Where was the promised Paradise as they labored in the earth, *"wanderers in a strange land"* (Alma 26:36)? Shut out from the Lord's presence, did they grieve over the state they found themselves in? Did they lament that somehow their situation *shouldn't have been*—that they had ruined something or something was ruined for them? Past spiritual experience can be little comfort when it can't be felt in the present. What good were promises they couldn't *now* feel? Would they ever taste joy again?

After "many days" of testing their obedience in the fallen world, the Lord initiated their return to His Presence. Adam's relief is obvious as his hope for joy in this life is renewed: *"Blessed be the name of God, for because of my transgression my eyes are opened, and in this life I shall have joy, and again in the flesh I shall see God"* (Moses 5:10). And Eve, comforted at the revelation and full of new Light, rejoices, *"Were it not for our transgression we never should have had seed, and never should have known good and evil, and the joy of our redemption, and the eternal life which God giveth unto all the obedient"* (Moses 5:11). Their suffering began to show purpose.

Adam and Eve made a deliberate choice in compliance with the plan of God,[8] acting in a conscious saving role for

---

8. Adam and Eve use here the word *transgression* rather than *sin*, suggesting the distinction between the two words. The prophet Joseph said that Adam did not commit sin in eating the fruit, because God had decreed that he should eat and fall but also promised redemption from the fall and from death (see *WJS*, 63). President Joseph Fielding Smith writes, "I never speak of the part Eve took in this fall as a sin, nor do I accuse Adam of a sin.... This was a transgression of the law, but not a sin ... for it was something that Adam and Eve had to do!" (*Doctrines of Salvation*, comp. Bruce R. McConkie, 3 vols. [Salt Lake City: Deseret Book, 1954–56], 1:114–15;

humankind; but that noble choice did not spare them the experience of spiritual death in their sorrowful separation from the Lord's presence. Did they wonder how long they would have to suffer, shut out as they were? The welcome Voice came to them: *"Behold I have forgiven thee thy transgression in the Garden of Eden"* (Moses 6:53). It appears that they did not need forgiveness for the transgression itself, but they did need a restoration of the Lord's presence in order to heal their sorrow and transcend the dreariness of separation. Forgiveness is primarily an issue of Presence, because with forgiveness comes the restoration of the Presence of God. "Forgiveness" may foreshadow here the ordinances that would alleviate the effects of the Fall and begin the reversal of spiritual death. Enoch describes that reversing event as Adam was caught away by the Spirit, carried down under the water, and brought forth again, *"born of the Spirit, and... quickened in the inner man"* (Moses 6:65). Then came the precious words, *"Thou art after the order of him who was without beginning... one in me, a son of God; and thus may all become my sons"* (Moses 6:67–68).

Where they may have deeply regretted their earlier situation in their own Wilderness experience, we find them even grateful at their subjection to telestial conditions, reconnected as they are now to heavenly joys. They see the purpose of their reduced circumstances and are led to rediscover Paradise, a more intimate one.

---

see also Elder Dallin H. Oaks, "The Great Plan of Happiness," *Ensign*, November 1993, 72.) President Smith taught on another occasion, "Mortality was created through the eating of the forbidden fruit, if you want to call it forbidden, but I think the Lord has made it clear that it was not forbidden. He merely said to Adam, if you want to stay here [in the garden] this is the situation. If so, don't eat it." (Unpublished address given at LDS Institute of Religion, Salt Lake City, January 14, 1961. Typescript approved by President Smith.)

Facing What Is

Is it possible that we too, like our First Parents, must discover the Paradise in the Wilderness? To our finite mind and eye, our primeval memory veiled, the Earth looks like a dangerously random place—we may not see either order or purpose in what we are subjected to. It seems that anything can happen, and we may be fearful and grieve over many things. Unable to see the larger purposes for the Wilderness experience, we resist the things that must be.

Looking to ourselves, how much do we insist on an ideal reality that cannot be realized in this world? Many things do not suit us: people are too much this way, not enough that way; they shouldn't do the things they do; the things that happen shouldn't have. We contract our physical and emotional muscles against greater and lesser circumstances, exhausting ourselves in the face of what comes upon the path. We get high blood pressure, we have heart disease, we get ulcers, in our refusal to accept what is; we may be shut down by an unrelenting sense of unworthiness, a debilitating self-pity, or depression; we may feel victimized, deprived, and helpless in the face of what presents itself in our world. If we're not beating on ourselves, we're beating on others that things have gone so wrong. We create hell for ourselves and for others too. "This is terribly wrong!" "I'm so angry!" "This shouldn't be!" "This is intolerable!"—and yet it has happened, and there is no changing what has happened. Is it God that is out of step? Is it I?

As Peter said in his grief at the Savior's revelation of His death in Jerusalem, *"Be it far from thee, Lord: this shall not be unto thee,"* and to whom the Savior replied, *"Get thee behind me.... Thou savourest not the things that be of God, but those that be of men"* (Matthew 16:22–23). Or as Amulek, who cried out, *"How can we witness this awful scene? Therefore let us stretch forth our hands, and exercise the power of God which is in us, and save them from the flames."* "No," Alma replied, *"The Spirit constraineth me"* (Alma 14:10–11). Or as Enoch, who weeping in bitterness of soul cried out: *"I will refuse to be comforted"* (Moses 7:44). Yet all of those unthinkable things had to be.

A new consciousness is possible that allows us to accommodate that which must be, and even to embrace it. Many of the causes that we think arise in this world were woven into the great plan of the Creator through arrangements and covenants entered into in the premortal world. But the Lord speaks to us as He did to the grieving Enoch when He showed him a new point of view: *"Lift up your heart, and be glad; and look..."* (Moses 7:44).

But what shall we look at that could change our view of life? Appearances can be deceiving, and to be free, we must insist on the Truth, which is always kinder than we might have thought. The poet Alexander Pope wrote:

> All Nature is but Art, unknown to thee:
> All Chance, Direction, which thou canst not see;
> All Discord, Harmony, not understood;
> All partial Evil, universal Good:
> And, spite of Pride, in erring Reason's spite,
> One truth is clear, "WHATEVER IS, IS RIGHT."[9]

And so let us look with eyes of greater awareness.

Cosmic Design

William Blake poses an age-old question in the epigraph at the beginning of this chapter: How can the God who made the gentle, harmless lamb be the same God who made the terrible tiger? Could both the lamb and the tiger be His?

---

9. *An Essay on Man*, Epistle 1:294.

It appears that there is a great, benevolent Ecosystem behind all the lambs and also all the tigers on the earth, provided by one wise Creator (e.g., see 2 Nephi 2:14). Scripture and Science indeed reveal that creation is not chaotic but that there is a marvelous intelligent order and purpose in all things above and within the earth. We observe the meticulous arrangement in the great macrocosmic universe and note the repeated design in the tiniest, even microscopic, details of Nature—One Governing Intelligence, operating not only in the vast macrocosm, but also in the details of our personal microcosm. We see system run into system, interrelated force fields in a constant dance of ever-configuring and re-configuring life. And not only is God the orchestrator of all this, He is also the in-dwelling Presence in His creation, filling all, connecting all, blessing all, in conscious, ceaseless divine activity. He is

> *the light which is in all things, which giveth life to all things, which is the law by which all things are governed, even the power of God who sitteth upon his throne, who is in the bosom of eternity, who is in the midst of all things.... There is no space in the which there is no kingdom; and there is no kingdom in which there is no space, either a greater or a lesser kingdom. And unto every kingdom is given a law and unto every law there are certain bounds also and conditions....*
>
> *[God] hath given a law unto all things, by which they move in their times and their seasons; and their courses are fixed, even the courses of the heavens and the earth, which comprehend the earth and all the planets. And they give light to each other in their times and in their seasons, in their minutes, in their hours, in their days, in their weeks, in their months, in their years.... The earth rolls upon her wings, and the sun giveth his light by day, and the moon giveth her light by night, and the stars also give their light, as they roll upon their wings in their glory, in the midst of the power of God.... Any*

man who hath seen any or the least of these hath seen God moving in his majesty and power. (D&C 88:13, 37–38, 42–45, 47)

As Alma testified to Korihor, *"All things denote there is a God; yea, even the earth, and all things that are upon the face of it, yea, and its motion, yea, and also all the planets which move in their regular form do witness that there is a Supreme Creator"* (Alma 30:44).

A perfect order operates in the tiniest details. Not only is there order in the structures and systems of Nature, in the life-spans and deaths of great stars, in the rhythm of times and sea-sons, but God has arranged even all the times appointed unto men (see Alma 40:10), and *"knoweth as well all things which shall befall"* (Helaman 8:8), and has determined the times and bounds of Man's habitation on earth. Yet throughout all this complexity, as the Apostle says, He is not far from us; in fact, in Him we live and move and have our being (see Acts 17:26–27), as He lends us breath and life and movement and choice from day to day (see Mosiah 2:21). Consider these three scriptures about God's relationship to us and to things as they are:

1. *O how great the holiness of our God! For he knoweth all things, and there is not anything save he knows it.* (2 Nephi 9:20)
2. *Know ye not that ye are in the hands of God?* (Mormon 5:23)
3. *But behold, all things have been done in the wisdom of him who knoweth all things. Adam fell that men might be; and men are, that they might have joy.* (2 Nephi 2:24–25) [10]

10. The question may arise in any discussion of God's omniscience as to how Man's freedom of choice can function. Neal A. Maxwell's com-ments help resolve the apparent conflict: "God's omniscience is *not* solely a function of prolonged and discerning familiarity with us—but of the stunning reality that the past and present and future are part of an 'eternal now' with God! (Joseph Smith, *History of the Church* 4:597). ... For God to foresee is not to cause or even to desire a particular occurrence—but it

By this last scripture we realize that the Fall, as well as all things that pertain to the Fall, have somehow played into the Divine intention for Man's joy, not just in some distant, other-world future, but now. Yes, Man was created to have a joy alive in himself even as he travels through straitened circumstances. Part of the purpose of the mortal probation is to turn Man's distracted consciousness from the outer world to the inner recesses of joy, to a Paradise, "happier far."

What Is, Is Right

Seeing into the nature of things, we discover the possibility of a great happiness veiled behind the most unthinkable turn of events. Brigham Young offers some mind-altering ideas:

> I am happy; I am full of joy, comfort, and peace; all within me is light, for I desire nothing but to do the will of my Father in heaven. I delight not in unrighteousness, but in righteousness and truth. I seek to promote the good and happiness of myself and those with whom I am associated. We have the privilege of securing to ourselves that eternal bliss that can never fade away....
>
> You need never expect to see sorrow, unless your own conduct, conversation, and acts bring it to your hearts. Do you not know that sorrow to you can exist only in your own hearts? Though men or women were in the mountains perishing—though they be in overwhelming depths of snow freezing to death, or be on a desolate island starving to death for want

---

is to take that occurrence into account beforehand, so that divine reckoning folds it into the unfolding purposes of God.... God has foreseen what we will do and has taken our decision into account (in composite with all others), so that His purposes are not frustrated." (*All These Things Shall Give Thee Experience* [Salt Lake City: Deseret Book, 1980], 8, 12.)

of food—though they perish by the sword or in any other way, yet, if the heart is cheerful, all is light and glory within; there is no sorrow within them. You never saw a true Saint in the world that had sorrow, neither can you find one. If persons are destitute of the fountain of living water, or the principles of eternal life, then they are sorrowful. If the words of life dwell within us, and we have the hope of eternal life and glory, and let that spark within us kindle to a flame, to the consuming of the least and last remains of selfishness, we never can walk in darkness and are strangers to doubt and fear.[11]

Perhaps to make his point, Brigham overstated to a degree in saying that no true Saint could have sorrow. The Savior Himself had sorrows, and many true Saints are called into situations where they feel pain, dismay, sorrow, confusion, and grief; and they are called to comfort each other as Love bids them do and as part of their baptismal covenant (see Mosiah 18:8–9). But still, he has made a profound observation that can change our life. Brigham teaches at least five important ideas here:

1. He is able to enjoy a fulness of happiness because he has given up his own will—he has been swallowed up in the Lord's will, and that has enabled him to find acceptance, even joy, in what the Lord puts on his path. We might understand from his words that it is often insistence on our own will that blocks our perception of joy.

2. The source of his joy rests in the intent of his heart to promote his own good and happiness, as well as that of his associates.

3. Sorrow can exist only in one's heart, suggesting that sorrow is a function of thinking, not of circumstances. It is how we interpret what is happening to us that either liberates us or

---

11. *JD* 6:40–41.

imprisons us. If we interpret what is happening as something that should not be happening, and we can't change it, then we will suffer. If we can accept that-which-cannot-be-changed as a reflection of what God would have unfold, then we can have peace. We might assume, "Of course, God is too benevolent to want or allow suffering." But have we misunderstood benevolence?

4. Possessing the fountain of living water, the principles, and the words of eternal life makes a cheerful heart possible even in the midst of the unthinkable, because it is in the nature of things that underneath it all, behind it all, there is a secret happiness. This is not just a clinging to positive ideas, but the transcending effect of the residence of the inner Spirit of happiness with its felt experience.

5. That is, the words of life kindle the flame of eternal life inside us as they consume the last remains of our selfishness (the greatest source of our suffering), allowing us to walk in the light—clean, trusting—and to have no doubt or fear.

On another occasion, Brigham commented on the price of freedom from the consternating darkness of the mortal probation, on the kind of mental and emotional adjustments we might make to enjoy the living Light in our soul. He spoke on the degree of submission we must achieve to things-as-they-are, to What Is:

> It is said that if we do right we shall overcome. I will tell you one mark you have got to come to in order to do right. If you can bring yourselves, in your affections, your feelings, your passions, your desires, and all that you have in your organization, to submit to the hand of the Lord, to his providences, and acknowledge his hand in all things, and always be willing that he should dictate, though it should take your houses, your property,

your wives and children, your parents, your lives, or anything else you have upon the earth, then you will be exactly right; and until you come to that point, you cannot be entirely right. That is what we have to come to; we have to learn to submit ourselves to the Lord with all our hearts, with all our affections, wishes, desires, passions, and let him reign and rule over us and within us, the God of every motion; then he will lead us to victory and glory; otherwise he will not.[12]

This passage provides additional details about what we would have to do to feel free:

1. We would have to acknowledge the Lord's hand in all things—to give up the idea that things happen randomly to us. *"And in nothing doth man offend God, or against none is his wrath kindled, save those who confess not his hand in all things, and obey not his commandments.... But learn that he who doeth the works of righteousness shall receive his reward, even peace in this world, and eternal life in the world to come"* (D&C 59:21, 23).

Job understood this principle of submission to What Is: *"Naked came I out of my mother's womb, and naked shall I return thither: the Lord gave, and the Lord hath taken away; blessed be the name of the Lord. In all this Job sinned not, nor charged God foolishly"* (Job 1:21–22).

2. We would have to submit to the Lord's hand in His testing of our level of consecration. The Lord's purpose seems to be from time to time to make it hard to stick with Him—so that, if we do stick, we gain something indispensable. Truman Madsen comments on the meaning of the call to sacrifice:

We are called upon to love God first and over all. The moment that pattern is followed he seeks in us the one thing that

---

12. *JD* 5:531–52.

we do not really want to give up. Many of us will say that we do not have that kind of faith. But I submit to you that you do not have that kind of faith *until* you pass that test [of giving up what you don't want to and putting God first].... It is the *love* of God that cries out for us to prove *our love* for Him. He cannot bless us until we have been proved, cannot even pull out of us the giant spirit in us unless we let him.[13]

3. We would see Him enmeshed in our own self as He is in the rest of His creation: *"He is above all things, and in all things, and is through all things, and is round about all things; and all things are by him, and of him, even God, forever and ever"* (D&C 88:41). We would have to realize that He is in us and we are in Him—and that that is never not so, not even for a moment.

John Taylor points to this same possibility of happiness even in severe trials. He quotes the poet Alexander Pope in showing us how "whatever is, is right," speaking with respect to the trials of the Church as a whole, but also of the individuals that comprise it:

> In relation to anything that has or may transpire, I feel that we are in the hands of God, and all is right.... We ought to feel that we are in the Church and kingdom of God, and that God is at the helm, and that all is right and will continue to be. I feel as easy as an old shoe.
>
> What if we should be driven to the mountains? Let us be driven. What if we have to burn our houses? Why, set fire to them with a good grace, and dance a jig round them while they are burning. What do I care about these things? We are in the hands of God, and all is right.... What is the position, then, that we ought to occupy—every man, woman, and child? Do

---

13. "Power from Abrahamic Tests," *Meridian Magazine*, www.meridian-magazine.com/articles/030902abraham.html, 2005. Italics in original.

our duty before God—honour him, and all is right. Concerning events yet to transpire, we must trust them in the hands of God, and feel that "whatever is, is right," and that God will control all things for our best good and the interest of his Church and kingdom on the earth. If we live here and prosper, all right; if we leave here, all right; and if we have to pass through affliction, all right. By and by, when we come to gaze on the fitness of things that are now obscure to us, we shall find that God, although he has moved in a mysterious way to accomplish his purposes on the earth and his purposes relative to us as individuals and as families, all things are governed by that wisdom which flows from God, and all things are right and calculated to promote every person's eternal welfare before God.[14]

We learn from President Taylor's words that, whereas we may be culturally conditioned to react to trials in a particular way, we actually have another, truer option: We can trust the Lord and trust also that everything is governed by Him and that whatever happens is designed to promote our personal eternal welfare.

So it seems that the Lord works in series of light and dark, and in the great, divine Ecosystem everything has its place. But He may let us wander around in the troubling and fearful dark until we begin to catch on to what is going on, until the mind opens to a new interpretation of our circumstances, and then His light begins to penetrate our situation. Dark and Light, Dark and Light in this world of high impact tutorials—but He's always there. He's always doing something with us, and He always knows what He is doing.

In a sense, then, each thing that happens is a test of our consecration and willingness to submit, because it is possible that there is nothing, no circumstance, that doesn't have God in it.

14. *JD* 6:113–14.

"Make up your minds thoroughly, once for all," says Brigham, "that if we have trials, the Lord has suffered them to be brought upon us, and he will give us grace to bear them."[15]

A clarification: When we say, "whatever is, is right" we mean to say that "what *is*" signifies that which *has happened* and is now unchangeable. It simply *is*. If we do not like "what is" and have the power to change it, then that is what we may do according to the Truth in us. It is when we cannot change something that we have the choice of either resisting it—which seems to make things worse—or accepting it, which is the beginning of peace and understanding of how things really are in the Wilderness. The Serenity Prayer is relevant here: "God grant me the *serenity* to accept the things I cannot change, *courage* to change the things I can, and *wisdom* to know the difference."[16]

All Things

If we were to take this subject of "what is" to the next level of appropriate response, we might have to acknowledge that everything and everybody in our life is our teacher, placed there by the Providential Hand for our blessing. That realization would require us to be grateful for everything that happens. That awareness takes us to a deeper spiritual state.

In 1831 the Lord told the Saints as they prepared to settle the land of Zion, *"Thou shalt thank the Lord thy God in all things. Thou shalt offer a sacrifice unto the Lord thy God in righteousness, even that of a broken heart and a contrite spirit"* (D&C 59:7–8). Surely it would take the deepest humility, the most broken heart and most contrite spirit to thank the Lord for the tribulations descending upon them. The next year the

---

15. *JD* 7:268–69.

16. Generally attributed to Reinhold Niebuhr and adopted by Alcoholics Anonymous; italics added.

Lord, knowing that trials were about to overflow upon the Saints, instructed them in how to get through them—in perhaps an unexpected way:

> *Be of good cheer, for I will lead you along. The kingdom is yours and the blessings thereof are yours, and the riches of eternity are yours. And he who receiveth all things with thankfulness shall be made glorious; and the things of this earth shall be added unto him, even an hundred fold, yea, more. Wherefore, do the things which I have commanded you, saith your Redeemer....* (D&C 78:18–20)

In 1833, the persecution raging on, the Lord reassured the Saints:

> *Verily I say unto you my friends, fear not, let your hearts be comforted; yea, rejoice evermore, and in everything give thanks; waiting patiently on the Lord, for your prayers have entered into the ears of the Lord of Sabaoth.... All things wherewith you have been afflicted shall work together for your good....* (D&C 98:1–3)

Instead of gratitude, we may each find that we have things on our personal lists of resistance that tempt us to curse, to grieve, or to retaliate: the driver who cuts us off on the highway, the man who is making us late, the sales clerk who could not care less, the mother who is unaccepting of what we do, the spouse who seems so unaware, the toxic sister-in-law. These are everyday abrasions. But the list gets much tougher: the husband who abandons the family, the wife who has an affair, the child who rebels, the loss of a limb, brain damage, cancer in a grandchild, blindness, sexual abuse, assault, fatal mistakes, and so on. Yet, what if each of these things and all things have a purpose? We realize that nothing ever happens just to us, but that every event affects others too. Who knows how a current trial may be a solution to something yet unseen? Everything in the mortal probation, no matter how bad or how good it seems, is a tangle of advantage and disadvantage. How often, for example, we are elated over an apparent windfall, only to find soon that it is turning sour in some way; or we fall into depression over a trial that with time produces an unexpected benefit.

But resistance, for some cosmic reason, just seems to make things worse. A wise man contrasts the effects of resistance with acceptance:

> Resistance is an inner contraction, a hardening of the shell.... You are closed. Whatever action you take in a state of inner resistance (which we could also call negativity) will create more outer resistance, and the universe will not be on your side; life will not be helpful. If the shutters are closed, the sunlight cannot come in. When you yield internally, when you surrender, a new dimension of consciousness opens up. If action is possible or necessary, your action will be in alignment with that whole and supported by creative intelligence.... [You experience] a state of inner openness. Circumstances and people then become helpful, cooperative. Coincidences happen. If no action is possible, you rest in the peace and inner stillness that come with surrender. You rest in God.[17]

Let us be clear that none of this is to condone evil intent in any degree, but as the Savior said, speaking not only of Himself, but with implications for all of us, *"it must needs be that offenses come; but woe to that man by whom the offence cometh!"* (Matthew 18:7). But the relevant question becomes, since the offense was permitted to happen, what is the hidden meaning? Not all meanings will be apparent, but one meaning will always

---

17. Eckhart Tolle, *A New Earth: Awakening to Your Life's Purpose* (New York: Penguin Books, 2005), 58.

be relevant, and that is the opportunity to trust in the love and wisdom and intent of the Guiding Power to exalt His children. Elder Scott said, "He would have you suffer no consequence, no challenge, endure no burden that is superfluous to your good."[18] So the perception of the Natural Mind will be at odds with God unless it puts off the Natural Mind through Christ and *"becometh as a child, submissive, meek, humble, patient, full of love, willing to submit to all things which the Lord seeth fit to inflict upon him, even as a child doth submit to his father"* (Mosiah 3:19).

This submission in gratitude and trust is our confession to the Lord that we do not understand all things. In thanks we withhold our puny judgment as we acquiesce to the infinite wisdom and love of Heaven. Healing energies seem to be released with this decision simply to give thanks in perfect trust. Some wise and comforting advice comes from a Frenchman, Jacques Lusseyran, blinded at seven years old and later a survivor of eighteen months in the Buchenwald Nazi prison camp. In a later chapter we will learn more about this man's extraordinary spiritual perception, but for our purposes here, he writes from his spiritual experience about quietly accepting What Is:

> One should not try to console either those who lost their eyes, or those who have suffered other losses—of money, health, or a loved one. It is necessary instead to show them what their loss brings them, to show them the gifts they receive in place of what they have lost. Because there are always gifts. God wills it so. Order is restored; nothing ever disappears completely.[19]

---

18. Richard G. Scott, "Obtaining Help from the Lord," *Ensign*, November 1991, 86.

19. *Against the Pollution of the I: Selected Writings of Jacques Lusseyran* (Sandpoint, Idaho: Morning Light Press, 2002), 29.

We wish to force our own conditions on life; this is our real weakness. We forget that God never creates new conditions for us without giving us the strength to meet them.... By all this, I learned at the same time that we should never give way to despair, no matter what brutal and negative events occur in our lives, [because] just as quickly the same sum of life is given back to us."[20]

His experience was that God always compensates with gifts and never requires difficult conditions without strengthening us. He says that when he remembers that God is there to support him, even in his blindness, "I have exactly the sensation of someone taking my hand, or that a ray of light—it is exactly this way—comes toward me and touches me. If I know where the ray of light is, I no longer have any problems."[21]

The secret to working a gratifying alchemy on trials is to give thanks for all circumstances—not just the obvious blessings, the good things, but the inconvenient events, the annoying, and even the very bad ones too. The reason is that heartfelt thanks opens us to the interior Light that always provides something in return for loss. A state of thankfulness becomes a purifying way-of-being that opens the soul to experiences of glory. It can soften grief. A Spirit-filled principle, it enables the soul to experience a universe richly endowed in the smallest details by the Great and Present Creator. A second-sight develops which permits us to see the Lord's love radiating in Nature, at work both in those around us and in life's daily details. As we express our thanks to Him and to each other, we create a peaceful, enlightened, and spiritual atmosphere. Our thanks replace the griping, the self-pity, the murmuring against events and people, the feelings of being overwhelmed, the wrenching fear,

---

20. *Ibid.,* 82.
21. *Ibid.,* 83.

also the pride, the arrogance, the self-righteousness. We give each other nourishing strength in our quiet acceptance and faith. We see everything with a new awareness through which we feel embraced by the Lord and supported in the whisperings of His Spirit: *"Wherefore, fear not even unto death; for in this world your joy is not full, but in me your joy is full.... And seek the face of the Lord always, that in patience ye may possess your souls, and ye shall have eternal life"* (D&C 101:36, 38).

Dear Reader, if you wish to feel the most penetrating power of the Spirit, try the experiment of giving thanks in the moment of disappointment, of tragedy, of the specter of ruin. When you are able to do it consistently, you will feel as though you have discovered and united with the mystery of life.

But it must be said that earth's challenges can seem very, very hard. They can hurt so very much. Even when we know that God won't give us more than we can bear, still, life can, in moments, seem unbearable. Elder Neal A. Maxwell comments:

> Even in the context of acknowledging His omniscience, the chastening experiences of life are difficult enough for us to bear. We could not trust in the perfectness of God's judgment if we did not first know that He foresaw and carefully calibrated our chastening and learning experiences accordingly.[22]

Once the stunned reaction to a grievous event has waned, one can find in a deep inner recess in his soul a joy that still breathes, undiminished.

We have treated here the way in which whatever is, is right. Could we go so far as to say, whatever is, is God? That would lend such a new spirit to our daily life. We could live in humility, trust, and gratitude, serving What Is. Then everything we seek would just seem to come to us.

---

22. *All These Things Shall Give Thee Experience*, 27.

Yes, we will on occasion grieve, it being a cathartic, purifying thing. And we will comfort and strengthen each other. But here in the Wilderness, we remember that each has a right to suffer; each, a right to loss; each, a right to find the inner Paradise, all in order to be fitted to live with the Gods. Thus, at some point, after the worst of the grieving has past, we can begin to sing, and to thank, and to praise our God who does all things well upon the Great Waters. And then, like our First Parents after Divinity came to visit, our eyes begin to open to the Paradise within.

CHAPTER THREE

THE SECRET SPRINGS OF POWER:
THE NATURE OF HOLY SPIRIT

If men do not comprehend the character of God they do not comprehend themselves. Joseph Smith[1]

ⱺ

Knowest thou not, that thou art a spark of Deity, struck from the fire of his eternal blaze, and brought forth in the midst of eternal burnings? John Taylor[2]

ⱺ

When I consider thy heavens, the work of thy fingers, the moon and the stars, which thou hast ordained; What is man, that thou art mindful of him? and the son of man, that thou visitest him? For thou hast made him a little lower than the angels [Hebrew: gods], and hast crowned him with glory and honour.

Psalm 8:3–5

---

1. *WJS*, 340.

2. "Origin, Object, and Destiny of Women," *The Mormon*, August 29, 1857.

PART ONE

"What is man?" the Psalmist wonders—*"for I am fearfully and wonderfully made"* (Psalm 139:14). One morning I caught a glimpse of the answer. It lasted only a moment, but sitting in my rocker by the window, the warm sunlight steeping on me, scriptures open on my lap, I saw of a sudden the truth of my being and felt the confirmation that we are indeed made of supernal stuff. *"Ye were also in the beginning with the Father; that which is Spirit, even the Spirit of truth"* (D&C 93:23). So brief, but in that flash, scripture became experience.

Let us consider here what Man brings with him from the eternal world. Our purpose will be to refresh us, Travelers in the Wilderness, with a vision of the luster of our own soul, that we may be strengthened in the truth of our being. Then, perhaps we can "by the power of the Spirit … catch a spark from the awakened memories of the immortal soul, which lights up our whole being as with the glory of our former home."[3] What might it mean to us to capture who we really are as we make our way through the Wilderness?

In this chapter we will explore Man's spiritual origin and physics.

Stuff of Life

> *In the beginning God created the heaven and the earth. And the earth was without form, and void; and darkness was upon the face of the deep. And the Spirit of God moved upon the face of the waters. And God said, Let there be light; and there was light.* (Genesis 1:1–3)

---

3. Joseph F. Smith, *Gospel Doctrine* (Salt Lake City: Deseret Book, 1956), 14.

The Spirit of God, this creative light, brooded over the vast abyss and, under the direction of the Gods, began its organizing work.[4] With a perfect and eternal love, the radiant heavenly lamps were hung in the firmament and began to beam their Light into the earth:

> The light which shineth, which giveth you light, is through him who enlighteneth your eyes... [and] your understandings; which light proceedeth forth from the presence of God to fill the immensity of space—the light which is in all things, which giveth life to all things, which is the law by which all things are governed, even the power of God who sitteth upon his throne, who is in the bosom of eternity, who is in the midst of all things. (D&C 88:11–13)

This radiant light-element streams visibly and invisibly from the throne of God, permeating all Creation as a subtle, refined, elastic, fluid-like element which is endowed with divine attributes of intelligence and love and the very powers of life. It infuses the entire Cosmos, holds Creation together, yet is fully integrated to one Will as it flows from the Divine Throne to manifest itself in an infinite variety of life forms. All of the dancing forces of Nature—heat, light, electricity, and all her varied and grand displays—"are but the tremblings, the vibrations, the energetic powers of [this] living, all-pervading, and most wonderful fluid, full of wisdom and knowledge,

---

4. Allusion to John Milton's *Paradise Lost* 1.19–22: "Thou from the first / Wast present, and with mighty wings outspread / Dove-like satst brooding on the vast Abyss, / And mad'st it pregnant: What in me is dark, / Illumine,..."; the poet calls on the great Creative Spirit to enlighten him at the outset of his inspired epic poem, in the same manner that the Spirit brought light to the creation of the earth. The *abyss* was that darkness of uncreated material which was "without form, and void" and which would become the earth prepared for Man.

called the HOLY SPIRIT."[5] That spirit "exists wherever there is a particle of material substance; that spirit is round about it, and in it, and through it."[6] It has greater powers of speed and penetration than other elements in Nature because its refined particles penetrate all other substances.[7] This infinite spirit is "an inexhaustible quantity of pure, living, intelligent, powerful Substance, diffused through all worlds in boundless space and capable of filling myriads of tabernacles."[8] Under its influence, all Creation vibrates as it arranges, combines, re-combines, harmonizes, and moves its materials, organizing them into "vegetables, animals, worlds.... These are some of the outward and more common exhibitions of its glory; while its invisible workings, its secret springs of power, and the fulness of its eternal glory, are withheld from the gaze of mortals."[9]

This holy substance is very fine matter: *"All spirit is matter, but it is more fine or pure, and can only be discerned by purer eyes"* (D&C 131:7). In fact, spirit is not only matter, but also energy. As science has demonstrated, all matter, in its most basic components, is energy. We live in a universe where even the most inanimate-seeming substance vibrates. We ourselves are vibrating energy systems capable of different levels of vibration, depending on decisions we make.

Inspired men have known since the foundations of the earth about the secret springs of the universe's power, while science has sought this knowledge in ingenious experiments, and then in elegant mathematical formulas when technology will take them no farther. With such means science searches

---

5. Orson Pratt, "The Holy Spirit," *Writings of an Apostle*, (Salt Lake City: Mormon Heritage Publishers, 1976), 56.

6. Charles W. Penrose, JD 26:24.

7. Parley P. Pratt, JD 1:8.

8. Orson Pratt, *Writings*, 56.

9. *Ibid.*, 49–50.

out things-as-they-really-are. A prominent physicist, seeking the most basic unit of matter and energy, explains the foundations of string theory and its apparently indivisible, vibrating components:

> Everything at its most microscopic level consists of combinations of vibrating strands.... Just as the strings on a violin or on a piano have resonant frequencies at which they prefer to vibrate—patterns that our ears sense as various musical notes and their higher harmonics—the same holds true for the loops of string theory.... Each of the ... mass and force charges are determined by the string's oscillatory pattern.... Everything, all matter and all forces, is unified under the same rubric of microscopic string oscillations—the "notes" that strings can play.[10]

Perhaps this theory begins to describe holy spirit in its enlivening work with the most basic units of creative material, as it sets it to vibrating. Everything in the Cosmos is playing music based on its particular configuration and vibration. The spheres are full of music. The elements of our physical world play the music given them by their Creator, but in the course of this chapter we shall see that Man can choose to a degree the energy by which he will vibrate and the music that he will play.

This holy spirit with its infinite sound and light is known by various names in scripture: the Light of Christ, the Light of Truth, the Light of God, the Spirit of God, the Spirit of Truth, even the Voice of God, as well as *holy spirit*, written here in lower case, to distinguish it from the third member of the

---

10. Brian Greene, professor of physics and mathematics at Columbia University, cited from http://www.pbs.org/wgbh/nova/elegant/everything. html; based on Greene's *Elegant Universe* (New York: Random House, 2005).

Godhead, known as *the* Holy Spirit or Holy Ghost.[11] It is, in fact, the Holy Ghost who administers this holy spirit in Man's behalf. The use in this chapter of *holy spirit*, *Light of Christ*, and even *Holy Ghost* will sometimes overlap, as they seem to do in scripture also, since they are in essence the same power.

Gifts of Holy Spirit

Manifesting itself in many grades and forms, from high to low, this omnipresent spirit may be compared to a spectrum of light where, as:

- as sunlight, it quickens life in the plant kingdom
- as the light of instinct, it quickens and governs life among animals, birds, and fish
- as the light of Man's physical functions, it operates to enable respiration, circulation, reproduction, etc.
- as the light of human reason, it quickens Man's intellect, giving him reason and analytical power, judgment, recognition of truth, and a conscience (see 2 Nephi 2:5).

Higher up the scale, holy spirit, as administered by the Holy Ghost, develops godly attributes and powers in Man.[12] The gift of the Holy Ghost is a greater quantity of holy spirit, perhaps

---

11. This distinction can be seen in comparing, for example, D&C 88:11–13, where what I am calling *holy spirit* is described as light flowing from the throne of God and filling the immensity of space, with 1 Nephi 11:11, where a personage is clearly indicated: *"He was in the form of a man; yet... I knew that it was the Spirit of the Lord."* Even in this example there has been a question as to whether it is the personage of the Holy Ghost or the spirit personage of Jesus Christ. Precise distinctions among the various references to this holy spirit, Holy Ghost, and the other members of the Godhead itself often seem to blur or overlap in scripture.

12. See Hyrum Andrus's discussion of the Light of Christ in *God, Man, and the Universe* (Salt Lake City: Bookcraft, 1968), 248–65.

even a higher form, than could be enjoyed without the laying on of hands for that gift. Conferred through the covenant process, the power of the Holy Ghost opens access to the fulness of Truth. Its functions also include not only the faith to bring things to pass, but also the power by which they are realized; it provides true understanding of scripture, as well as revelations and visions from the eternal world; it bestows myriad gifts of the Spirit; it is the power which enables Priesthood;[13] its enabling power is also known as *"grace,"* as in Moroni 10:32, which perfecting power flows from the Atonement. This Spirit is that which provides life *"more abundantly,"* as the Savior promised His disciples (see John 10:10). It is described in scripture both as fire and as water: as a flaming fire, it fills the heart with *"that joy which is unspeakable and full of glory"* (Helaman 5:44); as living water it fills the Seeker with the mysteries of the kingdom.[14]

In addition to its activity on the spectrum of life, holy spirit exists throughout the Cosmos as a sort of network and is used by the Holy Ghost "to order things according to the perfect will of God."[15] Through this network God enjoys unimpeded

---

13. The prophet Joseph taught: "The Holy Ghost is God's messenger to administer in all those priesthoods" (*HC* 5:555).

14. Examples of Spirit referred to as living water: John 7:37–39—*"If any man thirst, let him come unto me, and drink.... Out of his belly shall flow rivers of living water. (But this spake he of the Spirit....)"*; Revelation 22:1—*"And he shewed me a pure river of water of life, clear as crystal, proceeding out of the throne of God and of the Lamb"* (see also 1 Nephi 11:25 with Romans 5:5); Jeremiah 2:13—*"They have forsaken me the fountain of living waters"*; John 4:10—*"He would have given thee living water"*; Revelation 7:17—*"For the Lamb which is in the midst of the throne ... shall lead them unto living fountains of waters"*; Revelation 21:6—*"I will give unto him that is athirst of the fountain of the water of life freely"*; D&C 63:23—*"But unto him that keepeth my commandments I will give the mysteries of my kingdom, and the same shall be in him a well of living water, springing up unto everlasting life."*

15. *DS* 1:54.

communion with all particles and entities of the infinite micro- and macrocosm and sustains the most intimate communication with all Creation. The Psalmist senses the omnipresence of the Great Creator and exclaims with admiration and wonder, *"Whither shall I go from thy spirit? or whither shall I flee from thy presence?"* (Psalm 139:7).

Through this spiritual network that connects all the Heavens and Earth, God comprehends and embraces all things; it is the means by which *"all things are before him"* and *"round about him; and he is above all things, and in all things, and is through all things, and is round about all things;"* and the way in which *"all things are by him, and of him"* (D&C 88:41). As a result, He has a perfect knowledge *"of things as they are, and as they were, and as they are to come"* (D&C 93:24); His perceptions of past, present, and future converge in "one eternal 'now.'"[16]

Therefore, one definition of a God might be: *One who has obtained full control over all holy spirit, wherever it may be, by virtue of His perfect obedience to eternal law.*

---

16. *HC* 4:597; see also D&C 130:9. Science describes the conditions under which the future can be known. Alvin K. Benson, BYU physics professor, in writing on traveling into the future, shows that in Einstein's special theory of relativity knowledge of future events becomes available to an observer traveling at high speeds in a particular reference frame. He writes: "Thus, if spaceships were available to travel at relativistic speeds, a person could continually look into the future of the development of the earth by taking frequent flights." With reference to God's omniscience: "Being able to see the past, present, and future is a phenomenon associated with travel at very high velocities, approaching and exceeding the speed of light. These conditions [seeing past, present and future] are described only for the celestial glory. Although we, as telestial beings, may not comprehend some of these concepts, they are certainly food for thought and keys to further understanding" ("Joseph Smith on Modern Science," in *Joseph Smith: The Prophet, The Man*, ed. Susan Easton Black and Charles D. Tate, 158–60, available on Gospelink.com.).

Holy spirit composes the very matrix of the Lord's own being and radiates from Him as the Light of Christ. By this Light or Spirit the Lord sheds His love abroad throughout the spiritual network (see 1 Nephi 11:22; Romans 5:5), consciously extending Himself into all Creation, even moment to moment, to uphold it—and not only into Creation, but into us: *"I am the true light that is in you, and you are in me; otherwise ye could not abound"* (D&C 88:50).

Yet, He is little perceived. Man walks about in the midst of heavenly forces unaware; he does not know that his ability to move or think or breathe comes to him through the Spirit of Jesus Christ, that *"God... has created you, and has kept and preserved you, ... and is preserving you from day to day, by lending you breath, that ye may live and move and do according to your own will, and even supporting you from one moment to another"* (Mosiah 2:20–21). Man's life, wholly beyond his power to create, is sustained moment to moment by the Heavens through the free gift of the Love and Light of Christ.

It becomes apparent that all Man's functions are gifts of the living Light of Christ: reasoning, language, reading, invention, bright ideas, creativity, musical talent, even athletic ability. We may think that we perform these rational feats by our own prowess; but it can humble us and open our eyes to realize that all these are present-moment, revelatory gifts of the Light of Christ.

Indeed, this Spirit may have a primarily revelatory action; just by its very presence in the life around us, small and great truths can leak through from the other world. Truth shines, says the scripture (see D&C 88:7), radiating knowledge of things-as-they-really-are into Man's mind and environment. Therefore, we would not be surprised to know that through the history of the world many have picked up these signals and thus might know even years in advance of the coming restoration of the gospel, might even perceive the true origin and destiny of Man, might experience healings and great revelations. Even without the gift of the Holy Ghost, many have sought diligently in the Light of Christ to obtain the truth of unseen spiritual realities. We might expect to see marvels and miracles come from any quarter on this earth, since miracles are characteristic not only of the true Church, but also of the activity of holy spirit as it circulates in all life. Human experience abounds with occurrences in which the other world seems to penetrate this one with its Light. Often their divine origin is not perceived.

A simple example: I happened recently onto a conversation between two people talking about "ah-ha!" moments. The first person had been reading a popular book on the new physics. He said, "As I read, I had something of a conceptual breakthrough. I suddenly felt as if I understood in a holistic way what quantum mechanics and virtual particles and so on were all about." He then got interrupted, had to leave his reading, and wasn't able to return to his book until later. As he went back to his reading, he began to think about his revelation, but he couldn't for the life of him remember what it was. "I read the section I had been reading again and again, but I just could not recapture whatever insight it was I thought I had. I've never been able to." His friend said in response: "Yes! Sometimes I experience the same thing! I could be reading a book, eating, or in a conversation when suddenly my mind feels uplifted, and I feel happy, and then this feeling is followed by me making some great connection about the secrets of space and time. But once this state of euphoria is over (and these moments last only seconds, but feel like time has stopped), and I start to fully analyze my discovery, I can't remember what I discovered. I can only remember discovering something and my soul felt happy for this added knowledge." The feeling of happiness and elevated light coming into the mind are the sure sign of the activity of the Light of Christ.

There may be more than random activity at work in these moments when the light seems to break through from the other world. One of the purposes of the Light of Christ is to draw one's attention to the other world so as to provoke inquiry into spiritual things. We remember that the whole Creation is upheld by the redeeming love of the Lord Jesus Christ and is organized specifically for the salvation of the souls of men. Therefore, all spiritual activity works toward that end.

Elder Boyd K. Packer says that if we understand the reality of the Light of Christ in everyone we see and within ourselves "we will have courage and inspiration beyond that which we have known heretofore." Then he says with energy, "And it *must* be so! And it *will* be so! All of this is a dimension of gospel truth that too few understand."[17]

He may have been referring to the spiritual sensitivity that every child of God has because of the Light of Christ in his or her being, in that *"all men are instructed sufficiently that they know good from evil"* (2 Nephi 2:5). This innate "instruction" enables each one to recognize and experience Truth. This truth-discerning capacity may exist in very low levels in some people who live consistently against the truth of their being; but all possess it, and it is to this essence in Man that we may confidently address ourselves when we share Truth with others. Everyone's spirit knows the Truth in some part of his being, for as the poet observed, "We dance around in a ring and suppose, / But the Secret sits in the middle and knows."[18]

Spiritual Possibilities

Looking into the new physics for what it might teach us about reality, one school of thought among string theorists finds that

17. "The Light of Christ," *Ensign,* April 2005, 14.
18. Robert Frost, "The Secret Sits."

we live in a multi-dimensional universe; they identify ten (some find twenty-six) possible dimensions, seven or more of which exist beyond Man's current perception.[19] Elder Bruce R. McConkie opens our understanding about the many dimensions hidden from our gaze. Speaking to a group of BYU students, he says:

> Now for instance, this great fieldhouse in which we are assembled is full of revelation at this moment. All the revelations of eternity are here, but you and I who have assembled in the devotional are probably not receiving them. This fieldhouse is full of the visions of eternity, and yet we are not viewing visions at this moment, but we could.... Now analogously, this great fieldhouse is full of great symphonies. There are symphonies played here, and our ears are not hearing them. There are sermons that are being preached, but we do not hear them. Yet if we had the means and the ability, we could tune in and hear the symphonies and see the visions.[20]

It is undoubtedly a blessing for Man in his current reduction of powers not to perceive all these things at once, but the possibility of expanding our "means and ability" to tune in is continually held out before us in scripture. For example, the prophet Joseph writes:

---

19. Alvin K. Benson, speaking still of Einstein's theory of relativity, mentions the fourth dimension of time. He writes, "Every object, every planet, every star, every galaxy, every person exists in a four-dimensional (four-vector) realm called the "space-time continuum" ("Joseph Smith on Modern Science," 158). In 1895, in his novel *The Time Machine*, H.G. Wells writes, "There is no difference between time and any of the three dimensions of space except that our consciousness moves along it." He adds, "Scientific people ... know very well that time is only a kind of space" (New York: Pocket Books, 2004, 5–6). We begin to question our personal perception of reality.

20. "Seek the Spirit," BYU *Speeches of the Year*, 1964.

But great and marvelous are the works of the Lord, and the mysteries of his kingdom which he showed unto us, which surpass all understanding in glory, and in might, and in dominion; which he commanded us we should not write while we were yet in the Spirit, and are not lawful for man to utter; neither is man capable to make them known, for they are only to be seen and understood by the power of the Holy Spirit, which God bestows on those who love him, and purify themselves before him; to whom he grants this privilege of seeing and knowing for themselves; that through the power and manifestation of the Spirit, while in the flesh, they may be able to bear his presence in the world of glory. (D&C 76:114–18)

Under the right conditions, the "secret springs" of the barely perceived realities that circulate in and around us in this very moment can be tuned to. And the reason is that Man, with his two-part nature, straddles the spiritual and physical worlds; he has senses that operate in both spheres. His mandate and privilege here are to become more conscious, to wake up, and to discern more of the infinite world around him. Elder Parley P. Pratt inquires:

Who then can define the precise point … which divides between the physical and spiritual kingdoms? There are eyes which can discern the most refined particles of elementary existence. There are hands and fingers to whose refined touch all things are tangible. In the capacity of mortals, however, some of the elements are tangible, or visible, and others invisible. Those which are tangible to our senses, we call physical: those which are more subtle and refined, we call spiritual.[21]

---

21. *Key to the Science of Theology*, 10th ed. (Salt Lake City: Deseret Book, 1966), 50.

Elder Packer strengthens our faith that we can perceive more of the spiritual world even as we pursue our journey in the flesh:

> With the eyes of our understanding, we see things that are spiritual. With our spirits reaching out, we can touch things that are spiritual and feel them. Then we can see and we can feel things that are invisible to the physical senses.[22]

This knowledge about the nature and function of holy spirit could become life-changing as its personal implications are seen, because it could help us consciously to experience holy spirit, which, in view of its divinity, could fill our souls with a transcendent joy and a sense of connectedness to all life. All the attributes and ability to experience holy spirit already reside in our own soul because, as we have seen, they form the essence of our being. We realize that there is a fountain of the most exquisite energy flowing through us and giving us life. To what extent do our own decisions either open our awareness or block our perception?

If holy spirit has particular attributes such as love, intelligence, and truth, then we can immediately think of emotions and thoughts that will "quicken" our perception, that is, will enliven or actually raise the vibration of our being to greater perception levels. The Lord says, for example, that *the power of my Spirit quickeneth all things*" (D&C 33:16) and that *"no man has seen God at any time in the flesh except quickened by the Spirit of God"* (D&C 67:11). Our decisions actually affect what we can perceive of the activity of holy spirit and the holy love being shed around us.

In this life, many different kinds of stimuli vie for our attention and distract us from the experience of holy spirit. We tend to be sidetracked by such internal noise as anger, fear, desire, self-will, and depression, not to mention the commotion which

---

22. "The Light of Christ," 8–14.

may characterize much of our external life. Holy spirit, on the other hand, whether as Light of Christ or Holy Ghost, is subtle and aligned with more sensitive awarenesses. These more subtle perceptions and feelings might include

1. That there is an infinite intelligence operating in the hidden inner recesses of my being and in my environment, and that it loves me and is supplying what I really need, day to day; that holy spirit at work in me is not an anonymous, mechanical thing; but rather, through the immediacy of the network of holy spirit, God is always present and always in charge and always striving with me, even though His present activity may lie beneath my awareness; that His aims for me are to evolve toward Him, and that all of my life is arranged, day to day, to bring that to pass. I could accept what comes with greater trust, quiet, even gratitude.

2. That I am more spirit than I am flesh, and so is everyone and every living thing around me; that I am primarily a sojourner and a pilgrim in this world (see D&C 45:13). That as I make a decision to live a consciously spiritual life, true to my being, holy spirit begins to reveal itself in the many forms of life around me, through spiritual senses perhaps hitherto dormant. I would sense it as it is mediated through Nature and through the preciousness of my fellow human beings. I would understand what the poet means when he says that in Nature "there lives the dearest freshness deep down things."[23] Reverence for life and for the earth is deeply evocative of holy spirit.

---

23. Gerard Manley Hopkins, "God's Grandeur." Hopkins (1844–1889) was a very devout worshipper of God. Part of the poem reads, alluding to Isaiah 6:3 *("the whole earth is full of his glory"):* "The world is charged with the grandeur of God. / It will flame out, like shining from shook foil…. Nature is never spent; / There lives the dearest freshness deep down things…. Because the Holy Ghost over the bent World broods with warm breast and with ah! bright wings." His allusion in the last line is to Milton as cited at the beginning of the chapter.

3. That, though I may have covered up this inner current, I can uncover it by being very still inside, by strengthening my inner awareness of the life-force in all parts of my body in quiet meditation, as it silently flows only with love and reverence for me, growing in sensation and luminosity before my inner eye; that this Light exists in a realm of my being that might be termed the "timeless" part of me. That this "real me" is the part to become more consistently aware of. That I can practice stepping into the timelessness of my most quiet mind to that still point inside. That I could learn to do this in any setting until, indeed, spiritfulness might become my primary awareness, while the noisy activity of my current life might fade into a sort of background music.

4. That were I to feel holy spirit in its purity, it would make me weep, so tender, so pure, so exquisite is it. Then I would understand something about the essence of the Lord Jesus Christ Himself. Then I would know also my own essence and the truth of my own being.

Part Two

Traveling the Path of Light from Spirit, to Man, to God

> *For I, the Lord God, created all things, of which I have spoken, spiritually, before they were naturally upon the face of the earth ... for in heaven created I them.* (Moses 3:5)

In this section we will explore the organization of holy spirit into a spirit personage and then the way in which that spirit takes upon itself a body and, through a long journey of sanctifying body and mind, arrives at Godhood.

Holy spirit has great potential but must find kinetic expression through organization. "Now, this Spirit always existed; it always operated, but it is not understood, and cannot be comprehended except through organisms. If you see a living blade of grass you see a manifestation of that Spirit which is called God. If you see an animal of any kind on the face of the earth having life, there is a manifestation of that Spirit."[24] Brigham Young explains that its godly "attributes can be made manifest only through an organized personage. All [its] attributes are couched in and are the results of organized existence."[25] Elder John A. Widtsoe emphasizes that when we see any living manifestation of holy spirit, we also see God's will impressed upon this medium through which He works. "Without the medium God would be helpless to execute, while still retaining all his power to invent. Without God, the medium would remain changeless, inert, throughout all eternity, having no power of initiation within itself."[26]

This scintillating spirit can be found in all degrees of purity, that is, from electricity, which is one of the more gross forms of spiritual matter, "up through all the gradations of the invisible fluids, till we arrive at a substance so holy, so pure, so endowed with intellectual attributes and sympathetic affections, that it may be said to be on a par … in its attributes with man."[27] When a given quantity of this purest form of holy spirit element is organized in the size and form of Man, with every organ developed, formed, endowed, precisely after the pattern of Man's outward body, we have a "spiritual body," "an individual intelligence, an agent endowed with life, with a degree of independence, or inherent will, with the powers of motion, of thought, and with the attributes of moral, intellectual, and sympathetic affections and emotions."[28]

---

24. Penrose, *JD* 26:23.

25. *JD* 10:193.

26. *Joseph Smith as Scientist* (Salt Lake City: Eborn Books, 1990), 47–48.

27. Parley P. Pratt, *JD* 1:8.

28. *Ibid.*

Man, then, was organized in the premortal world out of the holiest and purest form of holy spirit. Begotten of loving heavenly parents (see D&C 76:24), we grew up in a heavenly environment. Love was the air we breathed. The organized spirit

> was born and matured in the heavenly mansions, trained in the school of love in the family circle, and amid the most tender embraces of parental and fraternal affection. In this primeval probation, in its heavenly home, it lived and moved as a free and rational intelligence, acting upon its own agency, and, like all intelligence, independent in its own sphere. It was placed under certain laws and was responsible to its great Patriarchal Head.[29]

We passed a long period of development in the spirit world. But we knew that our premortal state was transitory because we could witness throughout the sidereal heavens worlds organized and peopled with fellow spirits who left the premortal world, took upon them bodies, died, were resurrected, and received their exaltation on the redeemed worlds they once dwelt on.[30] Even though we were already highly developed beings, we learned that a body would give us power to advance and be exalted in the scale of intelligence, both in time and eternity.[31] We therefore knew that the next step on the journey was for us to come to the material world.

> *And I, the Lord God, formed man from the dust of the ground, and breathed into his nostrils the breath of life; and man became a living soul.... Nevertheless, all things were before created; but spiritually were they created.* (Moses 3:7)

---

29. *Ibid.*, 1:57.
30. See "Origin, Object, and Destiny of Women."
31. Parley P. Pratt, *JD* 1:7–9.

Elder John A. Widtsoe explains one reason why Man had to come to a material dimension:

> The universe is dual: spiritual and material, composed of "spirit-element" and "matter-element." These two realms are closely interwoven, perhaps of the same ultimate source; yet they are distinct in their nature. Mastery of the universe means acquaintanceship with and control of both of these elemental divisions of the universe in which we live.[32]

In spite of the fact that the body would be made of a grosser material than the spirit, it "was necessary as an habitation for it that [the spirit] might be clothed with a body, perfect in its organization, beautiful in its structure, symmetrical in its proportions, and in every way fit for an eternal intelligent being; that through it, it might speak, act, enjoy, and develop its power, its intelligence and perpetuate its species.... They [the spirits] had the intelligence before, but now they saw a way through which to develop it."[33]

The spirits knew that by the union of their spirit with a body of flesh they would be capable of continued increase, ultimate perfection, and eternal exaltation, "that the spirit, quick, subtle, refined, lively, animate, energetic, and eternal, might have a body through which to operate... [in order that the spirits not be left to] spend their force at random, or remain dormant, or useless, without those more tangible, material objects, through which to exercise their force. Thus, then, was the body formed as an agent for the spirit."[34]

---

32. *Evidences and Reconciliations* (Salt Lake City: Deseret Book, 1965), 72.

33. John Taylor, *The Government of God* (Orem, Utah: Grandin Book Company, 1992), 78–79.

34. *Ibid.*

Man's Body

In the eternal plan, the spirit is to rule the body as its tool of divine expression. But the body was also designed to be the instrument of Man's fullest joy as it was sanctified, redeemed by the power of the Atonement, resurrected, and exalted in the eternal world; for *"man is spirit. The elements are eternal, and spirit and element, inseparably connected, receive a fulness of joy; and when separated, man cannot receive a fulness of joy"* (D&C 93:33–34).

Through the history of Man on the earth, various philosophies and religions have regarded Man's body as unworthy and unspiritual, to be rejected, to be vilified, to be renounced. But in the revelations we find that all the organs our body uses here have their spiritual counterparts and have taken their place in this world of form impressed with the image of a glorified, material Heavenly Father and Mother.[35] The true needs of the body are the needs of the spirit, which uses the body as an instrument for its development and its ministry. The body, therefore, is a precious treasure and treating it well, increasing in it the enlivening powers of holy spirit, magnifies the soul's powers. The line between spirit and body is not always clear, composed as they are of varying forms of the same material, and so joy is often experienced through all parts of our whole being and vibrates along the entire continuum of material and spiritual. A feeling of joyful wholeness can come from moments of feeling fully integrated, body and spirit. Many ancient disciplines

---

35. "This organized spirit we call a body, because, although composed of the spiritual elements, it possesses every organ after the pattern, and in the likeness or similitude of the outward or fleshly tabernacle it is destined eventually to inhabit. Its organs of thought, speech, sight, hearing, tasting, smelling, feeling, etc., all exist in their order as in the physical body; the one being the exact similitude of the other. This individual, spiritual body, was begotten by the Heavenly Father, in his own likeness and image, and by the laws of procreation" (*Key to the Science of Theology*, 56).

teach how to develop greater spiritual perception through the integration of body and spirit.

Everything that we behold on earth has its unseen spirit body in the image of its physical form (see D&C 77:2), each creature reflecting in some way the beauty of its spiritual creation and purpose. Man's happiness will be greater as he identifies with his own spiritual origins and nature, as well as others' too. We can look through the physical to the spiritual beauty and purpose of each living thing and increase our own perception and joy by so doing. The enlightened person looks on Creation with love and with reverence for every creature that lives. He knows that his body is given him to increase his power to help others, that for this he was born, and that his life and happiness are inextricably entwined with others', and that this is the message streaming from the secret springs.

Elder Charles W. Penrose summarizes briefly the stages in Man's journey from his spiritual organization to his ultimate destiny:

> The perfection of [holy spirit's] manifestation is in the personality of a being called God. That is a person who has passed through all the gradations of being, and who contains within Himself the fulness, manifested and expressed, of this divine spirit.... If you see a man you behold its most perfect earthly manifestation. And if you see a glorified man, a man who has passed through the various grades of being, who has overcome all things, who has been raised from the dead, who has been quickened by this spirit in its fulness, there you see manifested, in its perfection, this eternal, beginningless, endless spirit of intelligence. Such a Being is our Father and our God, and we are following in His footsteps.... He is a perfect manifestation, expression and revelation of this eternal essence, this spirit of eternal, everlasting intelligence or light of truth.[36]

---

36. JD 26:24–25.

Man as spirit, as human being, or as God, will never outgrow his need for holy spirit.

The Heavenly Spirit Strives with Man in His Journey

Man arrives on earth with embryonic divinity. He is "a part of God," "a spark of Deity struck from the fire of his eternal blaze," as President Taylor writes.[37] He has "every organ, attribute, sense, sympathy, affection that is possessed by God Himself," says Elder Parley Pratt, but "these attributes are in embryo; and are to be gradually developed. They resemble a bud, a germ, which gradually develops into bloom, and then, by progress, produces the mature fruit, after its own kind."[38]

But even with all this potential, Man has only a basic set of life-functions activated here. This set is designed to sustain physical life and to provide rational powers that we might *"live, and move, and have our being"* (Acts 17:28), but these life-functions are not enough to exalt us in the eternal world. Elder Orson Pratt speaks of the greater workings of the Holy Ghost on Man:

---

37. John Taylor, *Government of God*, 80.

38. *Key to the Science of Theology*, 101. Included here are Elder Pratt's well-known words on the effect of the Holy Ghost on Man's faculties: "The gift of the Holy Ghost adapts itself to all these organs or attributes. It quickens all the intellectual faculties, increases, enlarges, expands and purifies all the natural passions and affections; and adapts them, by the gift of wisdom, to their lawful use. It inspires, develops, cultivates and matures all the fine-toned sympathies, joys, tastes, kindred feelings, and affections of our nature. It inspires virtue, kindness, goodness, tenderness, gentleness and charity. It develops beauty of person, form and features. It tends to health, vigor, animation and social feeling. It invigorates all the faculties of the physical and intellectual man. It strengthens, and gives tone to the nerves. In short, it is, as it were, marrow to the bone, joy to the heart, light to the eyes, music to the ears, and life to the whole being.... Such is the gift of the Holy Ghost, and such are its operations, when received through the lawful channel—the divine, eternal priesthood" (100, 102).

"So far as the operations of the Holy Spirit upon the mind are manifest, it is evident that it does not dwell in unholy temples; that is, it does not dwell in them to sanctify, to purify, to teach the mind in such temples; but it merely dwells in them to carry on those processes, generally ascribed to the laws of nature."[39] Holy spirit provides basic life forces, but the Holy Ghost adds greater dimensions.

Brigham Young provides an example of the way in which Man can, through his awareness, cultivate these enhanced spiritual forces. He likens Man's dependence on these to a tree's dependence on unseen nutrients in the atmosphere and sunlight. Man's consciousness of the existence of unseen spiritual nutrients in his environment gives him greater access to them. Brigham says, "The Elders of Israel, though the great majority of them are moral men, and as clear of spot and blemish as men well can be, live beneath their privilege; they live continually without enjoying the power of God. I want to see men and women breathe the Holy Ghost in every breath of their lives, living constantly in the light of God's countenance."[40] Basic life-forces, even morality, are not enough.

The fountain of Spirit can become for Man an eternal source of increase:

> I have often told you from this stand, if you cleave to holy, godlike principles, you add more good to your organization, which is made independent in the first place, and the good spirit and influence which come from the Father of lights, and from Jesus Christ, and from the holy angels add good to it. And when you have been proved, and when you have labored and occupied sufficiently upon that, it will become in you what Brother Joseph Smith told Elder Taylor, if he would adhere to the Spirit

39. Orson Pratt, *Writings,* 52.
40. *JD* 9:288.

of the Lord strictly, it should become in him...a fountain of revelation. That is true. After a while the Lord will say to such, "My son, you have been faithful, you have clung to good, and you love righteousness, and hate iniquity, from which you have turned away, now you shall have the blessing of the Holy Spirit to lead you, and be your constant companion, from this time henceforth and forever." Then the Holy Spirit becomes your property, it is given to you for a profit, and an eternal blessing. It tends to addition, extension, and increase, to immortality and eternal lives.[41]

Brigham comments on Man's powers of increase in the celestial kingdom:

It supposed by this people that we have all the ordinances in our possession...that can be administered in the flesh; but there are other ordinances and administrations that must be administered beyond this world.... We have not, neither can we receive here, the ordinance and keys of the resurrection. They will be given to those who have passed off this state of action and have received their bodies again, as many have already done and many more will. They will be ordained, by those who hold the keys of the resurrection, to go forth and resurrect the Saints, just as we receive the ordinance of baptism, then the keys of authority to baptize others for the remission of their sins. This is one of the ordinances we cannot receive here, and there are many more.... We have not the power in the flesh to create and bring forth or produce a spirit; but we have the power to produce a temporal body. The germ of this, God has placed within us. And when our spirits receive our bodies, and through our faithfulness we are worthy to be crowned, we will then receive authority to produce both spirit and body. But these keys we cannot receive in the

---

41. *JD* 2:135.

flesh. Herein, brethren, you can perceive that we have not finished, and cannot finish our work, while we live here, no more
than Jesus did while he was in the flesh. We cannot receive, while
in the flesh, the keys to form and fashion kingdoms and to organize matter, for they are beyond our capacity and calling, beyond
this world. In the resurrection, men who have been faithful and
diligent in all things in the flesh, have kept their first and second
estate, and worthy to be crowned Gods, even the sons of God,
will be ordained to organize matter.[42]

On the other hand, he says, "Every kingdom will be blot-
ted out of existence, except the one whose ruling spirit is the
Holy Ghost, and whose king is the Lord."[43] He suggests that
those who cultivate evil principles will ultimately undergo
some form of disorganization, they will be

decomposed, both soul and body, and return to their native element. I do not say that they will be annihilated; but they will be
disorganized, and will be as though they never had been, while
we will live and retain our identity, and contend against those
principles which tend to death or dissolution. I am after life....
If you wish to retain your present identity in the morn of the
resurrection, you must so live that the principle of life will be
within you as a well of water springing up unto eternal life.[44]

---

42. *JD* 15:137.

43. *JD* 2:124.

44. Ibid., *JD* 7:56–57. Elder John A. Widtsoe comments, "President
Brigham Young has suggested that the ultimate punishment of the sons
of perdition may be that they, having their spiritual bodies disorganized,
must start over again—must begin anew the long journey of existence, re-
peating the steps that they took in the eternities before the Great Council
was held. That would be punishment, indeed!" (*Evidences and Reconciliation*, 213).

Spirit is a dynamic element, either seeking a higher degree of organization in Man, or slipping backwards to a lower degree—all in accordance with the way in which Man uses his mind.

The Holy Ghost's work is particularly with Man's mind. Joseph teaches that this Spirit "has no other effect than pure intelligence. It is … powerful in expanding the mind, enlightening the understanding, and storing the intellect with present knowledge."[45]

Spiritual Frontier of the Mind

Man's spiritual frontier consists of his mind and spirit. These are the instruments of his transformation. Joseph explains that even though the "mind of man is coequal with God himself,"[46] "all mind and spirit God ever sent into the world are susceptible of enlargement." That is, although Man's intelligence cannot be created or made, it can be enlarged. We also note that the prophet equated *mind* and *spirit*. Heavenly Father's children are, then, primarily *mind*, and, considering their divine origin, even creative mind—with infinite potential to create, not only worlds, but to participate in creating themselves as Gods. The prophet elaborates, "You have to learn how to make yourselves God[s], Kings, Priests, etc., by going from a small to great capacity. Till [you] are able to dwell in everlasting burning and everlasting power."[47] These achievements become possible only as Man gets control of his own mind and shapes it as an instrument through which God can extend power to him.

Obviously, then, the Gods are committed to the development of Man's mind which must be enlarged according to

---

45. *TPJS*, 149.

46. *WJS*, 341. "Co-equal" is taken to mean "co-existent" or "co-eternal."

47. *Ibid.*, 341.

certain laws and principles in a relationship with Them: "The relationship we have with God places us in a situation to advance in knowledge. God has power to institute laws to instruct the weaker intelligences that they may be exalted with himself."[48] Joseph elaborates on this process—God's part and Man's part:

> We consider that God has created man with a mind capable of instruction, and a faculty which may be enlarged in proportion to the heed and diligence given to the light communicated from heaven to the intellect; and that the nearer man approaches perfection, the clearer are his views, and the greater his enjoyments, till he has overcome the evils of his life and lost every desire for sin; and like the ancients arrives at that point of faith where he is wrapped in the power and glory of his Maker, and is caught up to dwell with Him. But we consider that this is a station to which no man ever arrived in a moment. He must have been instructed in the government and laws of that kingdom by proper degrees.[49]

We see that to fulfill his destiny, Man must learn the laws of God and bring his mind into harmony with them; he must, Elder Widstoe says, be "permeated by the vibration of law" and come into possession of Truth through "the prehensile power of the soul."[50] Man is designed to reach for and grasp and fill himself deliberately with Truth and Light and thus to be quickened with the same energies as the Gods in their Heaven. For this purpose the energetic Word of God is provided, it having a quickening or vibratory effect on the human mind (see Alma 31:5) as it causes the mind to expand (see Alma 32:34); for

---

48. *Ibid.*, 346.

49. *HC* 2:8.

50. *Joseph Smith as Scientist*, 155.

the word of the Lord is truth, which is light, which is Spirit, *"even the Spirit of Jesus Christ"* (D&C 84:45).

Dr. Alvin K. Benson observes:

> By proper attunement to the source of truth, the knowledge and understanding carried by light from Christ can be absorbed by our bodies through a phenomenon analogous to quantum mechanical resonance. This attunement is like the light-matter interactions producing resonance phenomena in radio, television, and spectroscopy. When attuned to spiritual resonant frequencies through obedience, we receive more and more light (truth) until we are perfected. (See D&C 50:24, 93:28, 88:49)[51]

Perhaps we have been tempted in the past to complain about the exacting nature of the commandments we have been given; but, on reflection, we see how privileged we are to have received with the Restoration of the Gospel the Law which preserves, perfects, and sanctifies the person who obeys it (see D&C 88:34). Embracing this Law as fully as we can prepares us to be quickened by the power of the celestial glory, actually causing the vibratory changes in our spiritual physics that resonate with that power. On the other hand, to the degree that a person chooses a law in place of the Lord's, he must inherit a kingdom to which his lower vibration corresponds (see D&C 88:35). Thus we see how indispensable it is for the Seeker to keep searching into the Law and conforming himself to it.

The perfecting process takes Man from one dimension of perception to another, clearing and expanding his vision as he goes. It is apparent that certain dimensions become perceptible by us only as we reach their vibrational level through the conscious incorporation of Truth. The Savior deliberately magnified Light and Truth and Intelligence in Himself and

---

51. Benson, 164.

consciously filled His own inner being until He was brimming with these and was able to comprehend all things (see D&C 93:24; also D&C 88:67). The Seeker will do as He did.

Truth: Man's Sustenance

The Spirit of truth, Elder F. Enzio Busche declares, must become our "constant and infinite guide," and thus we come to see the "real me," or the spiritual child of God, created in innocence and beauty, but engaged in a battle against the misery-making forces of darkness. He continues:

> It is Jesus Christ who, through His light, is searching and finding each individual child of God who is yearning and fighting for righteousness and truth and who is crying for help.... Through the Light of Christ our minds are quickened with understanding (see D&C 88:11).
>
> The issue is truth, my dear brothers and sisters, and the only way to find truth is through uncompromising self-education toward self-honesty to see the original "real me," the child of God, in its innocence and potential in contrast to the influence from the other part of me, "the flesh," with its selfish desires and foolishness. [52]

Elder Busche touches upon the very issue that can provide relief to the Traveler in the Wilderness. Let him wipe away the film of unbelief and find refuge in the Truth of his own being. When he is tired, and hungry, and thirsty for he knows not what, he could remember the healing power of Truth.

So often, our suffering and bewilderment have to do with having left the path of the Truth in some way or other and then having come to doubt its power. We have in some way forgotten that our aim is not only to experience positive

---

52. "Truth Is the Issue," *Ensign*, November 1993, 24.

emotions, nor just to feel good by whatever means, but it is to be true to the Truth of our being. Sometimes the solution is as simple as coming into resonance with that Truth; then that yielding can restore our luster.

Man must feed on Truth; only then is he capable of union with God. Untruth in all its possible shades puts him out of harmony with divine forces. Thus the Holy Spirit leads the Seeker to be "a mind that feeds upon infinity," intent to hear the Voice carried on silent light into the abyss of his soul.[53] Thus Man's music increasingly resonates with the harmony of the spheres.

And feeding on such Truth, the Spirit may awaken him, "in a dream or vision, or by the spirit of prophecy...to a partial vision, or to a dim and half defined recollection of the intelligence of the past," says Elder Parley P. Pratt. "[Man] sees in part, and he knows in part; but never while tabernacled in mortal flesh will he fully awaken to the intelligence of his former estate. It surpasses his comprehension, is unspeakable and even unlawful to be uttered."[54] One day our former glories will be unveiled again; meanwhile, just the knowledge that we are full of unutterable wonders can light our way—yes, can cause us to question our current perceptions of reality and expand toward greater ones.

Meanwhile, the Lord has placed Man in a darkened world, but Man can awaken to the awareness that both he and the Wilderness in which he finds himself are permeated with living Light.

---

53. Reference to William Wordsworth, "The Prelude" (1850) 14.70–75.

54. *Key to the Science of Theology*, 58.

CHAPTER FOUR

THE WILDERNESS MIND

All men that are in a state of nature, or ... in a carnal state, are in the gall of bitterness and in the bonds of iniquity; ... they are in a state contrary to the nature of happiness.

Alma 41:10–11

&

Until you can govern and control the mind and the body, and bring all into subjection to the law of Christ, you have a work to perform touching yourselves.

Brigham Young[1]

&

Behold, all ye that kindle a fire, that compass yourselves about with sparks; walk in the light of your fire, and in the sparks that ye have kindled. This shall ye have of mine hand; ye shall lie down in sorrow.

Isaiah 50:11

---

1. *JD* 3:249.

Begotten in Light and reared in bliss, the premortal spirits continually beheld the splendors of eternal Beauty and Truth. In their infinite variety as organized intelligences, some perceived more than others, but all the spirit children enjoyed a vast consciousness, flourishing in the ocean of holy spirit. Still, a yet greater consciousness was needed to get them to their ultimate destiny. But, to ascend above all, they must descend below all.

And so it is that Man, trailing glory into a darker sphere, commences a course in deep impact training. The memory of his premortal powers and glories tucked away, he begins to interact with his new surroundings through a veiled consciousness. As he grows in his new world, his consciousness begins to develop anew, influenced now primarily by his fallen environment. "Shades of the prison-house begin to close upon the growing Boy."[2] His mind is shaped by both accurate and inaccurate interpretations of the nature of things. With no memory of who he really is, he fixes on his emotional and physical survival, thus fostering self-absorption and anxiety. Flawed ideas take root in his mind which cause him to react to life in unconscious, negative patterns. Conditional love and even hatred dog him. His perception is clouded by vain imaginings and faulty interpretations. He relates to the world through the lens of his own self-talk instead of perceiving reality directly. He sins and is sinned against. Fear threads its way through his life. His confused mind fashions his perception of a confused world. That is, the Natural Man suffers from a degree of insanity.

Purposes of the Natural Mind

Of course we agreed to this imposition, knowing that these limitations would serve the purposes of the Great Plan of

---

2. William Wordsworth, *Intimations of Immortality from Recollections of Early Childhood.*

Happiness in order that we might come to *know* good and evil and to experience bitter and sweet in the full spectrum of opposites available in this world. Without the darkened mind, Man would see through life's dilemmas to the greater reality, and his tutorials would lose their impact. Elder Charles W. Penrose explains the necessity of a veil:

> We are here to learn the laws that govern this lower world; to learn to grapple with evil and to understand what darkness is. We came from an abode of bliss to understand the pain and sorrow incident to this probation. We came here to comprehend what death is.... The knowledge of our former state has fled from us.... The veil is drawn between us and our former habitation. This is for our trial. If we could see the things of eternity, and comprehend ourselves as we are; if we could penetrate the mists and clouds that shut out eternal realities from our gaze, the fleeting things of time would be no trial to us, and one of the great objects of our earthly probation or testing would be lost. But the past has gone from our memory, the future is shut out from our vision, and we are living here in time, to learn little by little, line upon line, precept upon precept.[3]

We must have known, even as we agreed to all this limitation, that it would try us sorely. But that Man would begin the mortal probation amidst clouds and mists, a mystery to himself, constitutes an essential part of the Plan. Yes, he must make the descent into confusion and darkness and into vanity, fear, blindness, selfishness, and tribulation, for, as the Lord told His suffering prophet, *"Know thou, my son, that all these things shall give thee experience, and shall be for thy good"* (D&C 122:7). Brigham Young spoke on the benevolent purposes behind the telestial curriculum:

---

3. JD 26:28.

It is the Lord's design that His people should have an experience; ... it was the will of the Lord that we should be made acquainted with darkness, and subjected to vanity.... to descend below all things, that they might ascend to thrones, principalities, and powers; for they could not ascend to that eminence without first descending, nor upon any other principle.... The Lord has designed, from ages immemorial, that we should be in darkness and ignorance, and at the same time I believe it is His will that we should receive light and intelligence in order that we may understand true principles.... It is then the design of the Lord that mankind should be placed in this dark, ignorant, and selfish state, that we should naturally cling to the earth.... He has designed all this to prepare us to dwell in His presence ... to possess His spirit, which is right and intelligent, for nothing but purity and holiness can dwell where He is.[4]

Meanwhile, we find ourselves submersed with our fellows in these beclouded telestial opposites, *"For God hath shut [us] up on all sides in disobedience, that he might have mercy upon all."*[5] For His purposes, God has insulated Man in ignorance—until the revelation of Truth.

So, if we find that we have a sturdy Natural Man, that is to be expected—that's the Plan; we're not surprised. The Gods themselves developed their perfected consciousness in part through a Wilderness experience of limited and distorted views of reality. Even so, as there was extended to them in the midst of their journey, so there is extended to us the invitation to burrow with our spirit in the Light of Christ (see Moroni 7:19), to "receive light and intelligence," to find out who we are (see

---

4. *JD* 2:302–3.

5. This is a more literal translation of Romans 11:32, which says in the KJV, *"For God hath concluded them all in unbelief, that he might have mercy upon all,"* where the word for *concluded* means shut up or imprisoned.

John 10:34, *"Is it not written in your law ... Ye are gods?"),* and to penetrate the veils of illusion drawn before us (see Ether 4:15). And the reason for this struggle is that the very search for the Truth behind the veils is a sanctifying and consciousness-expanding journey.

The poet William Blake describes Man's faulty sense of reality: "If the doors of perception were cleansed every thing would appear to man as it is, infinite. For man has closed himself up, till he sees all things through narrow chinks of his cavern."[6] Nevertheless, the Truth leaks through, and the fretful Seeker knows that this fallen world is not all there is; his searches make him aware of glories that lie just beyond his perception, and his restiveness drives him on to penetrate the veil. He often finds the path obscure, fraught with conundrums, and the opposition to his transformation insuperable. Life can seem a hopeless tangle.

The scriptures abundantly describe the Seeker's felt experience in his fall from bliss in such words as "lost" and "fallen" (1 Nephi 10:6); "awful state of blindness" (1 Nephi 13:32); "nothingness ... worthless and fallen state" (Mosiah 4:5); "awful reality" (2 Nephi 9:47); "deep sleep" (2 Nephi 1:13); uncomprehending "darkness" (D&C 88:49), bitter taste (see Moses 6:55), "carnal, sensual, and devilish," "shut out from the presence of God" (Moses 6:49). These conditions are not amenable to simple remedies.

Hugh Nibley points out the ultimate futility of earthly solutions for fallen Man's distress: "Psychotherapy can cure you of the neurotic lies you live by to block out the real horror of your condition—we are all hiding in the broom closet. Freud said he could liberate you from that but only to face a worse

---

6. From *The Marriage of Heaven and Hell,* an illuminated book by William Blake (1757–1827).

horror—your actual condition."[7] So a veil has been mercifully drawn, not only to subject us to certain experiences, but also to keep us from a thorough awareness of our situation, which awareness would be unbearable were we able to perceive the full contrast. What great submission in humility and trust is required of us! (see Mosiah 3:19).

But even though God provided for the narrower consciousness for undertaking the journey in this world, He provided also the means for liberating this consciousness: *"I give unto men weakness that they may be humble; ... if they humble themselves before me, and have faith in me, then will I make weak things become strong unto them"* (Ether 12:27). The prophet Joseph writes of God's promise that His covenant people would not have to remain in weakness: "He will endow you with power, wisdom, might and intelligence, and every qualification necessary; while your minds will expand wider and wider, until you can circumscribe the earth and the heavens, reach forth into eternity, and contemplate the mighty acts of Jehovah in all their variety and glory."[8]

Man's Plan of Happiness, then, includes a two-part experience; to descend below all things in weakness that he might rise above all. How important then to understand the true nature of this life and the way in which the illusion it presents may be transcended.

Impact of Premortal Experience on the Mind

The shaping of Man's mind begins before this mortal probation. He brings with him certain dispositions. He arrives, for

---

7. *Brother Brigham Challenges the Saints*, vol. 13 of *The Collected Works of Hugh Nibley*, ed. Don E. Norton and Shirley S. Ricks (Salt Lake City: Deseret Book and FARMS, 1994), 396–97.

8. *TPJS*, 163.

example, with a heightened consciousness toward that which will comprise his earthly plan. This heightened awareness in specific areas acts as a steering mechanism. A child destined to play the violin will be drawn to everything about violins but may tend to avoid sports. The girl with intellectual gifts may be drawn to opportunities to use her mind at the expense of, say, homemaking skills. So the strengths and gifts he comes with will necessarily cause him to develop consciousness in those areas, but also predispose him to be weak in others. None of us gets the whole pie in this life, only a slice or two. Therefore, we can be philosophical about some of our weaknesses, and others', realizing that it just wasn't given us to be strong in some areas, in order that we would focus on other particular skills during our earth life. Since we can't do everything, our lives are necessarily full of both accomplishment and neglect.

Man brings premortal baggage and is shapeable by environment and nurturing only to a degree. Of course, attentive parents can nurture many aspects of a child's potential and teach many skills. But each person comes with plans and covenants and predispositions already in place. As nurturing efforts go forward, parents and teachers soon reach that core of the premortal spirit that will not respond to the most skillful shaping efforts. This girl is going to play basketball no matter how many dolls we give her. It is peaceful wisdom to realize the formative power of premortal events and to recognize the validity of many different attributes, strengths and weakness in the people who cross our path, as they work out their own salvation. Since we can never be sure what the Lord is doing with a person, it is our opportunity to consider staying out of the way.

However, in each of us, no matter our premortal endowment, there remains a good deal of developable consciousness and Christness. These powers develop largely according to our relationship with Truth.

Each person brings the results of some of the choices he made in the world before. He arrives here, in his infant state, innocent before God—his slate wiped clean (see D&C 93:38), but, nevertheless, also with certain tendencies. His choices in the premortal world had a shaping influence on his intelligence there and resulted in a particular relationship to Truth. To paraphrase the scripture, the intelligence that we attained to in the previous life through our diligence and obedience, we have brought with us to this life (see D&C 130:18). This thrust of our premortal spirit still shapes to some degree how we will respond to Truth as it is presented to us here. Since Truth always demands something of us, we make choices as to whether we will abandon our current practice in favor of the Truth or whether we will reshape reality to suit us. Our choices in every sphere tend either to reveal or conceal things as they really are.

Components and Characteristics of the Natural Mind

The apostle Paul writes that we see the world as reflected in a distorted mirror ("through a glass, darkly" [1 Corinthians 13:12]). Francis Bacon uses the same analogy: "All perceptions as well of the sense as of the mind are according to the measure of the individual and not according to the measure of the universe. And the human understanding is like a false mirror, which, receiving rays irregularly distorts and discolors the nature of things by mingling its own nature with it."[9] This carnal mirror causes Man much trouble in this world but can also serve as a potent instrument of his education.

To define the term, *carnal* comes from the Latin and simply means "of the flesh or of the body"; that is, it is the Carnal or Natural Mind that develops as one experiences life in a physical body. This mind is laid over and veils the Spiritual, disabling

---

9. *Novum Organum* (1620), Book 1, Aphorism 41.

many of the functions of the Spiritual Mind. For example, this Natural Mind does not process miracles or perceive realms beyond its own and is not inclined to spiritual things. Brigham Young describes this mind's affinities:

> How difficult it is to teach the natural man, who comprehends nothing more than that which he sees with the natural eye! ... Talk to him about angels, heavens, God, immortality, and eternal lives, and it is like sounding brass, or a tinkling cymbal to his ears; it has no music to him; there is nothing in it that charms his senses, soothes his feelings, attracts his attention, or engages his affections, in the least.[10]

This mind wants empirical proof, contending, as Korihor did, that *"ye cannot know of things which ye do not see"* (Alma 30:15), but even with proof may go into denial in self-protection against uncomfortable truth: *"The natural man receiveth not the things of the Spirit of God: for they are foolishness unto him: neither can he know them, because they are spiritually discerned"* (1 Corinthians 2:14). Paul identifies some of the characteristics of the Carnal Mind: *"For ye are yet carnal: for whereas there is among you envying, and strife, and divisions, are ye not carnal and walk as men?"* (1 Corinthians 3:3).

The Carnal Mind develops as an alternative to the mind and will of God. When in the early stages of Man's existence on the earth Satan came among men to recruit them to his worship, they accepted his lies and loved him more than God: *"And men began from that time forth to be carnal, sensual, and devilish"* (Moses 5:13). It was departing from the mind of God that created the thought-world of the Natural Mind and fostered its development. These men made a conscious

---

10. *Discourses of Brigham Young*, ed. John A. Widstoe (Salt Lake City: Deseret Book, 1941), 260.

decision. We, on the other hand, must become conscious of the diabolical lies we accept.

The Natural Mind necessarily reflects Man's telestial environment, which means that it tends to run in paths of negativity, such as the strife, envy, and division that Paul mentions. Unchecked, it produces various degrees of misery as this mind attaches to anxious or self-seeking thoughts. In fact, in the ongoing experience of the Natural Man there flows an underlying irritation and even suffering which he often tries to keep from his awareness through various attempts at escape. This undercurrent in his mind blocks his perception of the Infinite, disrupts his sense of wellbeing, and often causes him to treat others roughly. But the important thing to remember is that the Natural Man deals in illusions that do not represent reality nor the truth of his being.

We see then that this Natural Mind will run Man rather than serve him as his tool if he does not understand its limited spiritual scope and potential. He can begin to subject the Natural Mind to his spiritual purposes through discerning the characteristics of the two minds. Here are a few instructive examples of scriptural references to these two minds and their respective content:

1. *Remember, to be carnally-minded is death, and to be spiritually minded is life eternal.* (2 Nephi 9:39)

2. *But now mine own eyes have beheld God; but not my natural, but my spiritual eyes, for my natural eyes could not have beheld.* (Moses 1:11)

3. *And I would not that ye think that I know of myself—not of the temporal but of the spiritual [mind], not of the carnal mind, but of God.* (Alma 36:4)

4. *You do not remember the Lord your God; ... your hearts ... do swell with great pride, unto boasting, and unto great swelling,*

envyings, strifes, malice, persecutions, and murders, and all man-
ner of iniquities. (Helaman 13:22)

5. It is your privilege, and a promise I give unto you ... that
inasmuch as you strip yourselves from jealousies and fears, and
humble yourselves before me, for ye are not sufficiently humble, the
veil shall be rent and you shall see me and know that I am—not
with the carnal neither natural mind, but with the spiritual. For
no man has seen God at any time in the flesh, except quickened by
the Spirit of God. Neither can any natural man abide the presence
of God, neither after the carnal mind. Ye are not able to abide the
presence of God now, neither the ministering of angels; wherefore,
continue in patience until ye are perfected. (D&C 67:10–13)

We learn from the foregoing scriptures that living in the
easy drift of the Natural Mind promotes spiritual death with
this mind's jealousy, fear, and pride; but, on the other hand,
by stripping oneself of the characteristics of the Natural Mind,
and quickened by the Spirit, the spiritual eyes begin to open
and a new consciousness begins to operate.

Of course the Light of Christ is the very foundation of the
Natural Man's living and breathing and functions as a continual
monitor of right and wrong in his soul. Nevertheless, without a
conscious awareness of the Light of Christ or the Spirit, or an
understanding of his choice between the two minds, Man will
necessarily live in his Natural Mind, tainting his experience
with its distortions.

In studying the Natural Mind, we soon see that our
thoughts, emotions, attitudes, and behavior profoundly affect
our ability to perceive spiritual things. In order to unveil the
Spiritual Mind, it becomes necessary to discern the nature of
thought and feeling so as to bring sharply to our realization
that we can choose by which mind we will experience life.

The Nature of Thought

If we were to diagram the process of the arising of a thought, we would see that the most basic interaction between Man's mind and his outer world begins with awareness or consciousness—a pre-thought state. As he becomes *aware* of life through his senses, he begins to process and *interpret* that which he perceives; his interpretations form themselves into *thoughts*; his thoughts create various kinds of *emotion* or *feeling*. These are stored in the mind; hence, it is not necessarily the true reality of things that is stored in the mind, but the interpretations he has made. So we see that the Natural Mind is full, not necessarily of true perceptions, but of the things it has selectively perceived and interpreted, based both on seen and unseen influences.

This process that begins with awareness and ends with interpretation and emotion is a rapid and largely unconscious process, influenced by the thoughts, emotions, and interpretations already accumulated. In this way Man builds up the database of his personal programming. The mind in itself is a neutral tool—it just receives information through various avenues, colors it according to our interpretations, relegates things to the conscious or unconscious mind, and at the same time, eliminates much more data from our consciousness than we are aware of. This eliminative function keeps us from being overwhelmed by too many stimuli, but also keeps us from seeing the full reality around us. With a different filtering system, we might be able to see through our flawed perceptions and behold the Infinite.[11]

---

11. The reader could pursue this idea through Aldous Huxley's *Doors to Perception* (New York: Harper & Row, 1963), 22; he cites Henri Bergson: "The function of the brain and nervous system and sense organs are in the main eliminative and not productive. Each person is at each moment capable of remembering all that has ever happened to him and of

Man's primeval mind, his pure consciousness, has been likened to the infinite blue sky, and the thoughts that enter his mind have been likened to the clouds that cross the sky. This analogy suggests that Man's pure consciousness, with holy spirit as its essence, is infinite and connected to eternity, whereas thoughts are only transitory mental activity. But not discerning the nature of thought, most of us attach to these passing cloud-thoughts as though they had an inherent reality. Instead of letting them go their way, we are not only distracted by the ceaseless, random, mental activity, but also controlled by their often negative content. We are unaware that as we assimilate them, they veil the larger mind. From where do all these impulses and thoughts come? Neither Science nor Revelation has fully resolved that question, but we can explore some sources.

A Body of Thoughts

Man is not alone with his mind. He lives and moves in the midst of many unseen influences, forces, and beings which can and do distort his perception. Thoughts from various influences circulate spirit-like, seeking access to the undiscerning and unguarded mind. The Lord instructs us again and again as to what sorts of things must go around in our minds, and He does that because thought so powerfully shapes our inner and outer reality. Emotion itself is created, as we have seen, by what we choose to think, by the interpretations we place on ourselves,

---

perceiving everything that is happening everywhere in the universe. The function of the brain and nervous system is to protect us from being overwhelmed and confused by this mass of largely useless and irrelevant knowledge, by shutting out most of what we should otherwise perceive or remember at any moment, and leaving only that very small and special selection which is likely to be practically useful." Huxley calls each of us a "Mind at Large," hindered in our accessing all knowledge by the reducing valve of the biologic mind.

people, and events. We have likely thought on occasion that we could blame circumstances for our emotions, but in reality the circumstances only provoke what is already inside, a mindset that tends either to peace or to turmoil.

Scripture often describes thought as coming *into* the mind as though from somewhere outside us. The Lord puts thoughts into His servants' minds, as He did with Samuel (see Helaman 13:4–5). But often thoughts enter from a dark source, as seen in these three passages (my emphasis):

1. *Thus saith the Lord...I know the things that **come into your mind,** every one of them.* (Ezekiel 11:5)

2. *Thus saith the Lord God; It shall also come to pass, that at the same time shall things **come into thy mind,** and thou shalt **think an evil thought.*** (Ezekiel 38:10)

3. *Suffer none of these things to **enter into your heart.*** (3 Nephi 12:29)

We are likely not aware of thoughts entering from outside ourself or that they shape our interpretations of events or other people.

Let us explore the idea that there was a body of disturbing thoughts or mental impulses, both subtle and overt, that attached itself to the fallen world and began to circulate as Adam and Eve walked out of the Garden, and that these have been going around in the telestial world ever since. After all, as the Preacher observes, there is really *"no new thing under the sun,"* but just a recycling (see Ecclesiastes 1:9–10). We see in the scriptures, as in history, the endless cycles of the quest for power and gain, generation after generation—the same old thoughts reappearing in different people throughout the earth's history, the brutal and the noble, the sacred and profane. Nothing really changes in this dimension; they just keep coming around. These are the fuel for the Natural Mind.

The reason for the recycling of the same thoughts is to ensure that each person who comes to earth gets to confront in his laboratory the same elements as everyone before him; each person gets a well-rounded exposure to them. That is to say, there is a set curriculum in order that we may each be tempted "at all points," as was our Savior, He being the prototype for us: *"For we have not an high priest which cannot be touched with the feeling of our infirmities; but was in all points tempted like as we are, yet without sin"* (Hebrews 4:15).

This body of thoughts belongs to what we might call the world-mind, which is just the Natural Mind at large. These mists of darkness that drift across our mental paths play mostly on our fear, which generates pride, coveting, criticism, depression, selfishness, hatred, power ploys, and mental disturbance in general. These world-mind thoughts, beliefs, and attitudes, are aggressive. Sometimes they seem to be thinking *us* more than we are thinking *them*. Without being conscious of these thoughts as visitors to our inner space, we attach to them as though they were ours, as though they necessarily represent reality. Undiscerning, we subscribe to them, and they become our reality. One reason we attach to them is that, as they present themselves, we unconsciously personalize them, so they *seem* to be a true reflection of our circumstances. Therefore, our minds are mixed with many sorrow-producing thoughts, simply because we do not yet discern their nature. One teacher of meditation and spiritual insight writes on thoughts as visitors and what happens when we do not perceive their true nature:

> We know directly from our own experience that when certain states arise strongly within us, they have a tormenting quality—states like anger, fear, guilt, and greed. When they knock at the door and we invite them in, we lose touch with the fundamentally pure nature of our mind, and then we suffer. By not

identifying with these forces, we learn that these defilements or torments are only visitors. These forces are adventitious, not inherent. They do not reflect who we really are.[12]

They do not reflect reality or who we really are, yet they run our lives. We may indeed entertain a lot of disturbance in our minds since disturbance is characteristic of the Natural Man, and we all get to be a Natural Man; but this mental/spiritual disturbance affects our physical wellbeing, our behavior toward ourselves, our treatment of others, and our feelings toward the Lord.

James Allen, author of the classic *As a Man Thinketh*, writes in the same vein as millennia of wise men have written on the consequences of negative thought:

> Suffering is always the effect of wrong thoughts in some direction. It is an indication that the individual is out of harmony with himself, with the law of his being. The circumstances which a man encounters with suffering are the result of his own mental inharmony. Man has but to right himself to find the universe is righted. Let a man radically alter his thoughts and he will be astonished at the rapid transformation it will effect on the material conditions of his life.[13]

Primary Illusion of the Natural Mind

One of the great and elusive secrets of the mortal probation, the one that has the power to remove the most veils, yet the one that is hardest to accept and practice, is that selfless love has the greatest power to expand our consciousness, synchronizing us, as it does, with the energy of the Universe; and that the preoccupation with our own agenda creates the great majority of our

---

12. Sharon Salzberg, *Lovingkindness* (Boston: Shambhala, 1997), 23.
13. *As a Man Thinketh* (Camarillo: DeVorss & Company, 1979), 117.

stress and spiritual stagnation. The mind absorbed in its own ego interests is "driven by the wind and tossed," unstable and confused. The Natural Mind is largely concerned with seeking its own (see Moroni 7:45) in its efforts to alleviate the distress of the fallen condition.

We can readily recognize that nearly every negative thought and emotion arises from our anxiety over what will happen to "me." As a result, our thought processes vacillate among various negative options. A young Tibetan monk, Sakyong Mipham, writes with acute perception:

> Our mind is constantly volleying between irritation and desire, jealousy and pride. We are unhappy with who we are, and we are trying to destroy our own suffering.... As we indulge in this negativity, our mind becomes thick with contamination which manifests stress, lack of peace, fueled by fear of not knowing what will happen to "me." Our mind becomes very speedy; bewilderment rules.[14]

The "contamination" he refers to is what Tibetan philosophy calls *drip*. He explains that *drip* is like a dark, heavy goo that thickens our mind; it accumulates through cultivating negativity, and then life seems to get dark and difficult. This contaminated mental state causes us to engage in "nonvirtue," that is, unkind acts against ourselves and others—and then the *drip* gets thicker.

It is because of our primeval nature that nonvirtue creates this *drip*: the behaviors that cause *drip* conflict with the shimmering virtues that form the essence of our spirit, and our soul

---

14. Mipham, *Ruling Your World* (New York: Random House, 2006), 13. Sakyong, a high lama in Tibetan Buddhism raised in the U.S., writes on the training of the mind in which stability is created through meditation and lovingkindness. He has understood the Wilderness Mind.

reacts with distress. Thus we engage in an endless cycle of suffering, not knowing that it is all happening only in our own mind because of our focus on the demands and illusions of our Natural Man. This mental contamination comes about through lack of spiritual knowledge with its resulting gaps in awareness and discernment. And we can see that nearly all those around us are dealing with the same collection of thoughts and the same recurring contamination—until they see through them.

On reflection, we see that our gravest problem does not lie in our life circumstances, but in our lack of a truer perception of reality, a larger frame of reference, which could liberate our mind from self-will and self-absorption. Much spiritual change can come simply as we become aware of the truth that Natural Mind thoughts are illusory. So as we notice how the Natural Mind works, we can begin to make different choices. Instead of insisting on being right, or making demands of others, or drooping in a bad mood, or indulging in self-pity, or feeling wronged, or fearing that we are not liked, we can see the insubstantial nature of these thoughts, note how they make us feel, and begin a process of inquiry.

Inquiry has to do first with becoming aware of what is coming and going in the mind. It assumes that most disturbing thoughts carry some sort of illusion, some distortion of reality. Some thoughts seem to have teeth and claws. But setting aside a human tendency to be gripped by fearful or miserable thoughts, we can quietly, deliberately, and deeply entertain the possibility of the *opposite* of what the thought is tempting us to believe. What might be a truer way of looking at this situation? We consider an alternative, perhaps a complete turn-around of the thought. We are testing whether the disturbing thought is true and loosening its grip by allowing the mind to *experience* a possibly truer option. How would I feel if I didn't believe that thought? What if I were *unable* to think that thought—

then who would I be?[15] This inquiry allows the Spiritual Mind to gain ascendancy. There may, in fact, come a time when we decide that there are certain thoughts that we will no longer entertain.

Sometimes inquiry produces realizations about ourselves that call us to repentance and provide liberation if we will make necessary corrections. If we do not make corrections, we will not escape the convolutions of the Natural Mind. Our old behaviors will anchor our perception to the telestial world.

As our discernment between Natural and Spiritual sharpens, we notice finer shades of negativity, as perhaps in conversation—maybe just the wisp of a cloud casting a shadow. We begin to step out of our Natural Mind and say, "Oh, that's how my Natural Mind feels."

Catching our Natural Man in the very act requires some kindness and patience since we usually let go of the old ways only a little at a time. The Natural Man is serving us as a live-in teacher. It is appropriate to be grateful and correct gently. Just becoming aware can lessen the power of the negative feelings, as insight and release often go together.

Two spiritual teachers offer two additional ways of dealing with painful thoughts. Deepak Chopra says, "Watch this wave of feeling travel away from you—watch it grow fainter and fainter. Breathe.... Cross the invisible boundary between ego and the real self where the ego's needs begin to lose their grip. If you follow any emotion far enough, it will end in silence."[16] With such an exercise we create distance between the disturbing thought and the truer mind, thereby lessening the thought's impact. Eckhart Tolle suggests that when somebody

15. See Byron Katie's work on inquiry, *Loving What Is* (New York: Random House, 2003).

16. *Book of Secrets: Unlocking the Hidden Dimensions of Your Life* (Worcester: Harmony, 2004), 63.

LIGHT IN THE WILDERNESS

says something to you that is rude or designed to hurt, "instead of going into unconscious reaction and negativity, such as attack, defense, or withdrawal, you let it pass right through you" as though you were transparent, so that it no longer hits a solid "wall" inside you. That does not mean of course that you don't tell "that person that his or her behavior is unacceptable, if that is what you choose to do. But that person no longer has the power to control your inner state. You are then in your power—not in someone else's."[17]

As we experiment to find what works for us personally, we find more power to choose: "I want this experience, but not that"—and change occurs through awareness and choice.

We learn that we are either in our Natural Mind with its attendant consequences, or we are in our Spiritual Mind, enjoying the larger reality of love and faith. We receive wages and identity according to the voice we listen to (see Alma 5:41–42). As we can testify, the felt experience in the one mind is radically different from the other. Each mind develops different dynamics and, therefore, a different reality and perception.

The Holy Ghost Rescues and Redeems Man's Mind

Because of Man's limited power to untangle himself on his own, the Lord sends the Holy Ghost to rescue and redeem Man's mind from the distortions of the Fall. But for this to happen, Man has to know how this Spirit works.

In 1996, in a BYU devotional, Elder F. Enzio Busche spoke on the way in which thoughts and behavior either conceal or reveal the operations of the Spirit. He observed that many times in our life, even though we have received the gift of the Holy Ghost, these gifts of the Spirit rest dormant in us; often

17. *Practicing the Power of Now* (Novato, California: New World Library), 110.

84

we are not even aware of their existence because we do not fully understand the workings of the Spirit. Being unaware of the powerful gift that we have, we cannot activate its power. He explained that the Spirit, being a divine entity, is polite, modest, responsible, and loving and cannot be with us when we are not manifesting those qualities. He listed several states of mind in which we may know that we are not under the influence of the Spirit: grouchy, unhappy, slothful, sloppy, irresponsible, or light-minded about sacred things. Many subtle things can cause us to lose the Spirit, but we can learn how to regain this power of happiness and peace. He advised that we beware of frustration, hurt feelings, grumblings, fear, judgment and condemnation of another, negative thinking, rush and haste and uncontrolled words—all functions of the Natural Mind. We are not in a state of awakening with this behavior and cannot be successful spiritually until we learn how to behave or what to do so that the Spirit will endow us with power. He said:

> None of us has enough wisdom, enough intelligence, enough knowledge, enough skills, or enough courage, by ourselves, to master our lives and even to succeed in life unless we learn what it means to surrender ourselves into the arms of the Lord and be filled with the Spirit.... We ... should not be satisfied to be one single moment of our waking hours without the insightful, powerful influence of the Spirit.[18]

He points out that we lose the Spirit because we never thoroughly intended to have it. But having discovered the emotional tangles that the Natural Mind creates, a person can make the decision to lead a consciously spiritual life. Awareness and intention are potent in penetrating to the Spiritual Mind. With

18. "Unleashing the Dormant Spirit," *Brigham Young University Speeches of the Year 1995–96* (Provo, Utah: BYU Publications and Graphics, 1996), 223.

that intention, one can be caught up in wonderful changes beyond his own power.

Elder Busche mentions haste and uncontrolled words; he teaches that divine light develops in places of peace and quiet. It is helpful to know that the Spiritual Mind functions out of a deep quiet and is more still and perceptive, more centered, approaching finally a state of pure consciousness. It seeks the simplicity of fewer thoughts, having set its self-will aside, and perceives things as they are more directly.

This may, in fact, be the Lord's own way, as He says, *"For my thoughts are not your thoughts, neither are your ways my ways, saith the Lord. For as the heavens are higher than the earth, so are my ways higher than your ways, and my thoughts than your thoughts"* (Isaiah 55:8–9). Since the Lord's perception is perfect and His interpretations are aligned with things as they really are, perhaps He remains more in a state of perfect consciousness than in a state of formed thoughts—He simply perceives things directly as they truly are in His "eternal Now."[19] That understanding of the Lord's mind might help us to know more about how to use our own.

As the veils come off and the infinite in Man's soul is uncovered, there is a gradual, or sometimes an instantaneous, spiritual response. Alma describes the gradual rising of the discernible Light in the soul being visited by the Holy Spirit over an extended time:

> *Your understanding doth begin to be enlightened, and your mind doth begin to expand. O then, is not this real? I say unto you, Yea, because it is light; and whatsoever is light, is good, because it is discernible.... If ye will nourish the word ... by your faith with great diligence, and with patience ... ye shall pluck the fruit thereof, which is most precious ... sweet above all that is sweet ... white ... pure; and*

---

19. *TPJS*, 220.

ye shall feast upon this fruit even until ye are filled. (Alma 32:34–35, 41–42)

The Lamanite King under Ammon's watchcare experienced a more dramatic rending of the veil:

> *Ammon... knew that the dark veil of unbelief was being cast away from [the king's] mind, and the light which did light up his mind, which was the light of the glory of God, which was a marvelous light of his goodness—yea, this light had infused such joy into his soul, the cloud of darkness having been dispelled, and... the light of everlasting life was lit up in his soul, yea, he knew that this had overcome his natural frame, and he was carried away in God.* (Alma 19:6)

The Natural Man draws unbelief across his spiritual eyes. He does this to keep himself from experiencing God and the joy of his own being, even to hide himself from himself and from God, but he pays a price: *"Your minds in times past have been darkened because of unbelief, and because you have treated lightly the things which you have received"* (D&C 84:54).

The veils can be withdrawn and the mind can be opened to a different experience. When King Benjamin's people opened their ears, their hearts, and their minds *"that the mysteries of God"* be *"unfolded to their view"* (Mosiah 2:9), they experienced (even though already a commandment-keeping people) a sudden infusion of light and joy so beyond any of their previous experience, that they could not speak:

> *The Spirit of the Lord came upon them, and they were filled with joy, having received a remission of their sins, and having peace of conscience, because of the exceeding faith which they had in Jesus Christ.... [Benjamin explains:] He has poured out his Spirit upon*

you, and has caused that your hearts should be filled with joy, and has caused that your mouths should be stopped that ye could not find utterance, so exceedingly great was your joy. (Mosiah 4:3, 20)

They testified that they could see beyond the limitations of the Natural Mind to *"great views of that which is to come,"* so that they could *"prophesy of all things"* (Mosiah 5:3). They had been blessed to rend the veil of unbelief and to open to the vastness of the Spiritual Mind.

If the ego-mind took shape as it was diverted from the mind and will of the Lord, and learned to defend itself for doing this, we realize that ceasing *"to excuse yourself in the least point because of your sins"* (Alma 42:30) and returning our mental and emotional faculties to Him will begin to disperse the inner darkness. And so it is that the Lord intends a radical revision of our thought-system, as, for example, in this scripture: *"If your eye be single to my glory, your whole bodies shall be filled with light, and there shall be no darkness in you; and that body which is filled with light comprehendeth all things. Therefore, sanctify yourselves that your minds become single to God.... Cast away your idle thoughts"* (D&C 88:67, 68, 69) and, *"Let virtue garnish thy thoughts unceasingly"* (D&C 121:45). With the casting away of the Natural-Mind thoughts and the cultivation of virtue in the mind, revelation begins to flow, and not only revelation, but a sense of Presence which gently offers to live our life with us.

The Lord reveals what it is that He is doing in our Wilderness:

> *Behold, that which you hear is as the voice of one crying in the wilderness—in the wilderness, because you cannot see him—my voice, because my voice is Spirit; my Spirit is truth; truth abideth and hath no end; and if it be in you it shall abound.* (D&C 88:66)

We have seen here that the Natural Mind is nothing more than a delusional thought-system, based on fear, on felt vulnerability, on perceived aloneness, scarcity, and limitation. It is preoccupied with getting what it thinks it needs to be happy, not only physical gratification and material things, but also emotional reinforcements of approval, praise, appreciation, and love, and, as a result, is unsure of its own worth, and does not entirely like itself. It hasn't yet realized that its orientation isn't working. But let us not be discouraged as we contemplate our personal Natural Man. Let us be reminded that our spirit and our foreordinations are far greater than our mortal overlay.[20] Nevertheless, increasing our awareness of the distinctions between the two minds provides us with clearer choices as to how we might live, helps us to see the difference between Isaiah's sparks of the Natural Mind and that blaze available in the Lord Jesus Christ (see Isaiah 50:11).

In the following chapters we will consider additional means by which we can escape the Natural Mind's insulation and confusion.

---

20. "Mortal overlay" is Allen Bergin's term in P. Scott Richards and Allen E. Bergin, *A Spiritual Strategy for Counseling and Psychotherapy* (Washington, D.C.: American Psychological Association, 1997), 101.

CHAPTER FIVE

THE LAW OF THE SPIRIT:
THE KEY TO AWAKENING THE SPIRITUAL MIND

There is an answer to the passionate longings of the heart for fullness, and I knew it, and the answer is this: Live in all things outside yourself by love, and you will have joy. That is the life of God; it ought to be our life. In him it is accomplished and perfect; but in all created things it is a lesson learned slowly and through difficulty.

Robert Browning[1]

❧

And charity ... seeketh not her own.

Moroni 7:45

❧

In studying the Natural Mind, we soon realize that if we are ignorant of the principle of spiritual energy in mind and body, if we act as though we can use our mind in whatever way we want, our spiritual ignorance will lead us into confusion,

---

1. Quoted in *Stepping Stones to an Abundant Life*, comp. Llewelyn R. McKay (Salt Lake City: Deseret Book, 1971), 119.

bewilderment, and suffering; the reason is that the body and spirit react to every mental impulse and that there are laws that govern the effect of thought and action in the soul.

In the early stages of spiritual development, we are easily seduced by the low-energy thought-world of the Natural Man. It comes through our magazines, our TV, our movies—it saturates our environment. If we entertain enough of the world-mind by passively absorbing it from our environment, we will have limited powers of discernment, fragile faith in Jesus Christ, and weak spiritual energies to nourish us on our journey. We find that the world-mind continually leads us to self-absorption with its irritation, anxiety, and self-seeking. Therefore, we see the necessity of distinguishing between the energy of the world-mind or Natural Mind and that of the Spiritual Mind—and to choose according to what we really want.

We already know that with certain types of thoughts, toxic conditions arise in the soul; that is, certain types of thoughts leave undesirable emotional and physical residues in the mind and body. Sometimes we can actually feel the consequences in our bodies of our fear or our anger or our anxious self-promotion. Zeezrom is a good example of someone whose quest for power and gain, whose lies and spiritual resistance, produced a guilt and fear so intense that he was brought low with a burning fever and an "exceedingly sore" mind (see Alma 15:1–5). We have perhaps already seen that living with our own personal-gain agenda produces fear and stress and a depletion of life-force energy, increasing that dark "drip" which is the opposite of the intelligence, deftness, spiritual gifts, stability, and higher consciousness in the Spiritual Mind.

A Different Energy

Here is the law of the spirit, that secret principle hidden from the Natural Mind:

The law of the spirit is selflessness, whereas that of the body is selfishness.... The God-Man does not use the body as an end in itself, but as a vehicle for manifesting the spirit [which is] unselfish love, and he fills his body... with the highest energies.[2]

We learn that the highest spiritual energies have to do with unselfish love. As we become more adept in the proper use of spiritual energies, we distinguish that which is nourishing from that which is toxic:

When [one's] acts are always motivated by impersonal, unselfish love... [the] mind will be peaceful, balanced, and healthy.... Thoughts... are all powerful and forge our fate for better or worse.... With the aid of good and positive thoughts we can attract good and desirable conditions, whereas negative, bad thoughts, bad feelings, propel us toward evil, misery and sickness.... Never allow a grudge, hate, contempt, greed, jealousy or other base instinct to touch your mind. Such emotions set up dangerous currents, poison mind and body, and the result is sickness. Discipline your emotions; be happy and do not allow external circumstances to influence you! Always be conscious of the fact that in the sky of your mind, you are the sun!... The secret of happiness depends on the degree to which we dominate our mind and our body. Keep your eyes constantly on mental liberation [from negative thought].... I must manifest the highest, I cannot be satisfied with less.[3]

This wisdom takes a closer look at the sorts of energy that pass through our mind and body. Our toxic thoughts are founded in pure illusion; we can let them drift away. Meanwhile, we

2. Selvarajan Yesudian and Elisabeth Haich, *Yoga and Health* (New York: Perennial Library, 1972), 15.

3. *Ibid.*, 35, 164, 171.

cultivate emotions that resonate with the energies of holy spirit flowing in our deepest being, emotions like helpfulness and gratitude that lead us to manifest the highest in all situations. Through the discipline of a spiritual practice we achieve mental, emotional, and spiritual liberation, changing the lives of those around us too, creating a different radiation for them to respond to. How this will nourish us and others too!

We each inhabit a world of both nourishing and destructive energies, but each of us also represents an individual energy system. The quality of our life experience depends not so much on the energy outside as on what energies occupy our inner space. We are the guardians of our mind. That we alone can be ultimately responsible for this energy is the message of millennia of wisdom.

Part of our godly development involves working to gain that discernment that will free us into entire responsibility for our own state of mind and our own happiness. We can develop a keen awareness as negative energy tries to poison our well; we want to do that because what we do, we do to ourselves—100% of the time. In that way, we learn that things are the opposite of the way they appear; for example, giving is receiving and withholding love precludes its experience. The spiritual law of restoration teaches:

> Remember... whosoever doeth iniquity, doeth it unto himself; for behold, ye are free... to act for yourselves.... Ye can do good and be restored unto that which is good... or... evil, and have that which is evil restored unto you. (Helaman 14:30–31)

How could it be any other way? That God makes us responsible for what we think (because that is the level at which we have the most power to choose) is an acknowledgment of our divine creative power. Our thoughts create internal and external energies: *"If ye do not watch yourselves, and your thoughts, and your words, and your deeds...ye must perish. And now, O man, remember, and perish not"* (Mosiah 4:30). We realize that it is not so much that God punishes us for unloving thoughts, but that by these thoughts we create hell for ourselves and others.

We see that the principle of restoration is indeed a principle of creation, because what we do must return to us in some form. What we do, that is, our thoughts, our speech, our actions, these create what our present and future must hold: *"For that which ye do send out shall return unto you again, and be restored"* (Alma 41:15)—and at some level that happens immediately, for good or ill (see Mosiah 2:24; Alma 34:31). So we become increasingly wise as we go through life creating the conditions in which joy can flourish or darkness reign. Indeed, what if there are no idle thoughts? Perhaps the mind never loses its creative power, moment to moment, planting the seeds that must ultimately flower into acts and consequences.

Elder F. Enzio Busche speaks of the power of our choices:

> There is a simple lesson we each have the opportunity to learn in life. It is that in each of us is the potential for two opposing situations. A person can experience feelings of joy that become almost unbearable. Or a person can experience unhappiness to the extent that there seems to be no way out.... Some individuals reach such a state of depression—or become so empty and hollow—that they want this life to come to an end. Both extremes are within our reach. And both extremes *seem* to be based on circumstance. Many who have not come to a state of spiritual awakening, may, in fact, believe that circumstances are the *deciding factor* in happiness.... We alone decide where it is that we stand on the continuum between total frustration and complete fullness of joy.[4]

---

4. *Yearning for the Living God* (Salt Lake City: Deseret Book), 274–76.

Changing Energies through Awareness

With an awareness of our power to choose the experience we want, let us look more closely at the distinction between the two main types of energy: self-absorption and pure love.

Made of the substance of light, truth, and intelligence, as well as the love inherent in that holy substance (see D&C 93:23, 29, 33), we understand that at our deepest center there exists a reservoir of pure, selfless love which flows through each of us like a hidden, underground spring. We are love that does not yet perceive itself. The Natural Man has covered up the well and created a hard shell over the heart—but the love is still there.

Now, this hard shell, or hard heart, has been formed as a protection to keep pain out—but also God. So, at the outset, as we think about change, it must be asked: Is it possible that in our deepest recesses we sense the joy or love or light that forms our being, and that fearing these, we cover them over? Could it be that we are afraid of our own divinity? On introspection, do we find that we act to shut down feelings of joy—that we can't endure them for very long? If that is so, then we must ask, Do I really want to be happier than I am now? If the answer is that we do indeed want a different experience from the one we now have, that we want to experience the height of Man's possibilities, we then must be open to change toward the unknown, since *"it doth not yet appear what we shall be"* (I John 3:2); we must be willing to expand into the fearsome divine, trusting that the Lord knows where to take us. When it is understood, approaching change from Natural to Spiritual can seem like imminent death—which it is.

But with courage, we begin to see through the Natural Man. We soon realize that he has a sturdy sense of identity with his natural self—with his history, his physical and emotional characteristics, his successes, failures, desires, limitations, sins, image, opinions, judgments, even addiction to disturbance—which he protects and defends. It seems to give him a sense of security to have a concrete idea of who he is and to identify strongly with it. But this is a false security, given his imperfect thought processes and his impure heart. He is projecting solidity on something that is really more fluid and will give way in the light of persistent awareness. It will help him to realize that this self-idea is largely a telestial-world fabrication that limits him spiritually. He must relax his grip on "me"; as Paul says, he must *"put off... the old man... and be renewed in the spirit of [his] mind"* (Ephesians 4:22–23).

But this divesting of an old identity is more than just giving up the man of sin. An even greater freedom can come as he also gives up the parts of his "story" that are holding him back. One man said, "One day, I finally realized that I no longer needed a personal history, just like drinking, I gave it up, and that, and only that, has made all the difference."[5] As we loosen the net of beliefs and concepts that keeps our Natural Man intact, our soul begins to swell and our mind begins to expand.

While we consider changing energies, we do not think that we will force ourselves to feel love or to think happy thoughts; we do not have to pretend love. Rather, we find that quiet, neutral place in our mind, our state of simple being, and there we set up our gentle *intentions* to be compassionate to all—even when our expectations are not met; to be helpful, to be patient, to be generous; to not hurt ourselves or others; to befriend our present moments; to feel the inner Presence. This is a very high-energy exercise as we connect with who we really are. We do not have to *make* ourselves feel anything—since that doesn't

---

5. Don Juan Nagual, quoted in Wayne Dyer, *There's a Spiritual Solution to Every Problem* (San Francisco: Harper Paperbooks, 2003), 85.

work anyway. Rather, we take up residence in that part of us whose still waters and quiet goodness are always available and in which our fears melt away. It seems that the feelings take care of themselves as the hardness of the Natural Man's heart gently gives way to a different sort of energy, as he relaxes his grip. Nor do we become doormats; rather, uncluttered by the distortions of "me," we see clearly how to resolve each situation in the most skillful way.

Sakyong Mipham, the Tibetan monk and close student of the ways of the Natural Man, acknowledges that the road out of self-absorption may at first look boring, fearful, and without compensation. He writes about the experience of softening a heart accustomed to self-absorption and unlove. Opening our heart, he says, is like tilling a new garden: "At first it's rough, because the soil needs working and there are plenty of rocks to remove. We feel discouraged. We're so accustomed to putting ourselves first that thinking of others may seem arduous. But over time the soil softens up, and our heart naturally begins to sprout kindness, compassion, and joy. The more we help others, the softer and more fertile our heart becomes."[6] With a vision of how illusory our Natural Man is and how deep the sacred eternal in us is, we begin to see how flexible we are, how fluid, and how capable of taking new directions.

So at first, we may not like the looks of the path to happiness, may not even understand how it can be happiness. After all, even though there are some things about our Natural Man that we don't like, it does represent familiar ground for us. Nevertheless, "if we're using nonvirtue as fuel for living, we're going to feel all the bumps on the road."[7] The Natural Man is his own enemy, because when the law of restoration responds to nonvirtue, more negativity shows up. After a while it seems

6. *Ruling Your World* (New York: Random House, 2006), 115.

7. *Ibid.*, 55.

that there is nothing left to live for. We feel deserted. But the real problem is our mind that has deserted virtue.

But freeing the mind from "me," letting go of the relentless worry about not knowing what will happen to "me," ceasing to "seek our own," letting the "me" become soft, open, pliable, inquisitive, accepting what is, receiving others as they are, nothing to defend, nothing to protect—this is peace and freedom from the contracted Natural Mind with all its stresses. And what this letting go leads to is the faith that Providence will supply our needs to a much greater degree than we might have thought.

But the concept of filling up with love which we focus outside ourself does not imply that we do not care well for ourselves, seeing to our own needs, eating well, looking good. We do these things. But our mind is primarily directed toward a sense of ministry, of life purpose, of looking about to see how to help, how to make a difficult situation better, how to encourage another. Our joy arises not from a list of good deeds we do, but in a deep awareness of God and of the truth of our being and its desire to find expression. In fact, we notice, that the changes happen more easily when our attention is diverted out of ourself to something larger.

Since our new perception is that time is God's and that our life is unfolding in His hands, we might see what He would have us do next, what direction our personal ministry might take. The happiness that comes then is not just a psychological phenomenon but a deep relaxation in a gift of the Spirit that always carries with it the fragrance of eternal life.

Sakyong writes about the importance of practicing to bring about the changes we desire:

> True love is the natural energy of our settled mind, an inexhaustible resource that we must cultivate.... We are meant not to wait for moments of love to randomly arise but to be always

cultivating love like a garden, tilling the soil so that the seed of our love can open, sprout, and break through.... When we practice being in love, we are digging deeper into our jar of virtue, freeing our minds from "me" and plumbing the depths of our being; contemplating love gives us the biggest of minds; the farther our love extends, the bigger our heart grows.[8]

With Sakyong's mention above of "freeing our minds from 'me,'" we are reminded that to empty oneself of the Natural Mind in order to let the greater spirit arise has a divine precedent. In Philippians we read that Jesus, even though a God, *"made himself of no reputation, and took upon him the form of a servant"* (Philippians 2:7). The meaning of the Greek word for *"made himself of no reputation"* is "he emptied himself." In this passage, Paul asks us to let this same mind be in us also (see Philippians 2:5). That is, the Spiritual Mind empties itself of the fears and strivings of the Natural self and humbles itself to the depths, so as to make room for the greater Presence. The person with too much of his Natural Man left in him does not have enough freedom from the stresses of self-centeredness to be available to the loving workings of the Lord.

"Emptiness" is often used in our culture to mean desolate, but that is not the kind of "emptiness" meant here. This kind is empty of inner noise and distress, of judgments and resistance and fear—it is a state of watchful peace. And more than that, the wonderful thing about humility is that when we get to the bottom of it, we find that it is continuous with the Lord's own Presence. To stay at this place as much as possible makes spiritual practice and change go more smoothly and fills life with confidence and serenity. Elder Busche talks about the way in which the Seeker goes about his daily life in order to retain the peaceful motions of the Spirit:

---

8. *Ibid.*, 101, 103.

A disciple of Christ is therefore constantly, even in the midst of all regular activities, striving all day long through silent prayer and contemplation to be in the depth of self-awareness to keep him in the state of meekness and lowliness of heart. It is the prophet Moroni who points out that *"because of meekness and lowliness of heart cometh the visitation of the Holy Ghost, which Comforter filleth with hope and perfect love"* (Moroni 8:26).[9]

For most of us, meekness and lowliness of heart have to be deliberately contemplated.

A Spiritual Practice

Let us think more about a spiritual practice, without which, change is only a fantasy. Something transformative has to be allowed to develop inside, something that can ultimately take us over. We already know that that which is not continually held in the forefront of our mind will be neglected. No matter how much a particular truth compels us, it must be internalized, it must be repeatedly kneaded into the mind, both in quiet time as well as in the active minutes and hours of our day, reviewing, reviewing, practicing within our daily space with the people coming and going through our life—until the principle becomes permanently ours. "Our circle of friends, family, work associates is our treasure, because they provide a container in which we practice virtue."[10] But the heart and mind must be softened up first in a spiritual practice.

What are some of the elements of a spiritual practice? Part of such a practice is learning to let one's mind slow down and experience the richness of the present moment. For many of us, it is so tempting to live in a mind that operates in such

---

9. "Truth Is the Issue," *Ensign*, November 1993, 24.

10. *Ibid.*, 181.

high gear that it does not let itself down enough to experience the subtlety of the spiritual activity in and around us. In the high-gear state, we necessarily live superficially, which is not a state conducive to spiritual change. For most of us, if we do not practice letting the mind down peacefully in a quiet time, we will not be able to do it amidst the busyness of daily life—which is where we need our spiritual presence most. We have to exercise ourselves in quietness.

We think on the word *receive*. The Lord says:

> For strait is the gate, and narrow the way that leadeth unto the exaltation and continuation of the lives, and few there be that find it, because ye receive me not in the world neither do ye know me.
>
> But if ye receive me in the world, then shall ye know me, and shall receive your exaltation; that where I am ye shall be also.
>
> This is eternal lives—to know the only wise and true God, and Jesus Christ, whom he hath sent. I am he. Receive ye, therefore my law. (D&C 132:22)

Until we *receive* Him, we're dealing only in concepts and perfunctory religion. When we're tired enough of theory, we will receive Him. We will simply do it. This direct contact begins in the inner recesses of the soul.

Therefore, in a set-apart, quiet time the mind can be stilled, perhaps just breathing for a bit as thoughts settle down, letting the silent, more subtle energies of one's spirit begin to rise. We invoke a deep calm and look to the Lord. In this practice, we allow ourselves to get down underneath the mental ripples on the surface. As our breathing slows and our thoughts thin out, a phrase can be selected, perhaps a line of scripture, that is full of meaning. We may not even see all the way through it, but we sense that behind the words is a significance that we want to experience. We think on these words; or perhaps we choose an inspiring image or picture, letting it distill on our mind like quiet rain on thirsty ground. We sit with it. Feelings of love and devotion deepen. The Psalmist sings, *"My meditation of him shall be sweet: I will be glad in the Lord"* (Psalm 104:34). Perhaps we begin to see beyond the words or image, and inspired insights and feelings begin to gather, even an intuitive understanding of the way of things. If we are deep enough and quiet enough, we have an experience with these ideas that goes beyond the rational mind, engages our spirit, and begins to set up new movement in our soul.

Getting to a feeling level, through the distilling into every cell of inspired words or images, is more helpful than trying to make changes by struggling only with the rational mind. Feelings permeated with Spirit get to a pre-thought level and carry more power to the source of change. Outworn understandings and habits can begin to drop away. A new awareness can arise. Then with thorough intention, that which once seemed beyond us becomes, in time, our way of being.

The experience we have as we persist with meditation is fragile. So, as we carry our quieter self into the din of daily life, we find ingenious ways to be mindful of and reinforce our meditation. Perhaps we set words to the rhythm of our breath and our walking; maybe we deliberately slow down our interaction with every-day things; perhaps we keep and review a little notebook of inspiring ideas. We are training ourselves before the Lord. Without recurring focus on the Lord's things, divinity will not arise.

The form of meditation described above deals with quieting the mind and contemplating inspiring thoughts and feelings. There are many forms of meditation and many different methods. Some find that the practice of meditation in which one learns to still the mind in such a way that thought entirely ceases and a greater consciousness arises, allows the old negative behaviors to give way to readiness for a more Christlike nature and stronger sense of communion. But whatever method one chooses, meditation for receiving God seems to be an indispensable element in the Seeker's transformation.

About meditation, President David O. McKay observed: "In our worship there are two elements: One is the spiritual communion arising from our own meditation; the other, instruction from others.... Of the two, the more profitable... is meditation.... Meditation is one of the most secret, most sacred doors through which we pass into the presence of the Lord."[11] Meditation can take us past the Natural Mind into the realm of spirit. The Seeker will find the method that is right for him or her.

Another benefit of the consistent practice of meditation is that it can make us more aware through our feelings of subtle influences. Becoming more discerning of feelings can sensitize us to the voice of the Spirit because feelings are the avenue of spiritual experience and perception. Elder Packer reminds us:

> We do not have the words (even the scriptures do not have words) which perfectly describe the Spirit. The scriptures generally use the word *voice,* which does not exactly fit. These delicate, refined spiritual communications are not seen with our eyes, nor heard with our ears. And even though it is described as a voice, it is a voice that one feels, more than one hears....
>
> The voice of the Spirit is... "a still voice of perfect mildness, as if it had been a whisper," and it can "pierce even to the very soul" and "cause [the heart] to burn" (3 Nephi 11:3; Helaman 5:30; D&C 85:6–7). Remember, Elijah found the voice of the Lord was not in the wind, nor in the earthquake, nor in the fire, but was a "still small voice" (1 Kings 19:12).

---

11. *Conference Report of The Church of Jesus Christ of Latter-day Saints,* April 1967, 85.

The Spirit does not get our attention by shouting or shaking us with a heavy hand. Rather it whispers. It caresses so gently that if we are preoccupied we may not feel it at all....

Occasionally it will press just firmly enough for us to pay heed. But most of the time, if we do not heed the gentle feeling, the Spirit will withdraw and wait until we come seeking and listening and say in our manner and expression, like Samuel of ancient times, "Speak [Lord], for thy servant heareth" (1 Samuel 3:10).[12]

Below is a sampling of scriptures that the Lord has provided which concern the awakening of the Spiritual Mind, and could themselves serve as fertile subjects of contemplation. Scripture has particular penetrating power because as the words on the page become thoughts in the mind, they develop the energy of the Holy Spirit. Inspired words possess a spiritual energy such that, on entering the soul of the engaged reader, it must necessarily work a transformation there. The spiritual energy in certain scriptures keeps us tuned to a different dimension, without which we will lapse back into the Natural Mind—hardly aware that that has happened.

One purpose then behind the Lord's continual admonition that we study scripture and that we pray always is to promote this process of opening the Spiritual Mind in order to increase one's spiritual energy so as to be able to bear more and more of His presence. Just thinking of God, remembering Him, counseling with Him, these awaken spiritual processes and cause changes. Here are some examples of what the Lord is asking us to do in order to open the Spiritual Mind. The first one deals with fear, since it is fear that so often keeps us locked in a narrow thought-world.

---

12. "The Candle of the Lord," *Ensign*, January 1983, 51.

1. *Look unto me in every thought; doubt not, fear not.* (D&C 6:36)

2. *And if your eye be single to my glory, your whole bodies shall be filled with light, and there shall be no darkness in you; and that body which is filled with light comprehendeth all things. Therefore, sanctify yourselves that your minds become single to God, and the days will come that you shall see him.* (D&C 88:67)

3. *Pray always and I will pour out my Spirit upon you.* (D&C 19:38)

4. *Cry unto God for all thy support; yea, let all thy doings be unto the Lord, and whithersoever thou goest let it be in the Lord; yea, let thy thoughts be directed unto the Lord; yea let the affections of thy heart be placed upon the Lord forever. Counsel with the Lord in all thy doings.* (Alma 37:36–37)

5. *[Angels minister to] them of strong faith and a firm mind in every form of godliness.* (Moroni 7:30)

6. *[They that] are willing to take upon them the name of thy Son, and always remember, and keep his commandments which he hath given them ... may always have his Spirit to be with them.* (Moroni 4:3)

7. *Come unto Christ, and be perfected in him, and deny yourselves of all ungodliness.* (Moroni 10:32)

These scriptures use words like *"every* thought," *"no* darkness," *"pray always,"* *"all* thy support/doing," *"every* form of godliness," *"always* remember," "deny *all* ungodliness." The Lord is asking us to set aside a superficial, dabbling sort of relationship with Him and turn over to Him the whole mind in order to undo the Natural and strengthen the Spiritual. We can become keepers of an inviolate mind, considering anything foreign to loving purposes a contaminant.

With the aura of a prophet's sure witness, President Gordon B. Hinckley writes of a practice that might greatly strengthen us: "I wish for each of you a time, perhaps only an hour, spent in silent meditation and quiet reflection on the wonder and the majesty of this, the Son of God." He mentions the "peace that comes from Him, His infinite love which each of us may feel, and an overwhelming sense of gratitude for that which He freely gave us at so great a cost to Himself."[13] These meditations form the essence of the daily spiritual life.

We realize of course that meditation is not something new to us. We are always meditating on something. But if we are not choosing our meditations deliberately, our thoughts will run in their ordinary channels, and we will experience more of what we don't want in our lives. It seems that lower energies around us are always trying to derail us. However, when we choose well how we will use our mind, our words, our love, we clarify and stabilize our mind. We keep our contemplations close to our heart as we step out of our worship time into our daily life, letting them shed their fragrance again and again in our mind, seeing more deeply into them as we go about our day. And if our thoughts have to do with turning our mind and will over to the Lord, there seems to be even more substantial progress in spiritual things.

In my experience, these two daily rhythms are central to change: quiet time in some combination of meditation/con-templation/prayer/scripture,[14] and conscious practice in the "laboratory." As to what is permitted into his mind, the Seeker may find himself becoming increasingly choosey about what he views or reads. If we want a particular kind of experience out of life and a particular kind of relationship with the Lord, we have to be selective about how we furnish our mental space.

---

13. "The Wondrous and True Story of Christmas," *Ensign*, December 2000, 2.

14. Among many writers on techniques of meditation and contemplation, in addition to those already cited, the reader may enjoy the gentle writings of Thich Nhat Hanh, for example, *The Miracle of Mindfulness* (Rider: London, 2008).

As the Spiritual Mind expands, we sense more quickly the soft brushing of the Spirit against ours, encouraging us to achieve a state of quiet inside, an inner sanctum. Elder Henry B. Eyring speaks of learning to be quiet when we are trying to experience spiritual things, and the importance of working with our feelings:

> Now, I testify it is a small voice. It whispers, not shouts. And so you must be very quiet inside. And that is why you may wisely fast when you want to listen. And that is why you will listen best when you feel, "Father, Thy will, not mine, be done." You will have a feeling of "I want what you want." Then, the still small voice will seem as if it pierces you. It may make your bones to quake. More often it will make your heart burn within you, again softly, but with a burning which will lift and reassure.[15]

Here we get to the crux of the whole matter. Learning to live in the Spiritual Mind is not just a matter of a list of good thoughts to live by. In its truest unfolding, it has a living, revelatory component. The Spiritual Mind is ultimately the Lord's mind and through it, we have direct access to Him.

But, let us add two more components to our list on the process of change. The first is that there must be the discipline to pursue prayerful contemplation and practice; and the second, there must be the attending to what falls to our hand to do. In this way, meeting the will of the Lord as it is manifested in the smaller and greater details of the responsible life, we keep the Natural Mind at bay and allow the revelatory to flourish. Dishes have to be done, teeth have to be brushed, that phone call needs to be made; visiting and home teaching need to be done. If we want the Lord to take us seriously, we must be responsible. By showing up to do what we've committed to do,

---

15. "To Draw Closer to God," *Ensign*, May 1991, 65.

what we know would fulfill all righteousness to do, we retain a remission of our sins. As Seekers, we set aside the lethargy of the Natural Man. We cultivate enthusiasm, even when we're tempted to be too tired for spiritual things. Our dependability and integrity are fixed.

Perhaps the reader has noticed that straining to improve oneself can seem fraught with unproductive stress. Instead, understanding the effect that different energies have on our life and experience, we gently expand the limits of our comfort into new behaviors and feelings, going from strength to strength. We can turn our attention to the ample, subtle, revelatory beauties in the people and things around us. Those with second-sight have observed that everything shines with heavenly light. Knowing that that's true, we too can see it, that divine invisible spirit which seems to bring to our hearts a feeling of security. As our hearts expand, there is so much more to "see." Our spiritual senses open, and we touch the sacred many times a day.

Could it be that self-improvement is less of tension and more of relaxation into simple, loving being? Is it perhaps more like surrender than struggle and effort? Deepak Chopra makes this observation: "You can be as alive as you want to be through a process known as surrender. Open yourself up to what is in front of you rather than allowing yourself to be distracted. This is humility."[16]

Many find that they can actually be immersed in thoughts of love, or the feeling of love, as a way of life. As we convey those feelings to God, man, or even ourself, Elder Gene R. Cook says that a magnified portion follows from the Spirit. He says, "Righteous feelings generated by a man seem to precede

---

16. *The Book of Secrets: Unlocking the Hidden Dimensions of Your Life* (New York: Random House, 2004), 169.

the increase of those feelings from the Spirit."[17] He reminds us that the very *power* of God is found in His attributes of godliness,[18] and so it is with Man. In fact, in a person who extends pure love to those around him, a radiation can be felt, an energy field, that seems to nourish those around him and helps others to awaken to a higher plane. Another friend of mine mentioned once that he had the opportunity of greeting Spencer Kimball. He said that as he came near to the prophet, he felt a nearly tangible force-field of love around him, almost causing my friend to fall back and filling him with wonder; then President Kimball stepped forward and hugged him and kissed him. My friend continues to feel affected by the memory of this encounter with the power of love.

Don Miguel Ruiz, a spiritual teacher, testifies that life can be very easy when love is our way of being and that it changes our perception of everything. He suggests a little meditation for strengthening our awareness of love and identifies a way of getting to that feeling state which is so helpful in shaping our experience:

> Take a deep breath and feel the air as it fills your lungs. Feel how the air is nothing but love. Notice the connection between the air and the lungs, a connection of love. Expand your lungs with air until your body has the need to expel that air. And then exhale, and feel the pleasure again. Because when we fulfill any need of the human body, it gives us pleasure. To breathe gives us much pleasure. Just to breathe is enough for us to always be happy, to enjoy life. Just to be alive is enough. Feel the pleasure to be alive, the pleasure of the feeling of love.[19]

---

17. "Charity: Perfect and Everlasting Love," *Ensign*, May 2002, 82.

18. *Ibid.*, 7.

19. *The Four Agreements* (San Rafael: Amber-Allen Publishing, 1997), 132.

It may be that there is more than we know in his finding love in the air around us. Many with second-sight would testify that it is indeed there.

In this chapter we have distinguished between two classes of thoughts and their respective energies. We have been reminded that the law of the Spirit and of the Spiritual Mind is the principle of acting through pure love. It is our primeval nature, as well as God's.

We have seen that the Spiritual Mind must be cultivated and trained to serve as an instrument of love and revelation and oneness with God during our Wilderness journey. This is a process in which we begin again and again. But, this taking into our own hands our own transformation—instead of passively hoping for a miracle to come upon us in some distant future—constitutes our doing *"all that we can do"* (2 Nephi 25:23) while we apply for those changes that ultimately come only from God.

Again we cite Elder Busche as he speaks on the issue of choice, reminding us of the illusory nature of the telestial world, but of our need to see through it to the reality beyond:

> This world we live in is not the real thing. The actual world—which is closer to us than we sometimes realize—is full of truth and capable of bringing us to a higher level than we can understand. Indeed, it is more beautiful and majestic than a human can imagine. My spiritual insight let me see that we as human beings live far below our potential from day to day. One day we will be confronted with our true potential; and we will see what we have missed because we have not embraced the ultimate help offered to us from our Creator. Life is not worth living if we walk around in it without really knowing that every choice we make defines our lives in the eternities. Nothing can be hidden, and even every thoughtless spoken word will be brought to our painful awareness one day.[20]

---

20. *Yearning for the Living God,* 53–54.

Each person has a choice between these two minds and their respective energies, and each choice dramatically affects his experience and his perception of reality during his Wilderness journey.

In the next chapter we will learn how the Lord goes about waking up our spiritual senses in order that we might "see" the love in the air.

CHAPTER SIX

NATURE'S HOLY PLAN:
NATURE WAKENS MAN FROM THE DREAM

Are you sure
That we are awake? It seems to me
That yet we sleep, we dream.

Shakespeare, *A Midsummer Night's Dream*

ॐ

Prophets of Nature, we to them will speak
A lasting inspiration, sanctified by reason, blest by faith....
Instruct them how the mind of man becomes
A thousand times more beautiful than the earth
On which he dwells, above this frame of things....
In beauty exalted, as it is itself
Of quality and fabric more divine.

William Wordsworth[1]

---

1. *The Prelude*, Bk 14:446–448, 450–456. William Wordsworth (1770–1850), an inspired poet of England, appeared with about a hundred other spirits on August 21, 1877, to President Wilford Woodruff in the St. George Temple. He requested temple ordinances for himself, as recorded in the

He arrives, and by the Plan of Happiness, Adam falls into a deep sleep in the bosom of the fresh new earth. His posterity, we continue for a time asleep, dreaming. We think we wake, yet on we sleep, oblivious to the truths of our reality. And what is it the Gods intend in order to awaken this mind of Man, "of quality and fabric... divine," that is "a thousand times more beautiful than the earth on which he dwells"? It is this: that beauty shall awaken beauty.

So God created the earth, adorning it with *"the good things... made for the benefit and the use of man, both to please the eye and to gladden the heart... for taste and for smell, to strengthen the body and to enliven the soul"* (D&C 59:17–19). He prepared all this to nourish and delight and awaken Man; then He placed Man in Nature's bosom.

Throughout the history of the earth, Man comes and goes tending to his daily life in the midst of Nature and, though from time to time he is distracted by her beauty, he rarely sees into her secret; he is unconscious of the holy purposes of the spirit behind the pleasing of the eye and the gladdening of the heart and the enlivening of the soul.

But some have seen into Nature's purposes and have written their insights. Here is a small sample from some of those who have credentials as truth-seers. The first example is an inspired poem in which the poet Wordsworth, seated in a grove surrounded by Nature's ceaseless busyness, sees into the nature of things. What he sees is that Man and Nature are linked in a holy plan. He writes:

> I heard a thousand blended notes,
> While in a grove I sat reclined,

Journal of Wilford Woodruff 7:367–68. President Woodruff also refers to this event in JD 19:229, but does not list all the names.

In that sweet mood when pleasant thoughts
Bring sad thoughts to the mind.

To her fair works did Nature link
The human soul that through me ran;
And much it grieved my heart to think
What man has made of man.

Through primrose tufts, in that green bower,
The periwinkle trailed its wreaths;
And 'tis my faith that every flower
Enjoys the air it breathes.

The birds around me hopped and played,
Their thoughts I cannot measure: —
But the least motion which they made
It seemed a thrill of pleasure.

The budding twigs spread out their fan,
To catch the breezy air;
And I must think, do all I can,
That there was pleasure there.

If this belief from heaven be sent,
If such be Nature's holy plan,
Have I not reason to lament
What man has made of man?[2]

The poet feels the "sweet mood" in Nature but cannot help
but be saddened by the contrast between the happy innocence
of Nature and Man's lamentable treatment of Man. He sees with
second sight that the spirit of happiness and love flows through

---

2. "Lines Written in Early Spring."

all Nature including Man, giving life and nourishment, even joy, to all. But Man, in his dream, is largely oblivious to the revelations and messages of the Divine in and around Him. He is not comforted by them and he acts against himself and others in a way entirely contrary to that spirit. The poet laments "what man has made of man," finding it so perverse in the presence of such a nourishing spirit. But Man can awaken to the awareness that his true nature is nothing but bliss, through coming to know the Light of Christ in Nature.

Wordsworth sees "into the life of things."[3] He perceives a presence that disturbs him with the joy "of something far more deeply interfused, / Whose dwelling is the light of setting suns, / And the round ocean and the living air, / And the blue sky, and in the mind of man; / A motion and a spirit, that impels / All thinking things … / And rolls through all things."[4]

I can bear witness to his vision because I too have learned about this secret spirit in Nature. In a sacred experience in a morning study time, my gaze was drawn to the little green fuzz appearing on the early spring trees out the window of my sunroom. In that moment the spirit of the scripture came over me, and I knew, as we have these "knowings," that the force driving that green fuzz into view was the power and Spirit of the Lord Jesus Christ, and that It was alive in every twig and blade and blossom that I could see through the window, and that It was alive in me.

On another occasion, deep in the south of Argentina at the Llao-llao, in a beautiful natural setting, I was sitting in a rustic dining room looking out through a panoramic window at a turbulent twilight sky, and in a somewhat melancholy mood, I saw a lone bird shoot rapturously from down below up to

---

3. "Lines Composed a Few Miles above Tintern Abbey, on Revisiting the Banks of the Wye during a Tour. July 13, 1798," line 48.

4. *Ibid.*, lines 93–112.

the tops of the trees. As I watched him, I felt a rebuke for my moodiness as I learned that not only was the Lord Jesus Christ the power behind his flight, but that the bird was—happy.

In yet another experience, driving with my mission-president husband down the highway of Tunuyan, Argentina, the breeze blowing the trees along the road, they shimmering and swaying in response, their bi-colored leaves creating a vision of dancing color, I thought, They look happy, and I knew in that moment that there was a spirit of happiness in them. I turned to my romantic-literature husband[5] and said, "I just learned that those trees are—happy." He leaned toward me and said, "That's pure Wordsworth." When we arrived back in Mendoza, I said, "Show me." He pulled out the collected works, and I have never been entirely the same since, even though he had taught me those very things before. But now I knew it.

In fact, since that awakening I have many times watched from my study window the sun come up behind the mountains and illuminate the white-barked, silver-green leaves in a stunning display of glinting, living light and shadow and—well, you know—it can't be told. But like you, I have been brought to tears by the Love shining through it all. And more than enlivened, I have known that I was alive in Christ; I have known that I was beholding life expressing its joy in the "midst of the power of God" and that I was witnessing "God moving in his majesty and power" (D&C 88:45–47). I have begun to understand the purpose of the spirit in Nature.

One golden October afternoon, a friend and I drove through yellow-dappled trees to the grounds in front of the temple. We parked there to talk, and she told me of her troubled feelings and relationships. I listened carefully but at the same time, the amber-toned trees against the infinite-blue sky so arrested my

---

5. Gordon K. Thomas, retired Brigham Young University professor of English literature.

mind—they so happily revealing their secret, hidden as it was in plain sight—that at one point I said to her, "Dear Friend —" and I gestured to what was happening around us, *"This is the only reality that matters."*

> *Let the mountains shout for joy, and all ye valleys cry aloud; and all ye seas and dry lands tell the wonders of your Eternal King! And ye rivers, and brooks, and rills, flow down with gladness. Let the woods and all the trees of the field praise the Lord; and ye solid rocks weep for joy! And let the sun, moon, and the morning stars sing together, and let all the sons of God shout for joy! And let the eternal creations declare his name forever and ever! And again I say, how glorious is the voice we hear from heaven, proclaiming in our ears, glory, and salvation, and honor, and immortality, and eternal life; kingdoms, principalities, and powers!* (D&C 128:23)

Nature's role is to arrest Man's attention so he can hear that Voice from Heaven. And it has often worked as each of us has many times yielded to holy messages when absorbed by sounds or scenes in Nature. In those moments the rational processes pause, and a deeper consciousness awakens. In such moments one feels a transcendent sense of connectedness to divine origins. The sensation seems to have the power to transform every fear and every care. The mind becomes deep and still.

Attention to Nature's message then can open the Spiritual Mind, where not only the truth about Nature is revealed, but also our own true nature is stirred into wakening. We become conscious of spiritual realities that flow in and around us. To slow down and let Nature distill within us begins to open the unseen world where the secrets of happiness flourish, where abound *"the mysteries and peaceable things—that which bringeth joy, that which bringeth life eternal"* (D&C 42:61). To see, to slow down, to absorb, to let work in us the simple beauties of life and love—these open our awareness to the world of the Spirit. The inarticulate but vivid impressions lead us to peace and awareness of an attentive Creator and to a desire to love all the Lord's creations, including Man. But we find that if we live too superficially, too speedily, and too negatively, we will not uncover the treasures. All things testify of Him, but we must become aware.

In another example from Wordsworth, this prophet of Nature relates a formative encounter with this God who extends Himself into all His Creation and personally to His watchful children. Here the poet describes a sensitive boy, himself, whose heart had not yet tasted the pure delight of divine Love, but whom Nature had prepared to feel intensely, in order that at a preappointed moment, the budding poet might drink deeply of this love of God:

> For the growing Youth
> What soul was his, when, from the naked top
> Of some bold headland, he beheld the sun
> Rise up and bathe the world in light! He looked—
> Ocean and earth, the solid frame of earth
> And ocean's liquid mass, in gladness lay
> Beneath him:—Far and wide the clouds were touched,
> And in their silent faces could he read
> Unutterable love. Sound needed none,
> Nor any voice of joy; his spirit drank
> The spectacle: sensation, soul, and form,
> All melted into him; they swallowed up
> His animal being; in them did he live,
> And by them did he live; they were his life.
> In such access of mind, in such high hour
> Of visitation from the living God,
> Thought was not; in enjoyment it expired.

No thanks he breathed, he proffered no request;
Rapt into still communion that transcends
The imperfect offices of prayer and praise,
His mind was a thanksgiving to the power
That made him; it was blessedness and love![6]

Thought and senses stilled, the boy experiences God directly in his spirit. He describes a sensation common to such visitations, that of living *by* the Divine Presence, as though the Mighty Being is living his life with him, doing his life with him, even that he was *being* lived and breathed, while swallowed up in this unutterable love. These sensations are closer to things as they really are than the solitariness we often perceive. What he came to know recalls a similar description of the Lord from scripture: *"He is above all things, and in all things, and is through all things, and is round about all things; and all things are by him, and of him, even God, forever and ever"* (D&C 88:41).

Another author, the spiritual teacher, Deepak Chopra, describes Man's becoming conscious of his true nature as in quiet time he stills his mind, leaves aside past and future, and yields to the present moment, penetrating the layers of world-cares to touch this quick pure spirit underneath:

> If you embrace the present [moment], become one with it, merge with it, you will experience a fire, a glow, a sparkle of ecstasy throbbing in every living sentient being. As you experience this exultation of spirit in everything that is alive, as you become intimate with it, joy will be born within you, and you will drop the terrible burdens and encumbrances of defensiveness, resentment, and hurtfulness. Only then will you become lighthearted, carefree, joyous, and free.[7]

---

6. *The Excursion* 1:197–218.

7. *Seven Spiritual Laws of Success* (St. Albans: Motilal UK Books of India, 2003), 61.

Another example, this one from the classic novel by George Eliot, describes the prayer experience of a young woman who has given herself entirely to service. The allusions to Nature in this passage show that she is already aware of the worshipful spirit in Nature:

> She closed her eyes, that she might feel more intensely the presence of a Love and Sympathy deeper and more tender than was breathed from the earth and sky. That was often Dinah's mode of praying in solitude. Simply to close her eyes and to feel herself enclosed by the Divine Presence; then gradually her fears, her yearning anxieties for others, melted away like ice-crystals in a warm ocean.[8]

How could it be any other way than that God would fill His creation with His tender Love and, even while placing Man in a necessarily darker world, would cause the very trees, the flowers, and the sky itself to radiate this Love into Man's soul? Nephi and the angel saw the truth of it together as they beheld the Tree: *"Yea, it is the love of God, which sheddeth itself abroad in the hearts of the children of men;... the most desirable above all things... and the most joyous to the soul"* (1 Nephi 11:22–23). Paul adds that it is by the Holy Ghost that this love is shed (Romans 5:5). But available to all, through that holy spirit permeating all Nature, that Light of Christ, God's love streams through the myriad forms of Nature. Yet, because of his hardened heart, Man does not know that he is journeying in darkness at noonday (see D&C 95:6), yes, even walking about in paradise:

> *The light shineth in darkness, and the darkness comprehendeth it not; nevertheless, the day shall come when you shall comprehend even God, being quickened in him and by him. Then shall ye know*

---

8. *Adam Bede*, chapter 15.

*that ye have seen me, that I am, and that I am the true light that
is in you, and that you are in me; otherwise ye could not abound.*
(D&C 88:49–50)

The "darkness" is Man's un-seeing, layered-over soul, which
this endlessly patient Light seeks to penetrate.

Brigham Young described Man's ability to transcend those
physical senses which bind him to a narrow view of reality. He
shows us that Man's spirit can be awakened under the influence
of the Holy Spirit to a greater capacity for obtaining knowledge
than that which the physical senses and the rational mind can
provide:

> When a man is full of the light of eternity, then the eye is
> not the only medium through which he sees, his ear is not the
> only medium by which he hears, nor the brain the only means
> by which he understands. When the whole body is full of the
> Holy Ghost, he can see behind him with as much ease, without
> turning his head, as he can see before him.... It is not the optic
> nerve alone that gives the knowledge of surrounding objects to
> the mind, but it is that which God has placed in man—a system
> of intelligence that attracts knowledge, as light cleaves to light,
> intelligence to intelligence, and truth to truth. It is this which
> lays in man a proper foundation for all education.... We are at
> present low, weak, and groveling in the dark, but we are planted
> here in weakness for the purpose of exaltation.[9]

There is then in Man a system for obtaining knowledge
which is not tied to the senses. Echoing this insight, Jacques
Lusseyran, a blind Frenchman, relates from his own experience the way in which Man has access to knowledge and
happiness through his spirit, beyond the physical senses. In his

autobiography,[10] and later in a collection of personal essays,[11] Lusseyran tells his story which begins just before the Second World War in France, when seven years into a happy childhood, he suffered an accident at school in which he was totally and permanently blinded. What he relates helps us to understand better the unseen spiritual world we live in and how we might gain conscious access to it and to those principles that open spiritual awareness. He writes:

> Barely ten days after the accident that blinded me, I made the basic discovery. I am still entranced by it. The only way I can describe that experience is in clear and direct words. I had completely lost the sight of my eyes; I could not see the light of the world any more. Yet the light was still there.... All the world around me was convinced that I had lost it forever. But I found it again in another place. I found it in myself and what a miracle!—it was intact....
>
> I felt it [the light] gushing forth every moment and brimming over; I felt how it wanted to spread out over the world. I had only to receive it. It was unavoidably there. It was all there, and I found again its movements and shades, that is, its colors, which I had loved so passionately a few weeks before.[12]

This was something entirely new, you understand, all the more so since it contradicted everything that those who have eyes believe. The source of light is not in the outer world. We believe that it is only because of a common delusion. The light dwells where life also dwells: within ourselves.

---

10. *And There Was Light* (Sandpoint, Idaho: Morning Light Press, 1987).

11. *Against the Pollution of the I: Selected Writings of Jacques Lusseyran* (Sandpoint, Idaho: Morning Light Press, 2006).

12. *Ibid.*, 26–27.

Yet I had to make the effort to find my way between doors, walls, human beings, and trees. As happens to all blind persons, I hurt myself often. But I quickly learned that I knocked against things only when I forgot the light. When I paid constant attention to the light, I ran a much smaller risk.

The second great discovery came almost immediately afterwards. There was only one way to see the inner light, and that was to love.[13]

His blindness took from him the usual way of perceiving things and made possible his awareness of other avenues for knowledge of the true nature of things, pathways usually veiled by the more dominant physical senses. He also learned how sensitive the spirit of truth is to the emotions that Man allows himself. He learned that when he was overcome with sorrow, or let anger take hold of him, or felt envy for those who could see—the light immediately diminished. "Sometimes it even went out completely. Then I became blind. But this blindness was a state of not loving any more, of sadness; it was not the loss of one's eyes."[14]

He discovered that the light he was able to perceive changed with his own inner emotional state. When he was sad or afraid, everything became indistinct. But when he was joyous and attentive, the light would return. Anger, remorse plunged everything into darkness. But a magnanimous resolution, a courageous decision, radiated a beam of light. "By and by I learned to understand that love meant seeing and that hate was night.... Sadness, hate, or fear not only darkened my universe, but also made it smaller.... Outwardly I could not avoid running against doors and furniture. I was punished very

---

13. *Ibid.*, 26–28.

14. *Ibid.*, 28.

thoroughly and very quickly."[15] He found that impatience seemed to surround things by some sort of smoke or fog, but that joy clarified everything.[16] But he said that when he was content, "I had eyes all around my head, and then, truly, I was no longer blind.... And it was all because I was content."[17] He found, in short, that there were two possibilities open to him: "to reject the world—that meant darkness, reverses—or to accept it, and that meant light and strength."[18]

We learn here that love makes possible true seeing, that it is a more revelatory principle than we might have suspected, and that even subtle shades of its opposites return us to the narrow cell of the Natural Man. How appropriate it might be for us to ask continually that our spirit be kept clear and sweet so as to perceive the things of the loving Unseen World in the details of our daily life. Then we would see how sacred ordinary life is.

When we speak of slowing down, immersing ourselves in the present moment, we are able to exercise a new faculty. Lusseyran identifies this key to the world of spirit:

> Because of my blindness, I had developed a new faculty. Strictly speaking, all men have it, but almost all forget to use it. That faculty is attention. In order to live without eyes it is necessary to be very attentive, to remain hour after hour in a state of wakefulness, of receptiveness and activity. Indeed, attention is ... a state of being. It is a state without which we shall never be able to perfect ourselves. In its truest sense it is the listening post of the universe.[19]

---

15. *Ibid.*, 62.

16. *Ibid.*, 96.

17. *Ibid.*, 97.

18. *Ibid.*, 62.

19. *Ibid.*, 31.

He said that a really attentive person could understand every-thing because a certain kind of understanding is not tied to the senses. With attention, every object revealed itself to him in all its possible facets. In other words, he could, with sufficient at-tention, enter completely into its inner world. He learned that blindness simply allows another state of perception—which all people have, but usually do not discover.

Like any sighted person, he could choose to depend on his own light or on the greater light coming to him. He writes of the danger of preferring one's own current of power to the uni-versal current of power and of his continual need to depend on the inner light. In this inner light he found what he calls an en-chanted world that was a great delight to him and which he un-derstood came to him from God. He declares that everyone has such a world inside but that Man in general is too distracted, not only by his senses, but also by his fears, to find it.

Apparently, as we monitor our own emotional and spiritual state, we can increase or decrease the power of the inner Light. Elder Busche alerts us to the need to be aware of our moods since it is so easy to become neglectful and then find that we have drifted from the principles of happiness. Even the least seeming casualness with the laws of Truth can have an effect on our sense of connectedness:

> We all are prone, once in a while, to be in a state contrary
> to the nature of happiness, and not necessarily because we have
> pursued wickedness or iniquity to a full extent.... [Rather that]
> we may have become a little careless.... Perhaps we may have
> permitted small bad habits or attitudes to enter into our lives; or
> perhaps we have even lost to some degree an understanding of
> the importance of keeping a covenant with exactness. If so, we
> are in a dangerous state. We must become aware of it. We cannot
> afford to ignore the situation. We may observe that for some time

we are not really happy, that we must constantly force ourselves to smile, or perhaps that we are in a state close to depression.... When any child of God breaks any of the laws of God, which are the laws of righteousness, the Spirit of Christ, which, according to the scriptures, gives "light to every man," will be withdrawn to some degree. (See D&C 84:46; D&C 93:2; D&C 121:37; John 1:9.) Shadows of darkness will fall upon the soul, and, in this state, an *awareness* of what is happening to us is essential.... [The Lord] wants to sharpen our awareness ... as He calls us to a continuous process of repentance."[20]

Yes, our awareness is sharpened through continual repentance of our carelessness with the true nature of things. How enlightening it is to understand the degree to which our spiritual perception is influenced by the emotions that we allow to flourish. The scriptures mention godliness, kindness, pure love—*"For if these things be in you, and abound, they make you that ye shall neither be barren nor unfruitful in the knowledge of our Lord Jesus Christ. But he that lacketh these things is blind, and cannot see afar off"* (2 Peter 1:8–9). We may not have realized how literal the apostle's words are.

The purest beauty is always moral. Wordsworth had noticed what Lusseyran did—that the Light in Man and Nature were the same Light, were of one piece, and flourished only in love and moral goodness. Wordsworth writes that he had come to recognize in Nature "the anchor of my purest thoughts," "the soul of all my moral being."[21] Nature stirs us so deeply precisely because its Spirit is continuous with the soul of our moral being; it addresses an aspiration in us. The divinity in Nature calls to the divinity in Man to awaken to that beauty in himself which is "a thousand times more beautiful than the

---

20. "University for Eternal Life," *Ensign*, May 1989, 71.
21. "Tintern Abbey," lines 109–111.

earth on which he dwells," even as he must wade through the turmoils and pollutions of the earthly life; for Man's essence is "of quality and fabric ... divine."[22] We find Man placed in Nature's lap so as to delight him, enliven him, and awaken him to his divinity.

---

22. See epigraph at beginning of chapter from Wordsworth, *The Prelude*, Book 14, lines 449–54.

CHAPTER SEVEN

THE GATES OF ZION: A VISION

The building up of Zion is a cause that has interested the people of God in every age; it is a theme upon which prophets, priests and kings have dwelt on with peculiar delight; they have looked forward with joyful anticipation to the day in which we live; and fired with heavenly and joyful anticipations they have sung and written and prophesied of this our day; but they died without the sight.

Joseph Smith[1]

❧

That every man may improve upon his talent, that every man may gain other talents, yea, even an hundred fold, to be cast into the Lord's storehouse ... Every man seeking the interest of his neighbor, and doing all things with an eye single to the glory of God. This order I have appointed to be an everlasting order unto you.

D&C 82:18–20

---

1. *TPJS*, 231; May 2, 1842; punctuation altered for readability. See full text of the prophet's quote at end of chapter in Appendix One.

The Lord loveth the gates of Zion.

Psalm 87:2

ᢙ

The path through the Wilderness ultimately encounters the opportunity to build Zion. The Lord gives us the vision of Zion even as we journey in the Wilderness. This anticipation of Zion opens our minds to the vast cosmos. Many prophets and poets have seen Zion in vision. One of these was the poet-seer, William Wordsworth, who, on August 21, 1877 (with about a hundred other spirits), requested his temple blessings at the hands of President Wilford Woodruff in the St. George Temple.[2] Here is a brief description of the Holy City that he saw, based on fragments from the poem. The poet describes his experience as he hiked through a mist on the Langdale fells of northern England, when suddenly, with a single step, the skirts of the misty vapor opened to his view, revealing a vision: "Glory beyond all glory ever seen / By waking sense or by the dreaming soul!" He saw "a mighty city":

> A wilderness of building, sinking far…
> into a boundless depth.
> Far sinking into splendour—without end!
> Fabric it seemed of diamond and of gold,
> With alabaster domes, and silver spires,
> And blazing terrace upon terrace, high
> Uplifted; here, serene pavilions bright
> …there towers begirt
> With…illumination of all gems!…

These towers, he saw, "mutually inflamed" each other, "molten together." He saw "temple, palace, citadel" and

---

2. See Footnote 1, Chapter 6.

Right in the midst... appeared... a throne
Under a shining canopy of state...
Such [forms] as by Hebrew Prophets were beheld
In vision—forms... of mightiest power.[3]

In the heart of every true saint there burns a love for the
dream of Zion. Who of us wouldn't search out the truths and
powers to qualify himself to walk through such gates? Here we
shall consider some of the means by which we might prepare to
obtain entrance to Zion's bright courts.

A Little History and Doctrine

When the Lord peoples a world, He soon introduces the principles of Zion. Each world starts as a fallen world, but it seems
there are always some people in these worlds that get the vision
of Zion, feel a hunger for it, obtain power and authority, and
build it. In the case of the Zions previously perfected on this
earth (and we might suppose it is so on other worlds), they
were removed from the fallen world and joined with the great
Holy City in another dimension: *"Thou hast taken Zion to thine
own bosom, from all thy creations, from all eternity to all eternity"*
(Moses 7:31). However, the latter-day Zion, or the New Jerusalem,
will be built and perfected on this earth and ultimately joined
by Enoch's city (see Moses 7:62–63). Zion is, then, an eternal society, an eternal constant, a brother and sisterhood throughout
eternity, forming and perfecting itself on worlds throughout the cosmos.

Zion is a condition sought for by all holy men, many of
whom failed to find it because of wickedness on the earth (see
D&C 45:12). Abraham *"looked for a city which hath foundations,*

---

3. *The Excursion* 11:829–881. See the full text of the vision at end of the
chapter in Appendix Two.

whose builder and maker is God," he, with others, desiring *"a better country, that is, an heavenly: wherefore God is not ashamed to be called their God: for he hath prepared for them a city"* (Hebrews 11:16).

Zion is the objective of every major prophet in every dispensation: that is, to bring the covenant people to a purified condition and to build a city where they could live together independently above the influences of the earth in a divinely empowered society. The Zion society is the precursor of that society that flourishes in the celestial kingdom. The Zion perfected on the earth will become the core society from this earth that will endure through the Millennium and be joined by the other heavenly Zions whose inhabitants belong to this earth. This society will witness the celestialization of the earth and become a branch of the celestial kingdom on earth.

A Zion society has particular temporal and spiritual characteristics, which we will explore here, but in brief, such a society is made up of people who received the ordinances of the gospel, took them seriously, and in spite of earth and hell, used the powers of the gospel to qualify to live with other like-minded people. In short, they used their mortal probation to practice the principles of Zion.

But one thing is clear with respect to preparation—our current culture will not prepare us to live in Zion. Babylon cannot prepare Zion. There has to be a break, a setting apart of the people and a reaching for a separate and higher order. Babylon is not easy to separate from since we are required to live more or less in her midst; but if we persist in living as the world lives, thinking and acting as they do, we will not have the power to inherit a place in Zion.

The scriptures describe three groups whose prophets succeeded in preparing them to build Zion: Enoch's community, Melchizedek's, and the one described in Third Nephi that lasted only about 167 years. At least two previous Zion societies, Enoch's and Melchizedek's, were taken from the earth, placed in another sphere, and quickened with a terrestrial glory; their inhabitants are now ministering angels to the earth[4]—continuing their ministry on the earth from a higher level. Paul described this city as mount Sion, the city of the living God, the heavenly Jerusalem, with an innumerable company of angels, the "general assembly and church of the firstborn, which are written in heaven" (Hebrews 12:22–23).[5] Melchizedek's society, as described in JST Genesis 14:25–40, shows us a people who, while living on the earth, practiced the principles and obtained through their righteousness sufficient faith to be translated and were then taken up into the Holy City: *"They obtained heaven, and sought for the city of Enoch which God had before taken, separating it from the earth, having reserved it unto the latter days, or the end of the world."* As the Lord promised, that city will come again and will unite with our own Zion on earth.

It is important to notice that while Enoch established his Zion through a ministry that spanned more than three centuries, he did it in the midst of wars and bloodshed and ripening filthiness on the earth—something like our day. "Then he obtained power," Brigham Young observed, "to translate himself and his people, with the region they inhabited, their houses,

---

4. *TPJS*, 170–71.

5. There may be a merging in the scriptures of these terrestrial Zions with the celestial kingdom itself, as in D&C 76:66, where the inheritors of celestial glory are described: *"These are they who are come unto Mount Zion, and unto the city of the living God, the heavenly place, the holiest of all."* Elder McConkie finds two cities: the City of Enoch coming down after the Second Coming and the celestial Jerusalem, the Holy City where God and angels dwell, coming down from heaven "to be with men forever in that day when this earth becomes a celestial sphere," based on John's vision in Revelation 21:2, 10. (*A New Witness for the Articles of Faith* [Salt Lake City: Deseret Book, 1987], 588.)

gardens, fields, cattle, and all their possessions ... and he obtained power to take his portion of the earth and move out a little while, where he remains to this day."[6] One instructive thing we learn here is that external circumstances do not determine spiritual success; rather, the Zion revolution begins inside of people, of individuals, independent of circumstances. Moses, on the other hand, who had the Israelites to himself in the Sinai desert, separated from Babylon, labored to bring his people into the presence of God. But they would not (D&C 84:24): *"They hardened their hearts and could not endure [the Lord's] presence"* and the Lord forbade that they should *"enter into his rest while in the wilderness, which rest is the fulness of his glory."* We learn from the prophet Joseph that translation of people into a higher dimension is a function of the Melchizedek Priesthood;[7] without it there can be no translation. Therefore, with Israel's rejection of the fulness of the Melchizedek priesthood, they refused all these priesthood powers—that is, they rejected the gifts of the Spirit, sealings in the temple, calling and election, Second Comforter, the key of the knowledge of God, translation, and the authority to bring Zion. They refused the very powers that could have qualified them to be taken up into Enoch's Holy City. They chose Babylon over Zion. We see then that the Saints in each dispensation react differently to the opportunity to create Zion, and the choice is always the same—Babylon's culture or Zion's.

In this dispensation, of course, the prophets strive in the same direction—to prepare a Zion people. Four times during 1829 the Lord directed Joseph Smith and his associates to *"seek to bring forth and establish the cause of Zion"* (D&C 6:6, 11:6, 12:6; 14:6). From then until the day he was martyred, the prophet Joseph exercised the faculties of his whole soul and body

---

6. Brigham Young, *JD* 3:320.

7. *TPJS*, 170.

toward this end. He said: "We ought to have the building of Zion as our greatest object."[8] "The vision of a modern Zion was not a fanciful Utopian scheme, nor one of the contemporary communal experiments. The Prophet's vision came by revelation, making him intimately familiar with the glory of Enoch's Zion. He sought for the Saints of this dispensation the same approbation which the Lord had given to the Saints of Enoch's day."[9] Joseph understood Zion by revelation, by divine commission, and by literal vision of not only what could be but of what would be.

Even though the commandment to reestablish Zion was the central goal of the Church in Joseph's day, it was not realized because the Saints were not prepared. The Lord gives two of the major reasons it failed:

> *[The Saints]* **do not impart of their substance,** *as becometh saints, to the poor and afflicted among them; and* **are not united according to the union** *required by the law of the celestial kingdom; and Zion cannot be built up unless it is by the principles of the law of the celestial kingdom; otherwise I cannot receive her unto myself.*

And then a solemn warning:

> *And my people must needs be chastened until they learn obedience, if it must needs be, by the things which they suffer.* (D&C 105:2–6)

These two specific reasons recur repeatedly in the scriptures on Zion: They do not impart of their substance to the poor;

---

8. *HC* 3:390.

9. See William O. Nelson, "To Prepare a People," *Ensign*, January 1979, 18; a good article on the history of Zion in this dispensation.

they are not united according to the union required by the law of the celestial kingdom. The book of Moses says similarly: *"And the Lord called his people ZION, because they were of one heart and one mind [unity issue], and dwelt in righteousness; and there was no poor among them [sharing issue]"* (Moses 7:18). Obviously the "law of the celestial kingdom," that is, the law lived in the celestial kingdom, is characterized by a comprehensive unity which includes the sharing of all resources in a consciousness of infinite abundance. We learn then from these scriptures that Zion is an economic as well as a spiritual system.

Temporal and Economic Aspects of Zion

The Lord has his own economic order, which exists above earthly economic systems; the power of this order rests in the system of tithes and offerings and in the proper utilization of resources in what the scriptures call the Lord's Storehouse. This storehouse is to be distinguished from the Bishop's Storehouse, where commodities are kept. The Lord's Storehouse is the aggregate of talents and resources existing among the members of any church unit, ward or stake, and its use is based on the Law of Consecration (see D&C 42:33–34, 55; 70:7–10; 82:17–18; 83:6). In order to organize and utilize the resources in the Lord's Storehouse, priesthood and Relief Society leaders must work together in priesthood counsels in order to administer the Lord's Storehouse and get the real powers of Zion moving among them.

The Lord said, *"The redemption of Zion must needs come by power"* (D&C 103:15), implying that as the members follow the Lord's organization and work the program in these temporal-seeming affairs, He will extend miraculous power to create a Zion society. He promises priesthood counsels: *"Whatsoever ye shall ask in faith, being united in prayer according to my command, ye shall receive*" (D&C 29:6). In this way the leaders unlock the powers of Zion for their people. Joseph foresaw this work going forward on two fronts through the power and authority of the priesthood:

> And whilst we are thus united in one common cause [on earth], to roll forth the kingdom of God, the heavenly Priesthood are not idle spectators, the spirit of God will be showered down from above and it will dwell in our midst.[10]

The establishment of Zion is a partnership between the Kingdom of God on the earth and that in Heaven.

The Roots of Poverty

Often poverty is a function, not of lack of resources, but of lack of knowledge as to how to organize and develop resources, how to work together (the "unity" issue the Lord frequently mentions) to mobilize the resources in the Lord's Storehouse, and faith to set in motion the Lord's miraculous economic principles. President Hinckley reassures priesthood leaders: "I am satisfied, my brethren, that there is enough of expertise, of knowledge, of strength, of concern in every priesthood quorum to assist the troubled members of that quorum if these resources are properly administered."[11] He implies an interesting principle: that the Lord has, in His omniscience, put in every unit, distributed among its members, sufficient resources to help the members meet their needs and become self-reliant.

The scriptures are clear that the Lord has all riches under His control—that He makes the rich and He makes the poor,

---

10. *TPJS*, 232.

11. Gordon B. Hinckley, "Welfare Responsibilities of the Priesthood Quorums" *Ensign*, November 1977, 84.

LIGHT IN THE WILDERNESS

for His own purposes (e.g., 1 Samuel 2:7–8). Since temporal goods have so much to do with spiritual matters, He declares that everything must be done in His own way. He describes His own system, explaining that He blesses some of the people with abundance, which He then requires them to share with those who do not have enough: *"And it is my purpose to provide for my saints, for all things are mine. But it must needs be done in mine own way... that the poor shall be exalted, in that the rich are made low."* Then the Lord warns: *"Therefore, if any man shall take of the abundance which I have made, and impart not his portion, according to the law of my gospel, unto the poor and the needy, he shall, with the wicked, lift up his eyes in hell, being in torment"* (D&C 104:15–16, 18).

We understand from these verses that the Lord intends a redistribution of wealth in establishing Zion, that is, the *haves* will give to the *have-nots*—but in appropriate ways, which is to say, *"See that all these things [caring for those in need] are done in wisdom and order"* (Mosiah 4:27). One of the implications for the Church of "wisdom and order" is that help be given under priesthood direction to promote self-reliance, taking care not to create or enable dependence. Self-reliance to the extent of one's ability is a foundation principle of Zion. Church welfare work operates on this principle: "[God] never forsakes us, but he does not do for us what we can do for ourselves."[12] This principle is obviously basic to our development of Heavenly Father's divine attributes and powers and to the realization of a Zion society.

The application of this principle begins at home, where we teach children to take responsibility, to become problem-solvers, to do as well as possible in school. We can teach them manners and courtesy. They can learn to repair and beautify things.

---

12. *A Leader's Guide to Welfare: Providing in the Lord's Way* (Salt Lake City: The Church of Jesus Christ of Latter-day Saints, 1990).

They can learn to work and contribute. All of these skills find a place in making a Zion society successful. We take care not to do too much for them or give them too much, teaching them to become self-reliant so as to be contributors to the Lord's purposes.

If they can't take care of themselves, they can't serve others. The Lord requires us to practice that pure religion as described in James 1:27: we must visit the fatherless and the widows; and we must keep ourselves unspotted from the world. What we are trying to do for our children is to prepare them to give so they can purify themselves and enter into a purified society. In this way, we and our children will have confidence in the presence of the Lord (see D&C 121:45).[13]

It strengthens our faith to know that the spiritual world has an intimate relationship with the material world and seeks to help us improve what we have here. That is, when we increase our obedience to the Lord Jesus Christ to include all His commandments, our circumstances—temporal, emotional, intellectual, and spiritual—begin to improve. Temporal conditions are responsive to spiritual dynamics. Life is fluid and reconfigures according to our spiritual input. That does not mean, of course, that afflictions, trials, pain, and sorrows will not come, but it does mean that within the covenant of consecration everything is arranged to work for our experience and our good (see, e.g., D&C 90:24—*"Search diligently, pray always, and be believing, and all things shall work together for you good, if ye walk uprightly and remember the covenant wherewith ye have covenanted one with another"*). The Lord alleviates our afflictions and consecrates them to our gain (see 2 Nephi 2:2).

---

13. I'm grateful to Harold Brown of Welfare Services for these insights which he gave in an address to welfare missionaries in Salt Lake City, January 2005.

The Law of Prosperity

The Lord has His own law of prosperity in His perfect economic system and it works this way: as a consequence for payment of tithes and offerings, we have the promise that we will have sufficient for our own needs and also enough to help others, plus spiritual guidance and divine intervention in our lives.

When the Lord says repeatedly in the scriptures, *"If ye will keep my commandments ye shall prosper in land—but if ye keep not [my] commandments, ye shall be cut off from [my] presence"* (Alma 37:13), He uses *prosper* to mean both spiritual and temporal enlargement through His enabling presence in the details of our lives. That the Lord intends *prosper* to mean both spiritual and temporal prosperity is clear from the scriptures, and in this following example we see the dynamic between caring for the poor and the increase in material goods:

> *And now because of the steadiness of the church they began to be exceedingly rich, having abundance of all things whatsoever they stood in need.... In their prosperous circumstances, they did not send away any who were naked, or that were hungry;... therefore they were liberal to all...whether out of the church or in the church....And thus they did prosper and become far more wealthy than those who did not belong to their church.* (Alma 1:29–31)

We have yet another example of the Lord's interest in our temporal as well as spiritual welfare, since all things are spiritual to the Lord (see D&C 29:34–35). This scripture helps us realize the Lord's continual involvement in our wellbeing, down to providing the very food on our plate, the very clothes, the roof, even to His going before us to prepare what we will need. His hands are tied only by our carelessness in observing the eternal laws of abundance and prosperity.

If it so be that the children of men keep the commandments of
God he doth nourish them, and strengthen them, and provide means
whereby they can accomplish the thing which he has commanded
them; wherefore, he did provide means for us while we did sojourn
in the wilderness.... I will also be your light in the wilderness; and
I will prepare the way before you, if it so be that ye shall keep my
commandments. (1 Nephi 17:3, 13)

Debt and Self-Reliance

Perhaps it is self-evident that Zion has a citizenship that does
not have debt. To prepare to live in Zion, the Saints must reduce and ultimately eliminate debt, control their spending,
and give generously to the Lord's programs of building and
relief. This requirement pertains to the temporal and spiritual
independence of Zion (see D&C 78:14).

With respect to our accountability for our wealth, we find
a possibly disquieting scripture in D&C 42:39—*"For I will con-*
secrate of the riches of those who embrace my gospel among the
Gentiles[14] *unto the poor of my people who are of the house of Israel"*
(membership of the Church throughout the world). The Lord
has blessed His Saints in the North American Church with
much prosperity—obviously not so that we can buy more and
more stuff, but as a stewardship, as a resource, that the rest of
the world can draw on. The Church in North America supports the rest of the world Church, as well as many humani-
tarian projects for those who are not members. This is a great
opportunity and blessing for us.

---

14. In the Book of Mormon, "Gentiles" is the term the Lord often uses to
refer to the saints gathered out of the great gentile nations of the earth,
who are nevertheless the literal blood of Israel, but *cultural* gentiles. He
uses the terms "remnant of Joseph" or "remnant of Jacob" to refer to the
seed of Lehi in the Americas. For example, see D&C 109:58, 60. "House of
Israel" is a comprehensive term and can refer to any of the tribes of Israel,
members of the Church or not, throughout the world.

The Heavens watch what we do with our abundance: *"If thou obtainest more than that which would be for thy support, thou shalt give it into my storehouse"* (D&C 42:55). We see that the Lord has an ingenious program to eliminate poverty as well as to establish temporal and spiritual self-reliance among His people; as we work toward that, we qualify for Zion.

Who Shall Escape to Zion?

The Brethren have repeatedly reminded us of what's coming on the earth. President Henry B. Eyring spoke to a group of university students with these sobering words:

> The Lord is anxious to lead us to the safety of higher ground, away from the path of physical and spiritual danger. As the world becomes darker and more dangerous, we must keep climbing. It will be our choice whether to move up or to stay where we are. But the Lord will invite and guide us upward by the direction of the Holy Ghost, which He sends to His leaders and to His people who will receive it.[15]

President Eyring warned that the Indian Ocean tsunami of December 2004 and the earthquake that caused it are "just the beginning and a part of what is to come, terrible as it was."[16]

We are experiencing now a foretaste of the events precedent to the Lord's Coming. The Lord tells us that Babylon will fall. He, knowing the calamity which should come upon the inhabitants of the earth, restored the gospel of Jesus Christ with its broad-spectrum protections to preserve us as trouble on the earth deepens (see D&C 1:17–18). Zion, having become

---

15. *Church News*, February 5, 2005, report of Henry B. Eyring's devotional address at BYU–Idaho, January 15, 2005.

16. *Ibid.*

independent temporally and spiritually, will, the Lord says, be for *"a defense, and for a refuge from the storm, and from wrath when it shall be poured ou<u>t without mixture</u> upon the whole earth"* (D&C 115:6).

The Lord looks to the future on our behalf: *"If Zion do these things she shall prosper, and spread herself and become very glorious, very great, and very terrible. And the nations of the earth shall honor her, and shall say: Surely ... God is there.... Therefore, let Zion rejoice, for this is Zion—THE PURE IN HEART; ... while all the wicked shall mourn"* (D&C 97:18, 21).

But if some members choose not to follow the Lord's instructions for advancement and protection, they will not find their Church membership any safeguard for them:

> *For behold, and lo, vengeance cometh speedily upon the ungodly as the whirlwind; and who shall escape it? The Lord's scourge shall pass over by night and by day, and the report thereof shall vex all people; yea, it shall not be stayed until the Lord come.... Nevertheless, Zion shall escape if she observe to do all things whatsoever I have commanded her. But if ... not ... I will visit her ... with sore affliction ... with pestilence, with plague, with sword, with vengeance, with devouring fire.* (D&C 97:22–23, 25–26)

We have considered here the eternal nature of the Zion order and acknowledged that our current society can never prepare us to live in Zion. The previous societies that succeeded in establishing Zion did so in the midst of sorrows and bloodshed, but were able to keep themselves separate from the world's unclean things. But the Zion society attempted in the early part of this dispensation failed because the Saints were not able to abandon the ways of Babylon. They were not able to care for the poor and they failed to establish unity among themselves. The prophet Joseph warned that "party feelings, separate interests, exclusive designs should be lost sight of in the one common cause, in the interest of the whole."[17] But the Wilderness Mind overtook the Saints, and unity eluded them. Chastened and driven from their homes, the vision of Zion fading away, the Saints mourned; but the Lord reassured them:

> *Zion shall be redeemed, although she is chastened for a little season.* (D&C 100:13)

> *Therefore, let your hearts be comforted concerning Zion; for all flesh is in mine hands; be still and know that I am God. Zion shall not be moved out of her place, notwithstanding her children are scattered. They that . . . are pure in heart, shall return, and . . . with songs of everlasting joy to build up the waste places of Zion.* (D&C 101:16–18)

The full establishment of Zion was to wait for a later day.

---

17. *TPJS*, 231.

Chapter Seven
Appendix One

ZION
Joseph Smith

The building up of Zion is a cause that has interested the people of God in every age; it is a theme upon which prophets, priests and kings have dwelt with peculiar delight; they have looked forward with joyful anticipation to the day in which we live; and fired with heavenly and joyful anticipations they have sung and written and prophesied of this our day; but they died without the sight.

We are the favored people that God has made choice of to bring about the latter-day glory; it is left for us to see, participate in and help to roll forward the Latter-day glory, "the dispensation of the fullness of times, when God will gather together all things that are in heaven, and all things that are upon the earth," "even in one," when the Saints of God will be gathered in one from every nation, and kindred, and people, and tongue, when the Jew will be gathered together into one, the wicked will also be gathered together to be destroyed, as spoken of by the prophets.

The Spirit of God will also dwell with His people, and be withdrawn from the rest of the nations, and all things whether in heaven or on earth will be in one, even in Christ.

The heavenly Priesthood will unite with the earthly, to bring about those great purposes; and whilst we are thus united in one common cause, to roll forth the kingdom of God, the heavenly Priesthood are not idle spectators, the spirit of God will be showered down from above, and it will dwell in our midst.

The blessings of the Most High will rest upon our tabernacles, and our name will be handed down to future ages; our children will rise up and call us blessed; and generations yet unborn will dwell with peculiar delight upon the scenes that we have passed through, the privations that we have endured; the untiring zeal that we have manifested; the all but insurmountable difficulties that we have overcome in laying the foundations of a work that brought about the glory and blessing which they will realize; a work that God and angels have contemplated with delight for generations past; that fired the souls of the ancient patriarchs and prophets; a work that is destined to bring about the destruction of the powers of darkness, the renovation of the earth, the glory of God, and the salvation of the human family.

(*TPJS*, 230–32; May 2, 1842; punctuation altered by author for readability.)

CHAPTER SEVEN
APPENDIX TWO

[VISION OF THE HOLY CITY]

The Excursion
By William Wordsworth
Book II: 830–881

A step,

A single step, that freed me from the skirts
Of the blind vapour, opened to my view
Glory beyond all glory ever seen
By waking sense or by the dreaming soul!
The appearance, instantaneously disclosed,
Was of a mighty city—boldly say
A wilderness of building, sinking far
And self-withdrawn into a boundless depth,
Far sinking into splendor—without end!
Fabric it seemed of diamond and of gold,
With alabaster domes, and silver spires,
And blazing terrace upon terrace, high
Uplifted; here, serene pavilions bright,

In avenues disposed; there, towers begirt
With battlements that on their restless fronts
Bore stars—illumination of all gems!
By earthly nature had the effect been wrought
Upon the dark materials of the storm
Now pacified; on them, and on the coves
And mountain-steeps and summits, whereunto
The vapours had receded, taking there
Their station under a cerulean sky.
Oh, 'twas an unimaginable sight!
Clouds, mists, streams, watery rocks and
        emerald turf,
Clouds of all tincture, rocks and sapphire sky,
Confused, commingled, mutually inflamed,
Molten together, and composing thus,
Each lost in each, that marvelous array
Of temple, palace, citadel, and huge
Fantastic pomp of structure without name,
In fleecy folds voluminous, enwrapped.
Right in the midst, where interspace appeared
Of open court, an object like a throne
Under a shining canopy of state
Stood fixed; and fixed resemblances were seen
To implements of ordinary use,
But vast in size, in substance glorified;
Such as by Hebrew Prophets were beheld
In vision—forms uncouth of mightiest power
For admiration and mysterious awe.
This little Vale, a dwelling-place of Man,
Lay low beneath my feet; 'twas visible—
I saw not, but I felt that it was there.
That which I *saw* was the revealed abode
Of Spirits in beatitude: my heart

Swelled in my breast.—'I have been dead,' I
Cried,
'And now I live! Oh! Wherefore *do* I live?'
And with that pang I prayed to be no more!—
....
—there I stood and gazed:
The apparition faded not away,
And I descended.

CHAPTER EIGHT

TO ENTER ZION:
RENOUNCING ENMITY

Therefore, verily, thus saith the Lord, let Zion rejoice, for this is Zion—
THE PURE IN HEART.

D&C 97:21

෴

And the Lord called his people Zion, because they were of one heart and
one mind, and dwelt in righteousness.

Moses 7:18

෴

Purity of heart is to will one thing.

Søren Kierkegaard

෴

If Zion is the pure in heart, we read the opposites of that condition in scripture where the Lord reveals why Zion was not
redeemed in the 1800s: *"There were jarrings, and contentions,*
and envyings, and strifes, and lustful and covetous desires among
them; therefore by these things they polluted their inheritances"

(D&C 101:6). The "jarrings and contentions" point to a basic impurity in the human heart, that is, *enmity*, which can be defined as hostility, hatred, or contempt for another person. In this passage the Lord identifies the feelings and behaviors that make our heart impure and lead to war instead of unity among us. Truly the battle is engaged between the two great thought-worlds: Babylon—with its anger, hatred, battle cries, casualties, and misery—and Zion, with her soundness, stability, clarity, and power of redeeming love. In the world we have to live in the culture of war, but the Saints must learn to live in the world and not make war; they must establish a different culture. The time is coming, our scriptures tell us, when Zion will be the only people not at war (see D&C 45:69). Not being at war in any degree qualifies one to enter the gates.

The Lord is serious about the feelings in our heart toward one another. In the same section in which He condemns "jarrings and contentions," He says that when He comes again, and the veil over the earth is taken off, the powerful glory accompanying Him will consume every corruptible thing of man or beast, that is, will consume any being that has enmity of any degree in its heart: *"And in that day the enmity of man, and the enmity of beasts, yea, the enmity of all flesh, shall cease from before my face"* (D&C 101:26). Enmity makes us impure and corruptible. The reason that beings with enmity will be destroyed seems to be that enmity decreases a person's ability to endure holiness, being a contracted, self-absorbed, toxic, and blind state. The nervous system of a spiritually underdeveloped person cannot withstand the higher energy field of purified beings and conditions. Enmity then puts us at risk and makes us perishable in the presence of holiness.

Therefore, we realize the critical need for the Saints to let go of the enmity among them if we are to sit down together in Zion without becoming irritated, annoyed, impatient, critical, frustrated, or even outraged with each other.

But let us explore a little more the manifestations of enmity in our life. Few of us could say that our heart is free of enmity, even though we may want to hide it from ourselves and downplay its extent and impact in our lives. But we do not have to dig very deep to find it, the veneer of our spirituality being sometimes woefully thin. It may surface in us while we're driving along on the highway, or perhaps at a sporting event, or when someone disagrees with us, offends, criticizes, opposes, shows lack of respect for, or is abusive to us.

Under these conditions, we may manifest feelings of enmity in overt ways or in subtle ways: through blaming, accusing, trying to control another, subtle put-downs disguised as jokes, trivializing another's opinions or feelings or being, undermining, threatening, name-calling, forgetting things important to the other, ordering another around, and abusive anger. Enmity is contempt, manifested not only in words but also in subtle facial expressions like eye-rolling or narrowing of eyes, cold silences, "don't touch me," giving each other "the look." If the words or attitudes disempower, show disrespect, or devalue the other, then they are abusive.

Most of us have experimented with these forms of enmity, and, on reflection, we don't approve of them. But, to our dismay, we may find ourselves being irritable with the very people the Lord has put in our lives to love and be happy with. What is it about others' behavior that has such negative power over us? Why is it that we give others that power to afflict us, making us want to criticize, withdraw, reject, punish? Why are we so affected by little habits or mannerisms or foibles or even larger issues in other people such that we make ourselves suffer through feelings of isolation, unlove, even unworthiness, because of *our* attitudes towards others? Are we not conscious that when we are irritated or critical, we are experiencing a form of pain?

When another person does something annoying (or insulting, disrespectful, even cruel), our programmed response may be to receive a fiery dart into our heart: "I refuse to tolerate this," "He'll pay for this," "I'm offended and angry," "I really hate him." Maybe we have just assumed that we need others' behavior to please us in order to be happy and to love them. Nevertheless, they disappoint us and in some cases they seem to be ruining our lives. So we let them know in various ways that we don't want them, whether it's a husband, a wife, a child, a neighbor, or some other person. Perhaps we think these unloving behaviors are just to be expected as part of the mortal probation—even though we can feel that they damage our confidence in our own goodness, make our perception of the Spirit a little spotty, and blind us to God's love.

Enmity in all its shades forms the veil between us and a higher dimension. It colors our world gray, and though we may not know what the real problem is, we feel under its influence that we are only sort of alive. Someone offends us, so we think, and we respond—not with understanding or mercy, but with some flavor of resistance or enmity. The problem is we can feel so *justified* for mistreating and withholding love from others. I mean, don't they deserve it? But no matter how justified, we're the ones who don't feel good when we're in a conflict with someone else or when we treat others badly. No, *"Men are instructed sufficiently that they know good from evil"* (2 Nephi 2:5). The Spirit warns us—but we may override it.

While we are justifying ourselves in our attack, we do not feel the toll these behaviors are taking or what is happening in our own body, nor do we see the pain in the other person's face. Enmity exacts a price spiritually, emotionally, even physically. It creates a type of energy in the spirit and body which precludes spiritual experience, keeping us dissatisfied with life, unclear, restless in spirit, perhaps even sick. We don't feel worthy;

our faith is weak; we don't feel a divine connection. Peter says that such a person who has neglected pure love is *"blind, and cannot see afar off, and hath forgotten that he was purged from his old sins"* (2 Peter 1:9). In the eternal sense it won't matter how much tithing we pay, or how much visiting teaching we do, or how many meetings we attend, or how much scripture we read if we do not come to love the Lord's way. It is likely that we will not be prepared to enter the gates of Zion until we can see ourselves and others in a different light.

Thus we sin against ourself when we entertain enmity. When we are feeling hateful thoughts and we are immersed in the feelings of our conflict with another person, we are unaware that it puts us at war with our own self. And what are some of the evidences for that? We need only locate in our body where it is that we feel that unlove to find the literal distress that enmity creates. Experiments in laboratories have shown that under the influence of powerful negative emotions, man's physiology deteriorates from coherence to chaos. It seems that nothing afflicts our emotional brain and our physiology more than feeling emotionally cut off from those to whom we are most attached—spouse, children, or parents. It was found that a harsh word, or a tiny facial contortion of contempt or disgust—hardly visible to an observer—is enough to speed up the heartbeat in the person for whom the remark was intended. "After a well-aimed jab combined with a bit of disdain, the heart rate will suddenly climb to more than 110 (as opposed to normal 70–80)."[1] Researchers have discovered that every time we engage in unpleasantness with someone at the office, or with a loved one, or even in the street, our line of

---

1. David Servan-Schreiber, *The Instinct to Heal, Curing Stress, Anxiety, and Depression without Drugs and without Talk Therapy* (Emmaus, Pennsylvania: Rodale Press, 2004), 180.

defense against infections lowers its guard for several hours.[2] On the other hand, Dr. David Servan-Schreiber observes, "True empowering love makes us stronger physically, boosts our immune system, heals emotional wounds and fears and transforms troubled relationships."[3]

We know that we are predisposed by the Fall to feel enmity. We arrive from the premortal world, innocent and full of love, and find ourselves in a culture in which fear engenders enmity. The root of enmity is fear. Our culture feeds that fear, and enmity increases. The Adversary has a great investment in keeping us trapped in feelings of enmity and encourages us to respond the way the world responds to the everyday abrasions of life. As a result, we think we have to feel offended, we have to get even, we have to be touchy, we have to control, and we have to live with pain or bitterness over something that happened years before. We may not even question that we have to think and live this way. But by these means, Satan increases his power over us and hides the truth of our being from us; his purpose is to disable our *will* to love and to be happy.

Here are some similar assumptions we make that keep us addicted to disturbance, encourage enmity, and ultimately disqualify us from entering Zion:

1. We are insufficient in ourselves and have to get others to fill us up with love, approval, and appreciation. We can never be good enough and need frequent reassurance.

2. We are victims in a random world where anything can happen and we have to be stressed and afraid and try to control a lot of things and people in order to feel safe. My happiness depends on circumstances, on what other people do, and on what happens to me.

---

2. *Ibid.*, 60.
3. *Ibid.*, 178.

3. If something bad happens to me, I have to be emotionally damaged by it—maybe for much of my life.

4. If someone is offensive, I have to be offended; what is more, I am justified in doing back to my offender whatever he did to me, or at least some form of vengeance or payback.

5. I have to be angry and frustrated with stupid and incompetent and corrupt people.

6. Because of all the circumstances that didn't turn out the way I wanted them to in my life, there is a certain level of emotional pain I have to live with.

7. My unhappiness is all their fault.

Interesting, isn't it, that not one of the above statements is true? But human beings find that giving up their addiction to misery and suffering and self-pity is one of the hardest things to do. In fact, instead of giving them up by seeing through them, the mind attaches to miserable thoughts and then tries to find evidence that proves these thoughts are justifiable! These thoughts, bordering on insanity, can take on a reality that they do not intrinsically possess.

So, when we are not clear about spiritual things, we can get trapped in a particular way of thinking because we don't see our options—we hear about the joy of the Son—but where is it? We're not trying to be bad; we just don't know a better way. I had a friend say to me a few weeks ago, "We know what we're supposed to be and feel like, but we don't see how to get there."

We suffer from the limitations of the Natural Mind. If we try to solve spiritual problems, like enmity and lack of love, in the Natural Mind, we will fail, because this mind can't feel the spiritual way of things; we will find ourselves just going through motions, but not changing our heart at all. Soon we realize that half-measures will not produce the change we need.

We have to stop protecting our carnal behavior and totally renounce it.

The Father of King Lamoni asks Aaron a form of the same question that my friend was asking, *"What shall I do that I may be born of God, having this wicked spirit rooted out of my breast, and receive his Spirit, that I may be filled with joy?"* Aaron's answer was: *"If thou repent of all thy sins, and bow down before God, and call on his name in faith, believing that ye shall receive, then shalt thou receive the hope which thou desirest."* The king then said to the Lord, *"I will give away all my sins to know thee"* (Alma 22:15–16, 18). With that commitment, a profound change was wrought in this man. We learn that the person who wants to be freed from the effects of his carnal programming must commit himself to an abandonment of the Carnal Mind or he can never hope for anything but adjustments to his behavior. He must gain access to the powers of change in the Spiritual Mind through cultivating a fervent love of the Lord and the abandonment of ungodly behavior. Moroni describes the process:

> *Come unto Christ, and be perfected in him, and deny yourselves of all ungodliness; and if ye shall deny yourselves of all ungodliness, and love God with all your might, mind and strength, then is his grace sufficient for you, that by his grace ye may be perfect in Christ.* (Moroni 10:32)

We can come to discern clearly our own ungodliness and the way it has contaminated our mind, behavior, and experience.

We see the value of continuing to observe the particular workings of our own mind, because, to get the best out of this instrument, we must know how it functions. In general the thoughts of the Natural Man are dispersed, drawing him in disparate directions, fragmenting his soul. It is his very inability to focus on principles of Light that keeps him from breaking through to that which would nourish and heal his soul.

Renouncing Carnal Behavior

As we have seen, the Natural Mind, if left to its own devices, tends to run in negative paths; it likes to collect worries, fears, self-deprecating thoughts, and negative interpretations of other people, which ideas then taint one's feelings and behavior. We have a part of our brain that likes to spin negative stories that have no foundation in reality. We want to be clear that unloving thoughts come from the delusional mind; loving thoughts, on the other hand, are a product of our eternal being and the stream of Truth in us. Unloving thoughts about ourselves and others cannot endure in eternity because they do not perceive things as they really are; they are not true and cannot develop Spirit but only unhappiness. But loving, generous, merciful thoughts do belong to Eternity, are real, will endure, and will produce heavenly fruit. When we greet each situation with kindness, we bring a spiritual essence to it, empowering ourselves and the situation, allowing miracles to take place.

Man sins against himself when he indulges in enmity because he was not created emotionally neutral; rather, he has a deep, divine need both for inner harmony as well as connectedness with other people. Indeed, the Lord designed Man to carry within himself the power to nourish himself emotionally and spiritually. Therefore it will make sense to us that the Lord has put the responsibility for our own happiness in our own soul, not in the hands of our neighbors or in the circumstances of our lives. To realize our full development and our capacity for joy, we can become more respectful of these inner, primeval needs for harmony and connectedness in our soul. If we think of love and peace as our quintessential reality, we begin to realize how far afield we may have strayed.

We see then that Man, by his unloving thoughts and behavior, has cut himself off from the very thing he craves most—without knowing what he was doing. He has done it by excluding, criticizing, manipulating, and punishing those around him, not realizing that every time he has done that, he has insulated himself from the actual experience of love. He does not love himself when he acts without love, nor does he feel lovable, nor does he feel God's love. He cannot love the mind he has created with his unlove. He rejects others and he rejects himself.

The Spiritual Mind must be strengthened through a spiritual practice, and doing that, we can exorcise enmity by an energy exchange. The world-mind has its energy, and the Spirit has its own particular type of energy. If we are feeding too much, through whatever medium, on the world-mind and its thought-world, which is characterized by enmity and self-seeking, the Natural Man will be our reality and will run us. We will not have the inner power to abandon ungodliness and to be lifted up in Christ and filled with His love. We must do an energy exchange by chasing darkness with Light and consciously choosing the energy that will hum throughout our soul.

We can do this exchange when we realize that each type of energy, light or dark, follows the intention of the heart. We can cultivate a new intention by considering a new point of view; for example, we can begin to pick up, not on what we don't like in a person, but rather on a different set of stimuli. Terry Warner talks about becoming responsive:

> We are constantly receiving signals from others that reveal something of their needs and hopes and fears…. We are called upon by others' unspoken requests, expressed in their faces and gestures and voices, to treat them with consideration and respect…. To be a person in a family or community [e.g., Zion]

is to pick up from others such gently expressed imperatives as these. Our humanity consists in our ability to sense and respect and respond to the humanity of others.... The fundamental ingredient is an awakening of each individual to others and a willing effort to respond without any personal agenda in exactly the way that seems most right, considerate, and helpful.[4]

I notice that I can love the people that I respond to with respect, but have trouble loving the people I have sinned against. How powerful that realization is! Somehow it all starts in my own head and in my choice as to a way of being with others. "At the level of who we 'are'—our *being*—there are two ways only,"[5] says a little book called *The Choice*. It describes these two ways as (1) the Responsive Way, which means that we choose to be responsive to others—their concerns, hopes, needs, and fears. These become as real to me as I am to myself. Then there is (2) the Resistant Way, in which we see people as objects; we are resistant to their reality and see them as less than, or less relevant, or less important, or less real. In this way of being, I am false. As a result of my choice, they may suffer, and I will suffer. Our confidence can grow in the Responsive Way. In time we may experience that everything but love is suffering in some form, even though, in the moment, the pain of unloving behavior may be masked by an aspect of pleasure.

The way of being we choose will determine the quality of our responses to others. We respond to others according to what we have cultivated inside. As another author writes: "Regardless of how another person interacts with you, you can give away only what you have inside to give. Just like the proverbial

4. *Bonds That Make Us Free* (Salt Lake City: Deseret Book, 2001), 129–30.

5. *The Choice* is based on Terry Warner's work on self-deception, as in *Bonds;* this quote is from *The Choice,* Arbinger Institute, 2. Their books can be ordered at www.arbinger.com.

orange, when you squeeze it, you get what is inside—it has nothing to do with who does the squeezing, or the circumstances surrounding the squeeze. What comes out is what is inside.... If you respond to hate with hate, or anger with anger, it is not because of what was directed your way; it is because that is what is inside you. You can't give hate if you have only love inside, no matter how much squeezing comes your way."[6] In another place he counseled, "Let people see that you ... have only love to give them."[7]

Letting people see that I have only love to give them is easier to do when I understand the real truth behind judging another person. There are so many factors that may distort my perception of him: I can never know his mind or heart—or even what his intent was. I don't even always know my own mind and heart or why I am picking on him—but with honest introspection I'll see that I myself am in some way guilty of what I don't like in him. We are indeed likely to project our own faults onto another person. The great philosopher, Søren Kierkegaard, writes reflecting on the eagerness with which we may latch onto a fault in another:

> Scripture warns against judging and adds, "lest you be judged." It still seems as if at times one might judge without being judged in return. But this is not the case. At the very moment you judge another person or criticize another person, you judge yourself. For to judge another means ultimately only to judge oneself or to reveal oneself. Perhaps it escapes your attention; you perhaps do not notice how earnest existence is, how by showing you all these people it provides you, as it were, occasions for judging ... then it is existence which judges you.

6. Wayne W. Dyer, *Real Magic* (San Francisco: HarperCollins, 2001), 139–40.
7. *Ibid.*, 164.

However greedy a man might be for judging—if he knew what it is to judge, how slow he would become! However wildly he snatches at the smallest crumb in order to have the occasion to judge—it is an opportunity to ensnare himself.[8]

"Existence," as Kierkegaard says, sets us up with repeated opportunities to choose how we shall regard our fellowman; and in what we choose, we often reveal only ourself. We can come to know by the type of energy in our own soul whether our appraisal of him is astute discernment or whether only our own guilty projection gone underground. If I'm incensed over how controlling she is, I could take a look at my own manipulations. How arrogant, how self-righteous we can be! So, we notice, others look different as we practice retaining a remission of our own sins instead of taking an inventory of theirs. Repentance produces a different energy and a different reality.

We may realize after awhile that we've had it backwards if we look to another person to see if he provokes love in us. Waiting to be provoked into love, or its opposite, is not the way of the Spiritual Mind. No, we must first choose a way of being that affects our behavior to all, allowing each person to be as he or she is, since we find we have no power or authority to change another. The apostle Paul counsels a particular way of being:

> Put on therefore, as the elect of God, holy and beloved, bowels of mercies, kindness, humbleness of mind, meekness, longsuffering; Forbearing one another, and forgiving one another.... And above all these things put on charity, which is the bond of perfectness. (Colossians 3:12–14)

The Natural Man's thought-system is so defective that he can't really act in pure love; his acts will be tainted in some

---

8. *Works of Love* (New York: Harper & Row, 1964), 220.

way by self-interest: "*Wherefore, a man being evil cannot do that which is good; neither will he give a good gift*" (Moroni 7:10). We must become swallowed up in love itself and then that way of being affects our way of treating everyone else, including ourself. It's a decision we make as part of our spiritual practice. We find we can stop blaming and become instead more solution oriented. Then we find we have nothing to forgive because we just no longer blame. We begin to see how we can be increasingly grateful for the role that each person plays in our life.

The Role That People Play for Us

Let us think on the role that people play in our life. "Existence" is indeed paying attention to us, it being much more loving and devoted to our spiritual welfare than we ourselves generally are to our own or others'. With eyes to see, we find that we are participants in a highly interactive universe, a dynamic laboratory, in which the Governing Powers lead us and even provoke us to "*be conformed to the image of [God's] Son*" (Romans 8:29). To this end, the Lord, knowing what we do not yet understand about our own soul, what has not yet been healed or resolved in us, allows circumstances and events to provoke the tutorials which will set us free in love.

Therefore, as thoughts seek access to our mind, and people cross our path, we may be deceived into thinking that any pain we feel is their fault. But eternal law says we get to choose out of which mind, which way of being, we will respond. We can get angry and resist everything and blame everybody and find peace very elusive. Or, we can love them and thank them for being our teachers and helping us to get clear on what it is that perhaps we need to change. Byron Katie helps us to see what a blessing we have in the people who tell us the truth. Can we receive it without getting angry and defending ourselves?

Defense is the first act of war. If you tell me that I'm mean, rejecting, hard, unkind, unfair, I say, "Thank you, sweetheart, I can find all these in my life, I have been everything you say, and more. Tell me everything you see, and together we can help me understand. Through you, I come to know myself. Without you, how can I know the places in me that are unkind and invisible? You bring me to myself. So, Sweetheart, look into my eyes and tell me again. I want you to give me everything." This is how friends meet. It's called integrity. I am all things. If you see me as unkind, that is an opportunity for me to go inside and look at what appears in my life.... If you say one single thing that I have the urge to defend, that thing is the very pearl waiting inside me to be discovered.[9]

In fact, as Katie says, "The people we most need are the people we're living with now. Again and again, they will show us the truth we don't want to see, until we see it. Our parents, our children, our spouses and our friends will continue to press every button we have, until we realize what it is that we don't want to know about ourselves yet."[10] The great insight here is that we must search fearlessly until we see *our own part* in our conflicts with other people, because it is surely there. When we then go to the people we've judged and we apologize and we tell them what we've seen about ourself and how we're working on it now—freedom and clarity come; we have a deeper experience with what it means to be clean.

President John Taylor teaches us that our relationships, the way we treat others, have to do with what it is we really want:

If there be trouble existing between me and anybody else, I would meet them half way, yes, I would meet them three

---

9. *I Need Your Love—Is That True?* (New York: Three Rivers Press, 2006), 219.
10. *Loving What Is* (New York: Random House, 2002), 33.

quarters or even all of the way. I would feel like yielding; I would say, I do not want to quarrel, I want to be a Saint. I have set out for purity, virtue, brotherhood, and for obedience to the laws of God on earth, and for thrones and principalities and dominions in the eternal worlds, and I will not allow such paltry affairs to interfere with my prospects. I am for life, eternal lives and eternal exaltations in the kingdom of God.[11]

Obviously one characteristic of a Zion person is that he will have learned to be quite independent of what others choose to do, as he sidesteps enmity's recruiting power. I also learn from President Taylor that my kindness is at least as much for me as it is for you, since I am responsible before God for my own spiritual fitness.

I return to this question: who knows but that the people in our lives are there precisely to provoke this very realization, this very ordering of priorities, whether to yield to the Carnal Mind or to press on to Zion and all that lies beyond? Perhaps the essential purpose of all relationships is to create the laboratory in which we uncover our own divine nature and encourage theirs. Who knows, indeed, but that by some premortal agreement, these people were placed to provide these very learning opportunities for us here on earth? This possibility doesn't necessarily condone what they may do, but it gives me a different perspective on their role in my life. It helps me to look at a person who would have irritated me a while back and just love that person as a reflection of God's love for me.

A dear friend of mine, who through the years had been in conflict off and on with her beautiful daughter, dreamed in the early hours of the morning of an encounter with this daughter. The mother said reproachfully, "You are so critical of me!" The

---

11. *Teachings of Presidents of the Church: John Taylor* (Salt Lake City: The Church of Jesus Christ of Latter-day Saints), 26.

daughter answered, "But, Mother, you are so critical of *me*." Suddenly they felt a great love for each other. Then the mother understood that she and her daughter, knowing the stresses and strains that would beset their earthly association, agreed in their love to submit to these difficulties during their earth life for what each would learn from each other. Neither wanted to be the source of pain for the other, but, more than freedom from sin and pain, they wanted spiritual growth. Now she just puts her arms around her daughter.

The Lord commands us to love our enemies (see Matthew 5:44). How do we do that? Loving people does not necessarily mean taking them into our intimate society; it does not necessarily mean doing whatever they might want us to do. President Joseph F. Smith clarifies what it means to love one's enemies:

> I feel in my heart to forgive all men in the broad sense that God requires of me to forgive all men, and I desire to love my neighbor as myself; and to this extent I bear no malice toward any of the children of my Father. But there are enemies to the work of the Lord, as there were enemies to the Son of God. There are those who speak only evil of the Latter-day Saints. There are those—and they abound largely in our midst—who will shut their eyes to every virtue and to every good thing connected with this latter-day work, and will pour out floods of falsehood and misrepresentation against the people of God. I forgive them for this. I leave them in the hands of the just Judge. Let him deal with them as seemeth him good, but they are not and cannot become my bosom companions. I cannot descend to that. While I would not harm a hair of their heads, while I would not throw a straw in their path, to hinder them from turning from the error of their way to the light of truth; I would as soon think of taking a centipede or a scorpion, or any poisonous reptile, and putting

it into my bosom, as I would think of becoming a companion or associate of such men....

I do not want to become so blinded with love for my enemies that I cannot discern between light and darkness, between truth and error, between good and evil, but I hope to live so that I shall have sufficient light in me to discern.[12]

President Smith teaches us how to be clear about the way in which pure love is to be expressed. We take care not to fall into the error of putting a scorpion in our bosom in the name of love. Yes, always harmless as doves, we can be wise as serpents (see Matthew 10:16).

But speaking of pure love, lest we mistake its true nature, here is a helpful analysis by the psychiatrist and spiritual therapist, David Hawkins:

> Love as depicted in the mass media is not what this level is about. What the world generally refers to as love is an intense emotional condition, combining physical attraction, possessiveness, control, addiction, eroticism, and novelty. It's usually fragile and fluctuating, waxing and waning with varying conditions. When frustrated, this emotion often reveals an underlying anger and dependency that it had masked. That love can turn to hate is a common perception, but here, an addictive sentimentality is likely what's being spoken about, rather than Love; there probably never was actual love in such a relationship, for Hate stems from Pride, not Love.
>
> [Pure Love] is unconditional, unchanging, and permanent. It doesn't fluctuate—its source isn't dependent on external factors. Loving is a state of being. It's a forgiving, nurturing, and supportive way of relating to the world. Love isn't intellectual

---

12. Joseph F. Smith, *Gospel Doctrine* (Salt Lake City: Deseret, 1986), 337–38.

and doesn't proceed from the mind; Love emanates from the heart. It has the capacity to lift others and accomplish great feats because of its purity of motive.[13]

Love, then, has an irrational quality to it; that is, it is not based necessarily on *reasons* to love another person, but is rather a choice as to how we are going to encounter the world around us. It is an attitude that we are going to establish, a "state of being" that is independent of what others choose to do.

Every person in Zion will have come to understand that Zion can only survive if love and at-one-ment are the established dynamic in each heart. Dr. Hawkins continues his remarks on love, showing how pure love dissolves impediments to unity:

> It's then possible to "one with another," for there are no longer any barriers. Love is therefore inclusive and expands the sense of self progressively. Love focuses on the goodness of life in all its expressions and augments that which is positive—it dissolves negativity by recontextualizing it, rather than by attacking it.... As Love becomes more and more unconditional, it begins to be experienced as inner Joy. This isn't the sudden joy of a pleasurable turn of events; it's a constant accompaniment to all activities. Joy arises from within each moment of existence, rather than from any other source.[14]

His observations are reminiscent of that heavenly gift that the Nephites enjoyed in the wake of the Savior's ministry (see 4 Nephi). Their love made it possible for them to live in a different dimension, or glory, even as they lived on the earth.

---

13. David R. Hawkins, *Power vs. Force: The Hidden Determinants of Human Behavior* (Carlsbad: Hay House, 2002), 89–90.

14. *Ibid.*, 90–91.

Living in a higher glory while on earth is what living in Zion is all about, and two people, or a thousand people, can realize this elevating potential in love.

We want to be clear that the purifying of emotions through letting enmity fall away is not only a psychological adjustment that Man achieves by his own efforts, but is, in addition, the result of the power of the Spirit of the Lord. Otherwise pure love could not appear in this world, coming as it does from another realm. It has to be brought into the soul of a man by a God from a higher plane.

In speaking about the nature of Heavenly Beings and the power of love, Elder John Groberg offered a marvelous insight into the "essences of eternity," which he said are light, life, and love. This being so, he said, each of us must become a conduit of love, must each be a receptacle for these essences. He reminded us that anger and disturbance can close the conduit but that complete forgiveness and whole-hearted love open it again. He emphasized the importance of learning to love with the *whole* heart, as they do in Heaven. He led us into the book of Moses which reveals the atmosphere of Heaven:[15]

> *And it came to pass that the Lord spake unto Enoch, and told Enoch all the doings of the children of men; wherefore Enoch knew, and looked upon their wickedness, and their misery, and wept and stretched forth his arms, and his heart swelled wide as eternity; and his bowels yearned; and all eternity shook.* (Moses 7:41)

Thinking about Elder Groberg's whole-hearted love, we realize that not only do anger and disturbance close the conduit, but also our incomplete loving. We have wonderful people in our lives that we allow ourselves to love only partially, depriving them of a blessing and relegating ourselves to a lower degree of

---

15. Regional Conference, Provo, Utah, January 27, 2002.

glory. With a different intention, we could love them without reservation. Then we could be like celestial beings who have so incorporated these essences that they are defined by them. The Lord says, "I *am*... the light" (3 Nephi 15:9; italics added). Heaven is a place where people have *become* love, light, and life, and these attributes of holy spirit are full of feeling. Heaven is a place of greatly expanded feelings. It is this arrogant resistance to love in the heart of the Natural Man that hardens him against joy and love and against even his own divinity. As we watch the resurrected Christ in those luminous scenes with the Nephites, weeping and then rejoicing and then weeping again, we realize that the feelings of purified beings extend to greater heights and depths than the Natural Man can begin to experience. We too can tremble with love and mercy.

We too can allow love and joy to flourish in our being, catching ourselves as we try to cut them off, foiling the limits we have placed on them, and thus prepare our very nerves and sinews to endure the presence of Holiness. Moroni shows us how it is done:

> *Wherefore, my beloved brethren, pray unto the Father with all the energy of heart, that ye may be filled with this love, which he hath bestowed upon all who are true followers of his Son, Jesus Christ; that ye may become the sons of God; that when he shall appear we shall be like him, for we shall see him as he is; that we may have this hope; that we may be purified even as he is pure. Amen.* (Moroni 7:48)

Therefore, these divine attributes are first, an inspired choice; then, as our choice connects with the ready powers of Heaven, they become our felt experience, reflecting who we really are. These then lead us, the purified in heart, hand in hand with loved ones, through the shining gates of Zion.

CHAPTER NINE

SELECTIVE AT-ONE-MENT:
DISCERNING THE ENEMY

I was answered that I must join none of them.

JS—H 1:19

∽

Search diligently in the light of Christ that ye may know good from evil; and if ye will lay hold upon every good thing, and condemn it not, ye certainly will be a child of Christ.

Moroni 7:19

∽

And now Father, I pray unto thee... that I may be in them as thou, Father, art in me, that we may be one.

3 Nephi 19:23

∽

Our spirit seeks *at-one-ment*[1] with things. We tend to

---

1. *Atonement,* literally *at-one-ment,* is a word introduced into English in 1526 by William Tyndale as he translated the Greek New Testament into

appropriate things to ourselves that come to us through our senses, whether images, experiences, or people. We do this because we are continually trying to process what is happening to us; this seeking to grasp and integrate the meaning of things is the nature of our intelligence. So we merge our awareness with the spirit of the things about us as it makes its energetic rounds through myriad forms of life. Drawn to Nature as we are, we pause at the sight of a tree blowing and shimmering in the sun; or we're distracted by the faces of flowers luminous with vibrant color and scent; or arrested by illuminated silhouettes of mountains and water steeping in moonlight; or delighted as our ear is "rinsed and wrung"[2] by happy choirs of birds. We infuse the essence of those into our own soul; we at-one with them through our awareness of them and feel nourished. Or perhaps Life brings us a wonderfully loving and wise person and, wanting to be like that person, we absorb something of

English; specifically, he created the word *at-one-ment* to translate the Greek word (*katallasso*) which means "reconciliation" or "to come back into a relationship after a period of estrangement." *Reconciliation*, a word with Latin roots, means literally, "to be seated together again." This word points to what has happened to man—he has fallen from a relationship, even many relationships, and from a knowledge of the oneness of the premortal children and of divine society. The scriptures tell us that man came from a heavenly society and fell, by his birth, into a state of spiritual death (see Helaman 14:16), alienated from his Heavenly Father by the nature of the Fall. Christ wrought the atonement to *restore* us to the heavenly society. So we might say that the word rendered *atonement* by the early biblical translators could have been more accurately rendered *re-at-one-ment* or *reunion*. Christ wrought the great Reunion. ("Living the Spirit of At-One-Ment," in *Selected Writings of M. Catherine Thomas* [Salt Lake City: Deseret Book, 2000], 189.) The Hebrew word for *atonement* includes the meaning "reconciliation," but scholars find additional possible meanings such as "cover" (even "embrace").

2. "rinsed and wrung"—Gerard Manley Hopkins's phrase in his poem *Spring*.

his or her essence into ourself, which awakens in us those very qualities. We become what we are drawn to; in fact, we *are* what we are drawn to. We find out who we are as we are compelled by what is beautiful and pure; we make it our own.

As we slow down and let life distill in us, becoming aware of the movement of life around us, that life responds to us. Those with second-sight report that these beauties in Nature that catch our attention send out their spirit in response in order to at-one with us, drawn by our interest in them. Holy spirit in Nature circulates through all and quickens all life and responds to itself wherever it finds itself, whatever material form it may occupy. This is beautiful, even holy, as this characteristic in our spiritual nature also leads us to at-one with each other in whole-hearted acceptance and love. In time, this eternal at-oneing instinct folds us into the Lord's bosom.

Jacques Lusseyran, the blind Frenchman, perceived by his inner light this at-oneing movement in the things around him, enabling him by their various spiritual "pressures" on him to describe with surprising clarity the landscape he was in:

> Being attentive unlocks a sphere of reality that no one suspects. If, for instance, I walked along a path without being attentive, completely immersed in myself, I did not even know whether trees grew along the way, nor how tall they were, or whether they had leaves. When I awakened my attention, however, every tree immediately came to me. This must be taken quite literally. Every single tree projects its form, its weight, its movement—even if it was almost motionless—in my direction.... I discovered that the universe consists of pressure, that every object and every living being reveals itself to us at first by a kind of quiet yet unmistakable pressure that indicates its intention and its form.... Even stones are capable of weighing on us from a distance. So are the outlines of distant mountains, and the sudden depression of a lake at the bottom of a valley....

If all people were attentive, if they would undertake to be attentive every moment of their lives, they would discover the world anew. They would suddenly see that the world is entirely different from what they had believed it to be.[3]

Paying attention, then, amounts to a sort of at-oneing with things, loving them, letting them "touch" us. How interesting that as one comes out of the cell of self-absorption, a generally negative state, and establishes his attention in the life around him, he begins to perceive a reality that is deeply nourishing, revelatory, and responsive. Awareness of these principles can greatly enrich our experience in such a universe.

Being Selective

The principle of attention can also protect us. We draw some things to us; others we let go. We find that we must discern the influences around us and observe a certain independence of spirit, since many undesirable things also seek to at-one with us. We want to be selective and spiritually alert so that this tendency to at-one with things not cause us to join to ourselves that which would divert us as Seekers from our goals.

We have observed that our inner space is not easy to defend as the world-mind comes crowding in from the infinite images and influences that present themselves in our environment. Many of the influences that seek access to us must be investigated because they carry with them their anger, their lust, their resistance, their sadness, their vanity—recruiting us to their energy field. The Lord says, *"Behold ... there are many spirits which are false spirits, which have gone forth in the earth, deceiving the world. And also Satan hath sought to deceive you, that he might*

---

3. *Against the Pollution of the I* (Sandpoint, Idaho: Morning Light Press, 2006), 32–33.

overthrow you" (D&C 50:2–3). In warning the Saints against the spirit of the antichrist, for example, John the Revelator writes: *"Beloved, believe not every spirit, but try the spirits whether they are of God: because many false prophets are gone out into the world. Hereby know ye the Spirit of God: Every spirit that confesseth that Jesus Christ is come in the flesh is of God. And every spirit that confesseth not that Jesus Christ is come in the flesh is not of God: and this is that spirit of antichrist, whereof ye have heard that it should come; and even now already is it in the world"* (1 John 4:1–3).

In our dispensation the prophet Joseph was also preoccupied with this subject. Said George A. Smith: "There was no point upon which the prophet Joseph dwelt more than the discerning of spirits."[4] The Lord counseled, *"Put your trust in that Spirit which leadeth to do good—yea, to do justly, to walk humbly, to judge righteously; and this is my Spirit. Verily, verily I say unto you, I will impart unto you of my Spirit, which shall enlighten your mind, which shall fill your soul with joy"* (D&C 11:12–13).

Of course, it is easy for us to discern overt evil: the antichrist that John mentions, or that which promotes violations of chastity, or pornographic images, or other blatant evils. There is no difficulty in recognizing those more obvious things to be avoided. But we may fail to discern the spiritual effects of the seemingly "lesser" negative influences that seek to take up residence in our soul in the form of thoughts or feelings.

Lusseyran witnessed the power of negative emotions and energies in his soul. His inner light, which enabled him to see, even though he was physically blind, would seem to go dark when his mind indulged in negative feelings. For example, he found that when he was impatient (a form of sadness, he says), when he wanted everything to go faster, the objects in his environment would seem to change in their relationship to him, would seem to reflect his irritable negativity:

---

4. *WJS*, 21 n. 21.

All the objects immediately started to turn against me like fretful children. They changed their positions. I could no longer trust them. There was a glass which was on the table, and which I had seen just a moment ago at the tip of my napkin. It disappeared a moment later. It was behind a bottle, and of course in trying to reach for it, I turned over the bottle. Impatience moves objects in exactly the same way that sadness puts them in shadows, almost eclipses them, surrounds them by some sort of smoke or fog.[5]

But he says, on the other hand, that joy, which he learned he could intensify in himself at will, clarified everything. He said he could "light" himself. "That is to say, I could create a light inside me so alive, so large."[6] He could in the same way extinguish all, or almost all, the light inside by an act of will. He found that the degree of light in himself was based on his own decisions, on what he chose to experience. This power to choose, he learned, was independent of circumstances. Even when he was in a Nazi concentration camp he found that he could retreat from the brutality around him into the inner light and find refuge and refreshment there.

All of us have that same power to choose and to find refuge in the inner light, but because our physical senses and rational mind may so overpower the spiritual in our soul, and because we may be accustomed to allow ourselves negativity, we may not realize when something alien approaches us. As Seekers we want to use our powers to at-one only with those seen or unseen influences that feed the energies of life and joy. We must reclaim our power to choose what we will at-one with through discerning the nature of the dark side.

---

5. *Ibid.*, 96.
6. *Ibid.*, 82.

Chasing Darkness

If we don't purify our minds of negativity, we will be vulnerable and may not notice the inner disturbance that would otherwise alert us to something alien seeking access to us. To escape from the spiritual captivity to which we are subject in this life, discernment is essential. Our vulnerability comes from a lack of scriptural knowledge, as well as from our ignorance of the prevalence of the dark entities. The representatives of the dark side take advantage of our ignorance—it is what they thrive on: *"Therefore, my people are gone into captivity, because they have no knowledge.... Therefore, hell hath enlarged herself, and opened her mouth without measure"* (Isaiah 5:13). The prophet Joseph taught:

> A man is saved no faster than he gets knowledge for if he does not get knowledge he will be brought into captivity by some evil power in the other world, as evil spirits will have more knowledge and consequently more power than many men who are on the earth.[7]

We want to learn to interpret our experience in the Light of Christ lest hell catch us unaware, attach itself to us, and plunge us into darkness.

A friend of mine reported the unexpected visit of Elder Neal A. Maxwell to a Relief Society class some years back. He asked the sisters, "What is the key of knowledge?" Everyone sat forward eagerly to hear the answer, but no one dared to say anything. "Five words:" the apostle said, "the fulness of the scriptures." He said that one of his primary concerns with the Church membership was that we weren't using the scriptures or applying them enough to our lives. Today the question

---

7. *Ibid.*, 113–14.

remains: Are we writing a sufficient amount of scripture on our heart, at-oneing with it, such that the Word has taken on life in our inward parts and now lights our soul? If not, we may experience disturbances whose source we have not yet recognized.

Man may indeed be oblivious to the fact that many unseen malignant forces continually seek access to his mind. *"Be sober,"* Peter counsels; *"Be vigilant; because your adversary the devil, as a roaring lion, walketh about, seeking whom he may devour; whom resist stedfast in the faith"* (1 Peter 5:8–9).

President George Q. Cannon spoke in a similar warning voice to the Saints:

> We ... do not sufficiently realize the importance of keeping guard upon ourselves, and upon our feelings, and of resisting the influences that surround us.... There are influences in the atmosphere that are invisible to us that, while we are here upon the earth, we ought to resist with all our might, mind, and strength ... influences that are opposed to the Spirit of God.... If our eyes were open to see the spirit world around us, we should feel differently on this subject than we do; we would not be so unguarded and careless, and so indifferent whether we had the spirit and power of God with us or not; but we would be continually watchful and prayerful to our heavenly Father for His Holy Spirit and His holy angels to be around about us to strengthen us to overcome every evil influence.[8]

These warnings alert us to the fact that negative spirits or entities may come by to see if we are entertaining any energy that they might feed on.

Eckhart Tolle, a spiritual teacher whose story will be told in the next chapter, writes that most of us have inside an internal negative energy field formed from life's painful experiences; he

---

8. *JD* 11:29–30.

calls this negative energy a "pain-body." We might identify this pain-body with some sort of unclean spirits that can and do nest in a person. He says that they feed on our negative energy.

It is tempting for us with our limited senses and faith to see this life as largely empty of spiritual influences, as though we live in a sort of vacuum between two scripturally described worlds. But that is an inaccurate perception. Our environment is full of different kinds of influences, and many of them keep us from moving forward spiritually by insinuating themselves into our thought processes—and we are not aware.

It is part of our education here to experience these influences, and all of us do. Sometimes we are aware of them, sometimes we are not, but at one time or another we have acted unwittingly under their direction. Elder Erastus Snow taught about the influence they exert over each of us in their attempts to usurp Man's dominion in the earth:

> Lucifer, who fell from heaven ... set about ... to wrest the dominion from Adam, and he has been trying ever since, from the beginning till the present, to wrest the dominion of this earth from Adam and his posterity, and the only means by which he expects or hopes to accomplish it is, in short, to take possession of the tabernacles of Adam, which means a man and his wife— male and female, whom he called Adam, and rule the earth, and make the earth and the fullness thereof his servants.... The name of Jesus has power over all these evil spirits ... [who] have set up their abode in the tabernacles of men.... They [evil spirits] do not altogether get possession of the tabernacles of men, only in isolated cases.... But others, and this embraces all of us, are more or less influenced by evil spirits ... to do many things in violation of the true laws of life and health, and of peace and glory and exaltation, and these evils to which we are prompted through the influence of these spirits are designed, little by little, to bring us

into bondage, to sin and death, and to him who has the power of death, which is the devil.[9]

We have the option of belonging to one of two groups. Alma teaches about the sheepfolds of Christ and Satan, *"The good shepherd doth call you; ... and if ye will not hearken unto the voice of the good shepherd ... behold, ye are not the sheep of the good shepherd. And now if ye are not the sheep of the good shepherd, of what fold are ye? Behold, I say unto you, that the devil is your shepherd, and ye are of his fold"* (Alma 5:38–39). We choose which fold we will at-one with based on which signals we are taking. But it appears that there are only two folds. Only by conscious effort do we stay in the fold of the Lord Jesus Christ. Alma outlines the process:

> *Humble yourselves before the Lord, and call on his holy name, and watch and pray continually, that ye may not be tempted above that which ye can bear, and thus be led by the Holy Spirit, becoming humble, meek, submissive, patient, full of love and all long-suffering; having faith on the Lord; having a hope that ye shall receive eternal life; having the love of God always in your hearts.* (Alma 13:28–29)

We will likely not understand perfectly all the influences that act on us in this life or how they affect or store themselves in us. But as we learn from Elder Erastus Snow, the name of Jesus Christ has ultimate power over all these influences; at the same time, however, there are important things we can do to help ourselves.

For example, Tolle counsels us to pay attention to any influences that might awaken or feed or give place to this aggressive negative energy. He says that any sign of unhappiness in

9. *Ibid.*, 19:274–75.

oneself, in whatever form, may be the influence of a visiting negative entity or the awakening of the pain-body already embedded in a person. He describes the nature of these entities in their various manifestations, from simply annoying to extremely threatening:

> Some pain-bodies are obnoxious but relatively harmless, for example, like a child who won't stop whining. Others are vicious and destructive monsters, true demons. Some are physically violent; many more are emotionally violent. Some will attack people around you or close to you, while others may attack you, their host. Thoughts and feelings you have about your life then become deeply negative and self-destructive. Illnesses and accidents are often created in this way. Some pain-bodies drive their hosts to suicide.

This author says that if these entities succeed in taking up residence, they tend to cause their host to become either a victim or a perpetrator. This person then will want to inflict pain, or to suffer pain, or both.

> You are not conscious of this of course, and will vehemently claim that you do not want pain. But look closely and you will find that your thinking and behavior are designed to keep the pain going, for yourself and others. If you were truly conscious of it, the pattern would dissolve, for to want more pain is insanity, and nobody is consciously insane.[10]

Tolle comments on the evidence by which one may discern that he is under the influence or programming of these thought-entities:

---

10. *Practicing the Power of Now* (Novato: New World Library, 1999), 78.

This can take the form of irritation, impatience, a somber mood, a desire to hurt, anger, rage, depression, a need to have some drama in your relationship, and so on. Catch it the moment it awakens from its dormant state.

The pain-body wants to survive, just like every other entity in existence, and it can only survive if it gets you to unconsciously identify with it. It can then rise up, take you over, "become you," and live through you.

It needs to get its "food" through you. It will feed on any experience that resonates with its own kind of energy, anything that creates further pain in whatever form: anger, destructiveness, hatred, grief, emotional drama, violence, and even illness.... Pain can only feed on pain. Pain cannot feed on joy. It finds it quite indigestible.[11]

This possibility of unconscious identification with negative energy alerts us to the need to be selective both about what we take in and also what we express under its influence. But the way to extinguish the influence of the dark side in us is through depriving it of food, that is, depriving it of the negative energy it wants to feed on. Instead we consciously strengthen the powers of love, forgiveness, faith, and gratitude in our soul.

Even though we must be subjected to the dark influences all the days of our mortal probation,[12] we have been given the power to chase darkness with Light; we can reject unwanted influences. The prophet Joseph writes: "Satan cannot seduce us

---

11. *Ibid.*, 77–78.

12. Brigham taught, "We shall not be entirely free from sin for some time yet; but so long as it [the will] is in a state of perfect subjection, we are so far sanctified to keep up this warfare against the power of sin until we have obtained a perfect mastery over the evil that is within our organisms, and are able to control it constantly until death shall end the struggle: then shall we be prepared for a glorious resurrection" (*JD* 9:150).

by his enticements unless we in our hearts consent and yield—our organization is such that we can resist the devil; if we were not organized so, we would not be free agents."[13]

Obviously the key to our success lies in awareness. We are dealing with a subtle beast (see Moses 4:5) and we want to identify the beginnings of these negative influences in ourself. Heber C. Kimball describes the spiritual carelessness that seems innocent enough but, if unchecked, begins to feed more malevolent forces. The key lies in discerning the influences at work and making a new choice:

> It is the duty of everyone to labor day by day to promote each other's happiness, and also to study the wellbeing of mankind. When we take a course opposite to this, we become uneasy, unhappy and discontented; we are not satisfied with anything that is around us; our food, our raiment, our habitations and all that we possess becomes an annoyance to us; now what is the cause of this? It certainly does not originate with the Spirit of God, for that will never render any one unhappy. You all understand, when you are in the right, that it is the spirit of the world, or that spirit which controls the world, which causes people to feel in this way; and unless they drive it far from them it will lead them down to sorrow, misery and death. It is a spirit that inclines to kill and destroy, and that inclines the wicked to waste away everything there is upon the earth. The Saints should be particularly careful to avoid the influence of this spirit of destruction, for it is not of God, and we can all see how it leads mankind to destroy each other.[14]

Our emotional experience in this life is powerfully influenced by what we wittingly or unwittingly at-one with. How

---

13. *WJS*, 65.

14. *JD* 10:240.

important it is to realize that *like* is drawn to *like*: intelligence to intelligence, truth to truth, light to light (see D&C 88:40), but also anger to anger and pain to pain. We will draw to ourselves the sort of energy from unseen beings that we ourselves entertain. And we receive the consequences of our thoughts, even when we are unaware of the spiritual dynamics involved. But when we become aware, sometimes that awareness is all that is necessary to chase away an unwanted thought or entity. In other situations, depending on how deeply they have entrenched themselves, other more powerful means of exorcising are needed, such as prayer and fasting (see Matthew 17:21).

Or Priesthood. In 1831 the Lord gave counsel in the exercise of Priesthood power over an evil spirit: *"You shall proclaim against that spirit with a loud voice that it is not of God—not with railing accusation, that ye be not overcome, neither with boasting or rejoicing, lest you be seized therewith.... Power [is given you] to overcome all things which are not ordained of [the Father]"* (D&C 50:32–33, 35). In 1842 the prophet Joseph taught the Relief Society about the "keys of the kingdom" by which false spirits were to be detected. Soon after he spoke to a large congregation of the Saints about "certain signs and words by which false spirits and personages may be detected from true, which cannot be revealed to the Elders till the Temple is completed.... There are signs ... the Elders must know ... to be endowed with the power, to finish their work and prevent imposition."[15]

Spirits can be detected by the influence they radiate. Everyone radiates a particular spiritual energy, and everyone is affected by that radiation. President David O. McKay explains how influential each of us is for good or ill:

> There is one responsibility which no man can evade; that responsibility is his personal influence, a silent, subtle

---

15. *WJS*, 20–21.

radiation.... This radiation is tremendous. Every ... person who lives in this world wields an influence whether for good or for evil. It is not what he says alone; it is not alone what he does. It is what he is.... Every man has an atmosphere which is affecting every other man. He cannot escape for one moment from this radiation of his character, this constant weakening or strengthening of others.[16]

Each of us is a representative of one side or the other, one fold or the other. There is no time-out. Every moment we are radiating the energy of whatever mind we have chosen. Knowing this, we can deliberately and authentically radiate that which is nourishing for ourself and others.

The spirit of the dark side is aggressive and is always recruiting. Where others' radiations are concerned, it is good to pray for the gift of discernment so as to be spiritually warned.

We soon observe that the greatest temptation to surrender our peace comes through a subtle avenue, that is, from someone else who is under the influence of the Adversary. When another person is angry, how easy it is to at-one with that spirit! But as we mature spiritually, we learn to maintain a sweet independence of the person in front of us, who may be suffering from spiritual ignorance:

> If you and I keep humble, and keep a childlike spirit, and never have anything about us but that kind of an influence, then, if a spirit approaches that is not of the Lord, we shall know it. Let us control our tongues, for James says the tongue is an unruly member and sets all on fire; and I can tell you how you may escape. When an unruly spirit approaches you, just hold your tongue, and then the fire which is connected with that spirit

---

16. A fusion of two quotes on the same subject, from BYU, April, 1948, and *The Instructor*, October 1964.

won't hurt you. I tell you, those wicked persons that come to annoy and disturb the peace of the Saints of God will have the fire of hell in them....

When I go into the company of a man, I know what kind of a spirit he has about him; and you can know it also, if you will carry with you the right spirit.... Therefore, strive to have in you that spirit which will enable you to discern the evil from the good.[17]

Brigham Young identifies two classes of spirits among the negative influences that Man may be subject to, those cast out with Satan and those who have lived and died here:

And every person who desires and strives to be a Saint is closely watched by fallen spirits that came here when Lucifer fell, and by the spirits of wicked persons who have been here in tabernacles and departed from them, but who are still under the control of the prince of the power of the air. Those spirits are never idle; they are watching every person who wishes to do right, and are continually prompting them to do wrong. This makes it necessary for us to be continually on our guard—makes this probation a continual warfare. We do not expect to be idle ... in the flesh. It is a spiritual warfare. He [the Saint] contends against the spirits of darkness and against the workers of iniquity, and wars all the day long against his own passions that pertain to fallen man. It is therefore necessary that the people speak often one with another, encourage each other in every good word and work, sustain every one in every good act, operate against every evil act, and continue so to do through life."[18]

It is important to emphasize that when we speak of the influence of the Adversary, we are not talking just about

---

17. Elder John Young, *JD* 6:233.

18. *JD* 7:239.

temptations to overt sin, but also to negative states of mind. And it is also important to realize that these spirits do not bother only the wicked, but hound and influence the very best among us. As the prophet Joseph said to Brother Heber C. Kimball after his horrific experience with evil spirits in England, "The nearer a person approaches the Lord, a greater power will be manifested by the adversary to prevent the accomplishment of His purposes."[19]

The Lord allows these influences for our great blessing because they require us to become more spiritually sensitive and to distinguish more clearly the sanctification process. In some remarks on the Saints' preparation to entertain angels, Brigham said, "To be Saints indeed, requires every wrong influence that is within them, as individuals, to be subdued, until every evil desire is eradicated, and every feeling of their hearts is brought into subjection to the will of Christ."[20]

And so we have a work to do to strengthen each other and ourselves. Tolle likens negative, obsessive, painful thinking to pollution. Unhappiness, he says, spreads more easily than a physical disease. The negative entity of one person can trigger and feed on the negativity in others, unless they are immune through being highly conscious. He asks, "Are you polluting the world or cleaning up the mess? You are responsible for your inner space; nobody else is."[21]

Violence and Shame

But what happens when evil things are forced upon us? There are times when we cannot avoid appropriating what is

---

19. Orson F. Whitney, *Life of Heber C. Kimball* (Salt Lake City: Bookcraft, 1967), 132.

20. *JD* 19:67.

21. *Power of Now*, 79.

happening to us even though it is full of malevolence. When we witness something brutal or perverted, or something violent is perpetrated upon us, a strange thing can happen. In our attempts to make sense of what is happening, to produce the meaning of the event, we appropriate the experience into ourselves—it becomes part of us. Depending on the emotional weight of the thing happening, its violence, its perversion, or the strength of its assault on our mind or body, we tend to at-one with it because we are trying to get hold of it in our mind, and it then takes its toll. Because of this tendency to appropriate and at-one with things in order to process them, a person may feel unclean and unworthy even though he or she has been made an unwilling participant. The result of the violence is that the person may then begin to inflict additional violence on himself or herself and act in negative ways towards others in reaction to the feelings of violation, of shame, guilt, and hatred.

Terry Warner, a philosophy professor at BYU, writes about appropriation, getting free from it, and the involuntary sense of responsibility for trauma inflicted. This liberation comes through recognizing our own role, not in the initial event, but in our response in the wake of the traumatic event:

> There are people who in fact do escape from the deep psychological and emotional difficulties resulting from personal violence. They do so by courageously recognizing how they themselves have nourished their troubled emotions—even though they might not have been morally responsible for them. Such inner confessions bring to an end their habit of blaming these upon others or upon something evil in themselves. Suddenly they therefore find themselves free to forgive and seek forgiveness.[22]

---

22. C. Terry Warner, "Renouncing Violence, Altogether," 8; Utah Academy Tanner Lecture, 7 April 2006.

That is to say, after a traumatic experience, we, in our confusion, may prolong re-hashing the horror of it, may deepen our anger, even hatred, for those involved, and thereby deepen the damage to ourselves. We remember that no matter how justified we may seem to be in our hatred of someone who has harmed us or a loved one, it is the nature of the energy that passes through *us* that determines the pace of our healing. We were not responsible for the initial assault, but we nevertheless experience the consequences of continuing to process the event in negative ways. We can accept personal responsibility for our healing.

It seems that our blaming of others causes us more harm than anything they may have initially done to us. What we do to ourselves is more damaging than what another can do to us, in terms of spiritual energies.

Therefore, if we can acknowledge even the tiniest part of responsibility for our suffering, acknowledging that amount that we caused can set us free. If we can stop the blaming, the hatred, the negative acting-out towards others, we can heal through detaching from the at-oneing we ignorantly created. In other words, any victim, though innocent of the initial violence, does violence to herself as she visits and revisits the experience, hurting herself with blame, resentment, self-hatred, and hatred for others. These cause such damage in the delicate soul that they require repentance; then forgiveness can go forward, perhaps on several fronts, in order finally to dissolve the effects of the original assault.

At the same time we can see a powerful truth—that it is less painful to be the victim than it is to be a perpetrator of harm. The perpetrator may never repent, but the victim can repent of his little part in his self-damage, and then he can heal from the entire experience through the power of the Savior's Atonement, which has no healing limits. But it would seem that one cannot heal from what he has helped to produce *until he repents of it.* The realization that the perpetrator is suffering more than the victim may allow the victim to reframe and recontextualize the experience so that compassion may be extended at least internally, if not in person, to the perpetrator. It is the surging of mercy and compassion through one's own soul that promotes the healing.

Dark and Light

By eternal law, then, we draw darkness or light to us through whatever our thoughts entertain. With respect to the drawing of negative influences to us, we find that people who have been subjected to traumatic experiences seem to be especially vulnerable to negative thought-entities, thoughts of misery, thoughts of self-destruction; that is, after a person has had a health crisis, a death, an assault, a serious accident, or perhaps some form of sexual abuse, he or she may be especially susceptible to an invasion. We may become suspicious if we or our loved ones experience lingering and deepening trauma after these kinds of events. Often one is not aware in the aftermath of such experiences that if he remains immersed in darkness of spirit, he may inadvertently attract the dark side.

The Adversary takes advantage when, in spiritual ignorance, one's defenses go down. His cronies move in to feed on the negative energy. By way of general observation, Satan's tactics are characterized by temptation (1) to misery, (2) to sexual sin, and (3) to destroying another and/or oneself. Thus, the innocent victim of sexual abuse may find that his or her distress has been compounded by the intrusion of unclean spirits who then tempt him or her to endless versions of misery-producing behavior, even to attempts at suicide.[23] Changing the inner energy is essential.

---

23. An LDS approach to dealing with evil spirits is Dr. Melvin C. Fish,

It is the Atonement of Jesus Christ that has the greatest power to change a person's inner environment. This power enables a person, in time, to bring the energy of forgiveness to the event, to the participants, and to himself or herself, so as to *"look unto God with firmness of mind, and pray unto him with exceeding faith, and he will console you in your afflictions, and he will plead your cause"* (Jacob 3:1). Elder Richard G. Scott testifies to the power of Jesus Christ to heal from afflictions:

> Yet no matter what the source of difficulty and no matter how you begin to obtain relief—through a qualified professional therapist, doctor, priesthood leader, friend, concerned parent, or loved one—no matter how you begin, those solutions will never provide a complete answer. The final healing comes through faith in Jesus Christ and His teachings, with a broken heart and a contrite spirit and obedience to His commandments. That is why human reaction to a challenge in life that engenders hatred, despondency, distrust, anger, or revenge must be supplanted by the tender mercies of a loving Father in Heaven and His Beloved Son.
>
> When anguish comes from the evil acts of others, there should be punishment and corrective action taken, but the offended is not the one to initiate that action. Leave it to others who have that responsibility. Learn to forgive; though terribly hard, it will release you and open the way to a newness of life....
>
> In summary, do what you *can* do a step at a time. Seek to understand the principles of healing from the scriptures and through prayer. Help others. Forgive. "Submit cheerfully and with patience to all the will of the Lord" (Mosiah 24:15). Above all, *exercise faith in Jesus Christ.*

Healing the Inner Self: From Darkness into Light (West Pacos Lane Trust, 1999; www.drMFish.com).

I testify that the surest, most effective, and shortest path to healing comes through application of the teachings of Jesus Christ in your life.[24]

Forgiveness and repentance cause our inner life and inner light to change; they begin a healing process for the damage we have done to ourselves and help to create a more healing environment for those around us. Then the forces of Light can reassert their influence, the inner light can begin to glow more intensely, and the person can resume life in an even greater peace, tutored by the experience, having discovered how, through love, through Christ, our joy becomes independent of negative circumstances.

In fact, so eternal are love and joy in our soul that no experience can destroy them. Lusseyran speaks of "the joy of discovering that joy exists, that it is in us, just exactly as life is, without conditions, and which no conditions, even the worst can kill."[25] This joy was designed to exist in any place or in any time, in pain as in pleasure. No matter what we have experienced, we find an aspect of ourself that remains intact and unharmed. Alma's words suggest that joy is possible even when there are great burdens: *Then may God grant unto you that your burdens may be light, through the joy of his Son. And even all this can ye do if ye will*" (Alma 33:23).

If we will, we can detach from any addiction to disturbance and find instead that one form of at-one-ment has to do with quietly accepting a world of dark and light, knowing that it is somehow all right. Sharon Salzberg comments on this integration:

We may look for that which is stable, unchanging, and safe, but awareness teaches us that such a search cannot succeed.

---

24. "To Be Healed," *Ensign*, May, 1994, 7.
25. *Against the Pollution of the I*, 153.

Everything in life changes. The path to true happiness is one of integrating and fully accepting all aspects of our experience. Ying and yang, circle half dark and half light.... Unity, integration, comes from deeply accepting darkness and light, and therefore being able to be in both simultaneously. We must move from trying to control the uncontrollable cycles of pleasure and pain, and instead learn how to connect, to open, to love no matter what is happening.[26]

So, we inhabit the right world for us now with its dance of light and dark. But let us search diligently in the Light of Christ that our at-one-ment may increase in that stream of holy spirit that flows over the rocks of the wearying Wilderness like living water.

---

26. Sharon Salzberg, *Lovingkindness* (Boston: Shambhala, 1997), 12.

CHAPTER TEN

THE NATURAL SELF SWALLOWED UP IN CHRIST

*His spirit drank
The spectacle: sensation, soul, and form,
All melted into him; they swallowed up
His animal being; in them did he live,
And by them did he live; they were his life.*

William Wordsworth[1]

ে৯

*They were encircled about . . . as if in the midst of a flaming fire, . . . and
they were filled with that joy which is unspeakable and full of glory. . . .
And . . . the Holy Spirit of God did . . . enter into their hearts, and they
were filled as if with fire.* Helaman 5:44–45

ে৯

*And oh, what joy, and what marvelous light I did behold;
yea, my soul was filled with joy as exceeding as was my pain!*

Alma 36:20

---

1. *The Excursion*, lines 207–210. Cited at greater length in Chapter Six.

LIGHT IN THE WILDERNESS

As we have seen, the premortal plan for Man includes his seduction by the telestial thought-world, the fabrication of a false self, the eventual discovery of its falseness, and his consequent waking up to a spiritually enlightened state under the power of God. As he pursues his path and develops spiritually, reality keeps reconfiguring for him, and he learns and relearns that life is not what he once thought it was. He especially learns that *he* is not what he thought he was. As he wakens from the dream-like state of the mortal probation, he learns that he is designed to go through some shifts from a lower state of awareness to a higher. The scriptures refer often to the Mighty Change, a transformation in which the old false self is consumed finally by the Lord, and a new creature is revealed.

A series of transformations is offered to each of God's children in the long journey from premortal origins through the post-mortal worlds; but not all will yield to the full transformation. Nevertheless, God loves all His children and has a plan for the progress of each of them. These plans developed in the premortal world based on the capacity and desires of the individual spirits. Even though some of the spirit children by their choices and desires will fall short of exaltation, the Lord loves them and will work with them to bring them as far as they will come. Ammon declares, *"We see that God is mindful of every people, whatsoever land they may be in; ... and his bowels of mercy are over all the earth"* (Alma 26:37). According to the Lord's timetable each of the Father's children will be offered the full truth.

The Lord works with all His children in a great variety of ways, often giving them experiences and revelations that reveal only a taste of the full truth, but not, for example, the nature of eternal worlds, or Priesthood ordinances, or details of Himself. *"The Lord doth grant unto all nations, of their own nation and tongue, to teach his word, yea, in wisdom, all that he seeth fit that they should have"* (Alma 29:8). Therefore, we find a great deal of spiritual experience throughout the history of the world in traditions that did not recognize the Lord Jesus Christ; or if they did acknowledge Him, did not have the fulness of the gospel. The First Presidency wrote:

> The great religious leaders of the world, such as Mohammad, Confucius, and the Reformers, as well as philosophers including Socrates, Plato, and others, received a portion of God's light. Moral truths were given to them by God to enlighten whole nations and to bring a higher level of understanding to individuals....
>
> Consistent with these truths, we believe that God has given and will give to all peoples sufficient knowledge to help them on their way to eternal salvation, either in this life or in the life to come.[2]

We acknowledge that even in the Restored Gospel we do not yet have a fulness. Though there has been restored to us a flood of rich doctrines and a greater access to Truth, much yet remains to be revealed to each of us. The Restoration is still going on, dependent to some degree on our preparation and diligent seeking. Elder Bruce R. McConkie observes, "We are in process of receiving all that God has spoken by the mouths of all his holy prophets since the world began. Only a small portion has come to us so far; we do not, as yet, begin to know what the ancients knew."[3] In another place he exclaims:

> Oh that we might rend the heavens and know all that the ancients knew! O that we might pierce the veil and see all that

---

2. Statement of the First Presidency, February 15, 1978.

3. *The Joseph Smith Translation: The Restoration of Plain and Precious Things,* Religious Studies Monograph Series, vol. 12, ed. Robert L. Millet and Monte S. Nyman (Salt Lake City: Bookcraft, 1987), 13.

our forebears saw! O that we might see and know and feel what the elect among the Jaredites and among the Nephites saw and heard and felt! He who is no respecter of persons calls us with his own voice; if we will but attune our ears we shall hear his words![4]

Nevertheless, the Lord is generous with all His children. Brigham Young taught on several occasions that everything Man knows or has developed in any field of knowledge comes through the Light of the Lord Jesus Christ. For example, he said, "I ... believe positively that there is nothing known except by the revelation of the Lord Jesus Christ, whether in theology, science, or art."[5] On another occasion he taught:

> There are men of talent, of thought, of reflection, and knowledge in all cunning mechanism: they are expert in that, though they do not know from whence they receive their intelligence. The Spirit of the Lord has not yet entirely done striving with the people, offering them knowledge and intelligence; consequently it reveals unto them, instructs them, teaches them, and guides them ... though they know it not.[6]

Not only in the arts and sciences have people received revelations. A variety of spiritual experience reported by seekers from every time period and every corner of the earth fills the religious literature of the world. As Harvard philosopher and psychologist William James writes in his classic study of religious experience, religion among "more developed minds" has some elements in common:

---

4. *The Mortal Messiah: From Bethlehem to Calvary*, vol. 4 (Salt Lake City: Deseret Book, 1981), 372.

5. *JD* 12:207.

6. *JD* 5:124–25.

There is a certain uniform deliverance in which religions all appear to meet. It consists of two parts: ... 1. The uneasiness, reduced to its simplest terms, is a sense that there is *something wrong about us* as we naturally stand. 2. The solution is a sense that *we are saved from the wrongness* by making proper connection with the higher powers.

In those more developed minds which alone we are studying, the wrongness takes a moral character, and the salvation takes a mystical tinge.... Remember that for some men it ["salvation"] arrives suddenly, for others gradually, whilst others again practically enjoy it all their life. The practical difficulties are: 1. to "realize the reality" of one's higher part; 2. to identify one's self with it exclusively; and 3. to identify it with all the rest of ideal being. When mystical activity is at its height, we find consciousness possessed by the sense of a being at once *excessive* and *identical* with the self: great enough to be God; interior enough to be *me*.[7]

To paraphrase James, thinking people come to recognize their bi-partite nature and, in seeking to transcend their "wrong" self, they have a sense of merging a higher self with God. This higher self seems at the same time somehow part of God, so that finally determining what is God and what is one's self becomes difficult, but also unimportant.

From his investigations James gives a description of Man's inherent ability to shift his own consciousness from a lower to a higher plane:

Man can learn to transcend these limitations [of finite thought] and draw power and wisdom at will.... The divine presence is known through experience. The turning to a higher

---

7. *The Varieties of Religious Experience: A Study in Human Nature* (New York: Random House, 1929), 498–99. Italics in the original.

plane is a distinct act of consciousness. It is not a vague, twilight or semi-conscious experience. It is not an ecstasy, it is not a trance. It is not super-consciousness in the Vedantic sense. It is not due to self-hypnotization. It is a perfectly calm, sane, sound, rational, common-sense shifting of consciousness from the phenomena of sense-perception to the phenomena of seership, from the thought of self to a distinctively higher realm.... For example, if the lower self be nervous, anxious, tense, one can in a few moments compel it to be calm. This is not done by a word simply.... It is by the exercise of power. One feels the spirit of peace as definitely as heat is perceived on a hot summer day. The power can be as surely used as the sun's rays can be focused and made to do work, to set fire to wood.[8]

So we see that the Lord has manifested Himself in varying degrees to His children throughout the history of the earth. And on reflection, that God would reveal Himself to His children in greater and lesser manifestations seems self-evident; at the same time, this realization does not need to threaten the covenant people in any way. As a missionary Church we seek not to destroy the Light that people have already received but to build upon and expand upon that Light (see, e.g., D&C 10:52–54). But, of course, because of the incompleteness of the Light that others through the ages have received, many different religions have developed with disparate conclusions and false ideas; yet also at the core of the Light they received were many common ideas about morality and goodness and proper human behavior and development.

Many people, then, have had genuine spiritual experience, but even so could not have described the full nature of the God or the divine forces that they experienced. Such is the case of three people whose accounts I present here. My purpose in

---

8. *Ibid.*, 507.

sharing these stories is not that they are necessarily duplicat-able, but that they can heighten our consciousness of Natural and Spiritual states as these come into bolder relief in their stories. The dual nature of Man is revealed in these accounts, as well as his capacity to live in a different awareness. In their stories we can ponder some aspects of the transformation that a child of God is capable of, as we ourselves strive for that more complete transformation available in Jesus Christ.

First, some preliminary observations about these particular accounts. Before their experiences each of these three people was deeply depressed, even suicidal, and in the course of the events described here, each was transformed from his or her misery into a person of peace, love, and radically new spiritual insight. Each went into the experience as one kind of person and came out entirely changed. They have in common the dis-covery that their suffering self was self-created through igno-rance; they experienced the annihilation of that false self and the uncovering of the loving, peaceful, clear self that forms the essence of each person who lives in this world.

A second awareness these three people share, common to spiritual experiences of dramatic shifts in awareness, is that they saw that their own being, which once had felt separate and isolated, was in some way actually at one with all animate and even inanimate things. The ordinary objects of life took on a brilliant sheen for them which filled their souls with joy. They were able to feel, as their only perception, the wonder that all things are part of One Great Being and that they themselves were in a spiritual sense separate from nothing; that all things were somehow part of them, and to extend it, somehow part of God. They saw that it is the sense of separateness and isola-tion that underlies suffering. Apparently the great delusion of the telestial world is that we are all separate. When the spiritual senses are awakened and the false self diminished, we see the

truth of our oneness with each other in God. Each author refers to the false self as an obstacle to perceiving the oneness of
all things.

The reader will notice that each author has trouble describing what he or she experienced. Our finite language does not
include an adequate vocabulary for spiritual experience or for
perceptions that transcend our own experience. Here we enter a
non-verbal realm that our spirit already begins to understand.

After their experience, they each found it a challenge to
integrate themselves back into normal daily life since they now
saw things so differently from the way everyone else around
them did. They had to tone down their ecstasy in order to minister among those they felt called to help.

Three Accounts

Following are excerpts from their own stories.

Byron Katie Reid Mitchell[9]

Byron Katie, a wife and mother in Barstow, California, entered
a ten-year depression that led her into rage, paranoia, and suicidal despair. For the last two years of her depression she spent
most of her time in her bedroom hardly able to care for herself or her family. When she checked into a halfway house for
women she was placed alone in an attic because the other resi-
dents found her so frightening. Katie slept on the floor because
she didn't feel worthy to sleep on a bed.

---

9. Byron Katie with Stephen Mitchell, *Loving What Is: Four Questions That
Can Change Your Life* (New York: Random House, 2002); Byron Katie
with Michael Katz, *I Need Your Love—Is That True?* (New York: Random
House, 2005); and Byron Katie with Stephen Mitchell, *A Thousand Names
for Joy* (New York: Random House, 2007).

One morning, a week or so later, lying on the floor, she woke up and realized that she was a completely changed being. The reconfiguration of her reality came with an instant realization that led her to develop what she calls The Work, the work of inquiry into thoughts, in the awareness that many thoughts in this world aren't true. Unwilling to use "I," because of her new awareness of being one with everything, she switches to "it" to refer to herself:

> For the first time in my life, I was seeing without concepts, without thoughts or an internal story. All my rage, all the thoughts that had been troubling me, my whole world, *the* whole world, was gone. There was no me. It was as if something else had woken up. *It* opened its eyes. *It* was looking through Katie's eyes. And it was crisp, it was bright, it was new, it had never been here before. Everything was unrecognizable. And it was so delighted! Laughter welled up from the depths and just poured out. It breathed and was ecstasy. It was intoxicated with joy: totally greedy for everything. There was nothing separate, nothing unacceptable to it. Everything was its very own self. For the first time I—it—experienced the love of its own life. I—it—*was amazed!*[10]

In another place, she writes more about what she learned:

> I saw clearly, irrevocably, that everything was backward, upside down from what I believed. My thinking had opposed everything as it truly was and reacted with stories of how I thought it should be. "My husband should be more honest." "My children should respect me more." Now I saw that instead of seeing what was happening, I was placing conditions on what was happening—as if I had the ability to dictate reality. It was clear

---

10. *A Thousand Names*, 197.

to me now that the truth was the extreme opposite. My husband should not be more honest—because he wasn't. My children shouldn't respect me more—because they didn't. Instantly I became a lover of reality: I noticed that this felt more natural, more peaceful.[11]

She walked to the bathroom and looked into her eyes in the mirror. She felt shot through as though with electricity. "It was like God giving itself life through the body of the woman —God so loving and bright, so vast—and yet she knew that it was herself.[12] She said that it was as if she were love which had been split apart, and now it was joined. "I remember tears of gratitude pouring down the cheeks as it looked at its own reflection. It stood there staring for I don't know how long."[13]

She felt nothing remaining of the previous Katie, her story was gone; she felt intense joy in the consuming and transforming of her previous, miserable self. Her family was astonished as she began listening to them and loving them and being delighted in them. The anger was gone. For many months tears would stream down her face and that would alarm people, but it was only because she felt so moved, so grateful.

People began to notice her light and to come to her house for help. She was a woman who had seen something. She would help them investigate their thinking, and they too would experience a degree of change and relief. She became a spiritual teacher and now travels the world helping people with The Work of inquiry (based on a set of questions to help see through one's thinking). She teaches that suffering is optional.

---

11. *I Need Your Love*, xvi.

12. *A Thousand Names*, 199.

13. *Ibid.*, 199.

Eckhart Tolle[14]

Eckhart lived in a nearly continual state of anxiety interspersed with bouts of suicidal depression until he was nearly thirty. But one night soon after his twenty-ninth birthday, he woke up in the very early morning with an intense feeling of dread. This was something he had done many times before, but this was worse. Everything in the room seemed hostile, alien, and frightening. He began to feel a deep loathing of the world, but especially of his own existence. He could find no reason to struggle on with his miserable and burdensome life. He wanted to cease to exist.

He was struck by the realization that if he couldn't live with himself any longer, there must be two of him—the "I" who couldn't live any longer and the "self" that he couldn't live with. "Maybe," he thought, "only one of them is real."[15]

He said that he was so stunned at this thought that his mind stopped and he felt as though he were being drawn into a "vortex of energy," at first slowly and then more rapidly. He was seized with fear but he heard the words in his chest, "resist nothing." He could feel himself being sucked into a great void inside himself. All at once there was no fear, and he allowed himself to fall into the void. He had no memory of what happened after that, but the next thing he knew, it was morning and he awakened to the sound of a chirping bird outside his window.

> I opened my eyes. The first light of dawn was filtering through the curtains. Without any thought, I felt, I knew, that there is infinitely more to light than we realize. That soft

---

14. *The Power of Now* (Vancouver: Namaste Publishing, 1999); *A New Earth: Awakening to Your Life's Purpose* (New York: Penguin Books, 2005).

15. *The Power of Now*, 4.

luminosity filtering through the curtains was love itself. Tears came into my eyes. I got up and walked around the room. I recognized the room, and yet I knew that I had never truly seen it before. Everything was fresh and pristine, as if it had just come into existence. I picked up things, a pencil, an empty bottle, marveling at the beauty and aliveness of it all.[16]

He writes that for the next five months he lived in a state of continual deep peace and bliss which then subsequently seemed to become second nature to him. In trying to understand what had happened to him he wondered whether the intense pressure of his suffering had caused his agonized self to collapse, and what was left was his true nature. He says that after this experience, due to circumstances in his life,

> I was left with nothing on the physical plane. I had no relationships, no job, no home, no socially defined identity. I spent almost two years sitting on park benches in a state of the most intense joy.[17]

As he returned to more normal activity, people would come up to him and tell him they wanted what he had and asked him to give it to them or show them how to get it. He would answer: "You have it already. You just can't feel it because your mind is making too much noise."[18] But he did begin counseling people about how to dis-identify with their mind.

He is a spiritual teacher who travels and lectures extensively, helping people toward the state that he experienced.

---

16. *Ibid.*, 4.
17. *Ibid.*, 5.
18. *Ibid.*, 6.

David R Hawkins, M.D., Ph.D.[19]

David Hawkins was from his childhood spiritually sensitive
and had on occasion already felt the presence of an infinite love
which he perceived as indistinguishable from his own being.
As his life went forward he became fascinated by the complexities of the mind and he studied psychiatry. He began a successful career, but when he was thirty-eight years old he came
down with a progressive and fatal illness that did not respond
to treatment, and he knew he was going to die. His spirit was
in a state of extreme anguish and despair, and as he could feel
his final moment approaching, a thought flashed through his
mind, and he called out, "If there is a God, I ask Him to help
me now." He went unconscious and when he awoke "a transformation of such enormity had taken place that I was struck
dumb with awe."

> The person I had been no longer existed. There was no per-
> sonal self or ego left—just an Infinite Presence of such unlimited
> power that it was all that was. This Presence had replaced what
> had been "me," and the body and its actions were controlled
> solely by the Presence's infinite will. The world was illuminated
> by the clarity of an Infinite Oneness, which expressed itself as all
> things revealed in their immeasurable beauty and perfection.[20]

He writes that that stillness persisted for nine months. "I
had no will of my own; unbidden, the physical entity went

---

19. *Power vs. Force: The Hidden Determinants of Human Behavior* (Carlsbad: Hay House, 2002). Dr. Hawkins is a controversial figure because
of his promotion of kinesiology as a means for ascertaining truth. Using his experience here does not imply endorsement of his subsequent
theories. However, I am accepting his personal experience as authentic and
instructive.

20. *Ibid.*, 12.

about its business under the direction of the infinitely powerful, but exquisitely gentle, will of the Presence."[21]

He reports that "everything and everyone in the world was
luminous and exquisitely beautiful. All living things became
radiant, and expressed this radiance in stillness and splendor....
Most people live their lives as though they're sleepers unawak-
ened to the perception of who they really are. Everyone looked
as if they were asleep, but they were incredibly beautiful—I was
in love with everyone."[22]

He observed the same thing that Katie and Eckhart had
experienced: that people who felt the compassion of what he
called the "Presence" reframed their reality so that they experienced healing on a level that transcended the world-mind. He
saw that one way of looking at pain and suffering is that it is
caused in people's minds, but not realizing that, people blame
God for what their false mind has actually done to them. He
learned that people who undergo a shift in consciousness like
his realize that they aren't at the mercy of the world but rather
are affected only by what their minds believe.

People have come from all over the world for help from this
spiritual teacher.

Dr. Hawkins offers counsel to people who want to experience what he has. One thing to notice is the benefit of quieting
the mind and an increasing detachment from the old thoughts
as a person draws nearer to God:

People wonder, *How does one reach this state of awareness?* I
can only share my own experience with you and note that few
follow the steps *because they're so simple.* First, the desire to reach
that state was intense. Then came the discipline to act with constant and universal forgiveness and gentleness, *without exception.*

21. *Ibid.,* 12.
22. *Ibid.,* 14.

One has to be compassionate toward *everything,* including one's own self and thoughts. Next came a willingness to hold desires in abeyance and surrender personal will at every moment. As each thought, feeling, longing, or deed was surrendered to God, the mind became increasingly silent. At first, I turned over entire stories and paragraphs in my mind, then ideas and concepts. As one lets go of the desire to own these thoughts, they no longer reach such elaboration, and begin to fragment while only half-formed. Finally, it was possible to turn over the energy behind thought itself, before it even became thought.

The task of constant and unrelenting fixity of focus—allowing not even a moment of distraction from meditation—continued while doing ordinary activities. At first, this seemed very difficult, but as time went on, it became habitual, automatic, and effortless. The process is like a rocket leaving Earth: At first, it requires enormous power, then less and less as it leaves the earth's gravitational field; and finally, it moves through space under its own momentum.

Suddenly, without warning, a shift in awareness occurred, and the Presence was there, unmistakable, all-encompassing.[23]

Anyone who tries making these adjustments in his own mind—for example, turning his will over to the Lord—may find that the exercise produces a few self-revelations as he confronts his urge to control and shape what is happening; he may also notice how many distracting desires keep his mind too busy for spiritual awareness. Quieting the mind, turning over self-seeking thoughts, letting the Natural Man yield to the Spiritual is an exercise in deep humility and trust, and it produces, if pursued in Christ, a quickened faith and enhanced consciousness of Divinity.

Dr. Hawkins's steps harmonize with teachings in our scriptures. As we add them to the context of the Lord Jesus

23. *Ibid.,* 22.

Christ, they take on even greater significance; as for example, in Omni:

> *I would that ye should come unto Christ, who is the Holy One of Israel, and partake of his salvation, and the power of his redemption. Yea, come unto him, and offer your whole souls as an offering unto him, and continue in fasting and praying, and endure to the end; and as the Lord liveth ye will be saved.* (Omni 1:26)

These three accounts are useful because, even though they are incomplete and not equivalent to the Mighty Change described in scripture, they give more detail about what the rebirth experience in Christ might be like. For example, these people experienced the goodness of God in an immersion so powerful that they actually became in some ways *like* God. Or perhaps we might say, when the veils of the false self were removed, what was left was God-like. They knew to the level of their deepest being of the reality of God and His love, and they knew that they themselves were love, and they found themselves unable to act in any other way but in love. Katie writes, "Love is so big that you can die in it—die of self and be fully consumed in it. It's what you are, and it will have all of you back to itself again."[24] Of course, there were some things they did not know, but of the love of God and man, they could testify.

We also see, following the pattern of the Savior Who could do nothing but the Father's will as it streamed into Him, that they just wanted to be aligned with God's will. Their felt experience was that the Divine Will had become alive in them, had completely absorbed them, and was, indeed, their very life, their breath, their perception. In this way like Jesus, they felt they could no longer do anything separate from the will of God without experiencing suffering. Yes, they knew they were

---

24. *Loving What Is*, 42.

still themselves, but they couldn't find the exact line between themselves and God, He being so intermixed in them and they in Him (see D&C 88:49–50). Their sense of "I" shifted to the sensation of being swallowed up in Something much more beautiful, loving, and powerful than themselves. As we read in their accounts, even though they felt fear at the imminent prospect of being swallowed up in the void, when it actually happened, they were released into an incomprehensible joy. That is, their old sense of identity thinned almost to extinction, but their sense of fulness and joy and oneness with God exceeded anything they had before felt or imagined.

What is arresting is that this relationship of oneness between Father and child had always been there. It was the relationship by which they had lived and moved and had had their being without knowing Who their Life Source was. And so it is with each of us.

The three accounts presented above describe the old self, the Natural Man, being swallowed up and dissolved in the Eternal Being. The prototype for this experience is the Son who allows the will of His flesh to be *"swallowed up in the will of the Father"* (Mosiah 15:1–7). And so the great plan, portrayed again and again in myriad ways, is that all that is false in the self be consumed in Christ and that each person become an entirely new creature in Christ. The angel echoes this pattern as he teaches Benjamin that each person must put off the characteristics of his Natural Man, through the power of the Savior, and become entirely submissive to the Father's will (see Mosiah 3:19).

Two additional scriptures describe this shift in identity, that is, from clinging to the old separate self to embracing the self made one with the Lord. The Lord Himself says, *"For whosoever will save his life shall lose it; but whosoever shall lose his life for my sake and the gospel's, the same shall save it. For what shall it profit a man, if he shall gain the whole world, and lose his own soul?"* (Mark 8:35–36). And Ammon, who himself had experienced a dramatic change, exclaims:

> *My joy is full, yea, my heart is brim with joy, and I will rejoice in my God. Yea, I know that I am nothing; as to my strength I am weak; therefore I will not boast of myself, but I will boast of my God, for in his strength I can do all things.... Therefore, let us glory, yea, we will glory in the Lord; yea, we will rejoice, for our joy is full.... Behold, I say unto you, I cannot say the smallest part which I feel.* (Alma 26:11–12, 16)

Alma too describes the liberation from the Natural Man and the expansion into redeeming love:

> *Behold, he changed their hearts; yea, he awakened them out of a deep sleep, and they awoke unto God. Behold, they were in the midst of darkness; nevertheless, their souls were illuminated by the light of the everlasting word; yea, they were encircled about by the bands of death, and the chains of hell.... Were the bands of death broken, and the chains of hell ... loosed? ... Yea, they were loosed, and their souls did expand, and they did sing redeeming love.* (Alma 5:7–9)

Joy is the common element in the experiences of those who cross this threshold from Natural to Spiritual into the Divine Will.

There are more insights to glean from these accounts: the nature of the light in a shining world, the quintessentially loving nature of Man, the falseness of our thought-system, the acceptance of seeming-reality as it presents itself, and perhaps more. But let us turn more directly to experiences in which the participants in the transforming experience come to know more comprehensively both the Transformer and the path to Him.

CHAPTER TEN

Transformation in Christ

One challenge for the Spiritual Seeker is to distinguish between *adjustments* he's able to make in his daily behavior and that radical change of heart the scriptures describe, that is, a totally new way of feeling and responding to life, a new consciousness. The old self must be dissolved and a new self unveiled. *"Marvel not,"* Alma declares after his transformation, *"that all mankind, yea, men and women, all nations, kindreds, tongues and people, must be born again; yea, born of God, changed from their carnal and fallen state, to a state of righteousness.... And thus they become new creatures"* (Mosiah 27:25–26).

Alma's rebirth experience reveals three main components of the Mighty Change: the pain, then the joy, and then the continuing effects of that change:

> As I was thus racked with torment, while I was harrowed up by the memory of my many sins ... I remembered ... to have heard ... of one Jesus Christ.... As my mind caught hold upon this thought I cried within my heart: O Jesus, thou Son of God, have mercy on me, who am in the gall of bitterness.... When I thought this, I could remember my pains no more.... And oh, what joy, and what marvelous light I did behold; yea, my soul was filled with joy as exceeding as was my pain!
>
> I stood upon my feet, and did manifest unto the people that I had been born of God. Yea, and from that time even until now, I have labored without ceasing, that I might bring souls unto repentance; that I might bring them to taste of the exceeding joy of which I did taste; that they might also be born of God, and be filled with the Holy Ghost. (Alma 36:17–20, 23–24)

First he experienced acute remorse which then gave way to inexpressible joy. After that, his only labor was to bring others to that same experience by the gifts and power of God, sensing that his life was no longer his but belonged now to the Lord Jesus Christ and His purposes. This rebirth was so profound that it seems not to have faded from him, as spiritual experiences often will, but to have woven itself so intimately into the fibers of his being that he carried its effects with him every day and forever after. Ultimately he was translated, yet another transformation. But we see that he went into the experience of spiritual rebirth one kind of person and came out an entirely different person. The old Natural Man had been swallowed up in the Lord Jesus Christ.

The Lord works in a variety of ways even among the covenant people. We read examples of people who strove for and received this change, as well as examples of those who apparently had not prepared themselves for it; people, in fact, who may even have been living against the light they had, as in the case of Alma the Younger. We have also the example in the account of Nephi and Lehi in prison with Lamanite and Nephite dissenters, who likely had not prepared for, nor could they have foreseen, the experience that was about to envelop them. After the shaking of the earth and the walls of the prison, after the awful solemn fearful cloud had come upon them, after the voice above the darkness, after the crying unto the voice until they obtained faith in Christ, they were encircled about as by a flaming fire and were filled with *that joy which is unspeakable and full of glory*" (Helaman 5:44). They received the baptism of fire associated with the spiritual rebirth.

We see that this change comes to people, not by the will of Man, but by the will of God. He works by His own infinite purposes, and we are left, often without explanation, simply to work away at qualifying as He has outlined. John reminds us, *"But as many as received him, to them gave he power to become the sons of God, even to them that believe on his name: Which were born, not of blood, nor of the will of the flesh, nor of the will of man, but of God"* (John 1:12–13). When we receive Him in the fullest sense, He gives us the power.

Dramatic or Gradual?

Our examples here, both scriptural and non-scriptural, describe rebirth experiences that happened suddenly and dramatically. Elder McConkie comments on the more common, gradual experience:

> We say that a man has to be born again, meaning that he has to die as pertaining to the unrighteous things in the world. Paul told us to "crucify the old man of sin and come forth in a newness of life" (Romans 6:6). We are born again when we die as pertaining to unrighteousness and when we live as pertaining to the things of the Spirit. But that doesn't happen in an instant, suddenly. That also is a process. Being born again is a gradual thing, except in a few isolated instances that are so miraculous they get written up in the scriptures. As far as the generality of the members of the Church are concerned, we are born again by degrees, and we are born again to added light and added knowledge and added desires for righteousness as we keep the commandments.[25]

President Spencer W. Kimball, a personal witness in these matters, shares his sacred experience with the process of rebirth, illustrating also a more incremental ascent to higher and higher states in his relationship with God:

> I have learned that where there is a prayerful heart, a hungering after righteousness, a forsaking of sins, and obedience to

---

25. Mark McConkie, comp., *Doctrines of the Restoration: Sermons and Writings of Bruce R. McConkie* (Salt Lake City: Bookcraft, 1989), 52.

the commandments of God, the Lord pours out more and more light until there is finally power to pierce the heavenly veil and to know more than man knows. A person of such righteousness has the priceless promise that one day he shall see the Lord's face and know that he is.[26]

Most of us go forward by gradual steps in the preparatory phases of the Mighty Change, with perhaps a more dramatic change taking place toward a culminating point. That is, we have to make progressive preparations to be able to receive certain kinds of spiritual growth and experience. These preparations include periods of proving and testing to make sure that a person can accommodate greater spiritual experience and not be impeded or even destroyed by it. But the objective of the mortal probation for the covenant person is to be born again to the highest degree of the Mighty Change that is within that individual's capacity. The problem with the word "gradual" is that it may produce too relaxed an approach to what is possible.

The Book of Mormon holds out many possibilities for those who will not be deterred. Jacob says, for example, that through searching the scriptures he and his people received gifts of the Spirit and an unshaken faith by which they could, in the name of Jesus, command the trees, mountains, or waves of the sea (see Jacob 4:6). Once we take the Book of Mormon deeply into our souls, we might be surprised at what could happen—perhaps things for which there are no known precedents. Who can say what is foreordained for us or even covenanted before this life? The Lord works in infinitely miraculous ways with those who will give themselves to Him.

Let us conclude with the account of the baptism of fire of Lorenzo Snow, fifth president of the Church. His sister, Eliza

---

26. *Ensign*, March 1980, 2. President Kimball was commenting on D&C 93:1.

R. Snow, tells the story of the beginnings of her brother's spiritual rebirth and enlightenment. She describes an occasion on which he was present at what was called a "blessing meeting" where the prophet Joseph's father was giving patriarchal blessings. Lorenzo was acquainted with some of the people receiving blessings, of whom he knew the patriarch was entirely ignorant. "He was struck with astonishment to hear the peculiarities of those persons positively and plainly referred to in their blessings. And, as afterwards expressed, he was convinced that an influence, superior to human prescience, dictated the words of the one who officiated.... That was the first time Lorenzo had met [the patriarch, the father of the prophet Joseph]. After the services, they were introduced, and Father Smith said to my brother that he would soon be convinced of the truth of the latter-day work, and be baptized; and he said: 'You will become as great as you can possibly wish—EVEN AS GREAT AS GOD, and you cannot wish to be greater.' "²⁷

President Snow said he had no idea of becoming a Latter-day Saint on that occasion. He continues his own story, expressing his confusion over what Father Smith meant:

> I could not understand this, but years after in Nauvoo while talking upon a principle of the gospel, the Spirit of God rested powerfully upon me and showed me more clearly than I can now see your faces a certain principle and its glory, and it came to me summarized in this brief sentence: "As man is now, God once was; as God is now, man may be." The Spirit of God was on me in a marvelous manner all that day, and I stored that great truth away in my mind.²⁸

---

27. Eliza R. Snow, *Biography and Family Record of Lorenzo Snow* (Salt Lake City: Deseret News Co., 1984), 9–10.

28. *Teachings of Lorenzo Snow* (Salt Lake City: Bookcraft, 1984), 2.

To become as God is requires some obvious changes. President Snow describes one of the first major changes in his becoming. Soon after his baptism, he realized that he had not experienced the witness or baptism in the Spirit he found promised in the scriptures. He lay aside his books with an uneasy feeling, left the house, and wandered around through the fields in a gloomy and disconsolate mood, enveloped in an indescribable cloud of darkness. His custom was to retire to a grove a short distance from his lodgings for secret prayer, but the spirit of prayer had departed and the heavens were "as brass"; as a matter of habit only, he went at the accustomed time to pray. He writes:

> I had no sooner opened my lips in an effort to pray, than I heard a sound, just above my head, like the rustling of silken robes, and immediately the spirit of God descended upon me, completely enveloping my whole person, filling me from the crown of my head to the soles of my feet, and O the joy and happiness I felt! No language can describe the almost instantaneous transition from a dense cloud of mental and spiritual darkness into a refulgence of light and knowledge, that God lives, that Jesus Christ is the Son of God, and of the restoration of the Holy Priesthood, and the fullness of the Gospel. It was a complete baptism—a tangible immersion in the heavenly principle or element, the Holy Ghost; and even more real and physical in its effects upon every part of my system than the immersion by water; dispelling forever, so long as reason and memory last, all possibility of doubt or fear in relation to the fact handed down to us historically that the "babe of Bethlehem" is truly the Son of God ... [and] that He is now being revealed to the children of men, and communicating knowledge, the same as in the apostolic times....
>
> I cannot tell how long I remained in the full flow of the blissful enjoyment and divine enlightenment, but it was several

minutes before the celestial element which filled and surrounded me began gradually to withdraw. On arising from my kneeling posture, with my heart swelling with gratitude to God, beyond the power of expression, I felt—I knew that he had conferred on me what only an omnipotent being can confer—that which is of greater value than all the wealth and honors worlds can bestow. That night as I retired to rest, the same wonderful manifestations were repeated, and continued to be for several successive nights. The sweet remembrance of those glorious experiences, from that time to the present, brings them fresh before me, imparting an inspiring influence which pervades my whole being, and I trust will to the close of my earthly existence.[29]

His sure witness resulted in his traveling the path to missionary, apostle, and prophet in the great dispensation of the fulness of times. But his story can remind us that we're raw spiritual material with unexplored possibilities.

One final point to ponder. History records that the rabbis of the intertestamental period looked back on the Golden Age of Israel and lamented the loss of the sacred gifts and powers. And after the New Testament Church had fallen into apostasy, those who remembered the vibrancy of the apostolic period wept over the Spirit's having taken flight. Now we stand in the full blaze of the restoration of the gospel. If people in other spiritual traditions and philosophies, even without the restored gospel, obtain such marvelous manifestations as those recorded in the world's spiritual literature, it may be that many of us have hardly begun to plumb the riches and powers of the restored gospel of the Lord Jesus Christ.

We have spoken here of things that the Seeker deeply desires; and the Lord, desiring it also, draws him ever on, urging

---

29. Quoted in Preston Nibley, *Presidents of the Church* (Salt Lake City: Deseret Book, 1968), 140–41.

upon him the Book of Mormon as the manual for the Mighty Change. Over and over again the book reveals the means by which transformations are brought to pass. Nephi, for one, points out the path and the promise:

> *I, Nephi, was desirous also that I might see, and hear, and know of these things, by the power of the Holy Ghost, which is the gift of God unto all those who diligently seek him ... For he that diligently seeketh shall find; and the mysteries of God shall be unfolded unto them, by the power of the Holy Ghost, as well in these times as in times of old, and as well in times of old as in times to come; wherefore, the course of the Lord is one eternal round.* (1 Nephi 10:17, 19)

"May we be convinced," President Ezra Taft Benson urged, "that Jesus is the Christ, choose to follow Him, be changed for Him, captained by Him, consumed in Him, and born again."[30]

How many varied and beautiful accounts there are of God touching Man and causing the layers of the old self to fall away. May each of us have our own story in Christ to tell.

---

30. Ezra Taft Benson, "Born of God," *Ensign*, July 1989, 22.

CHAPTER ELEVEN

THE PREDOMINANT PRINCIPLE IN MAN:
A NEW IDENTITY

As the living Father hath sent me, and I live by the Father: so he that eateth me, even he shall live by me.

John 6:57

༼༽

Someone [is] watching deep within.... There is inside each of us someone watching deep within. Someone who sees.... A power to help, to assist everything that is, or better yet, to convey in itself everything that is: the power that the spirit possesses to contain the whole universe—our link with the Principle, with God ... that fountainhead at the bottom of us: I have called it someone watching deep within, also joy.

Jacques Lusseyran[1]

༼༽

You are the oracle of the Spirit, the repository of the intelligence that comes from another state of existence invisible to the natural eye ... There are spiritual agents, invisible to the natural eye, not only in us,

---

1. *Against the Pollution of the I* (Sandpoint, Idaho: Morning Light Press, 2006), 100, 103, 104.

but in the elements, in the heavens above, and in the earth beneath, who are continually producing effects, the cause of which we cannot comprehend.

Brigham Young[2]

నా

We considered in the previous chapter the experiences of people who slipped the bonds of the Natural Man. Their old identity and personal will consumed in God, they became aware of Him as a living Presence in their souls. The three epigraphs above also bear witness to an indwelling Presence in Man.

One of the secrets that eludes the Natural Man is that he is born with something of God in him and that he lives by a divine life-support system. Forces beyond his perception set him in motion on the earth. He goes about his daily life under the illusion that he is entirely autonomous, a principle of life unto himself, self-willing and self-determining. But there is a reality that he does not perceive, and it is this: *"I am the true light that is in you, and… you are in me; otherwise ye could not abound"* (D&C 88:50). Intimately intermixed in Man's being is the presence of conscious Deity. This hidden reality puts Man on a continuum with all the Gods that have preceded him. He can awaken to his foreordained place and elect to increase in his own being this Presence, this Light and this Life.

Ascent of Man

Let us consider the nature of Life itself and its tendency to seek greater elaboration in Man. A human being, placed on the vast spectrum of Life above the animals, but below the Gods, is designed to move upward from a lower to a higher degree; the more he ascends in that Life, the greater his consciousness,

---

2. *JD* 1:88.

vigor, intelligence, godlike qualities and powers. The Savior alludes to Man's capacity to ascend in the scale of Life when He says: *"I am come that they might have life, and that they might have it more abundantly"* (John 10:10). "Abundant" life refers to a more highly organized and greater power of Life than Man could otherwise have. It refers to the quality of Life the Gods themselves enjoy.

The Lord teaches that He is the true Light or Life in us and that it is He Who causes us to abound or flourish; this Light or Life is a degree of the presence of the Lord Himself. Man can increase this Presence and power of Life until a fulness of "Christ be formed" in him (see Galatians 4:19).

As Elder Orson Pratt observes, Christ's presence in us increases according to the degree that we receive the truth into our being: "Hence we see that wherever a great amount of this intelligent Spirit exists, there is a great amount or proportion of God, which may grow and increase until there is a fulness of this Spirit, and then there is a fulness of God."[3] Jesus showed us how this was done as He Himself ascended from grace to grace until he received the fulness of God (see D&C 93:12–14, 17). Then He says to us, *"For if you keep my commandments you shall receive of his fulness, and be glorified in me as I am in the Father; therefore ... you shall receive grace for grace"* (D&C 93:20). That is, He promises that we too can be filled incrementally, as a vessel is filled with water, with the fullness, or presence of God.

But Jesus, like each of us, had a choice as to whether to be filled or left on His own. He could have cultivated an alter-ego, a self-willing Natural Man, as we have each done to some degree. But instead, He chose so to align and identify Himself with the divine attributes and will of His Father, that He became those attributes; indeed, with so much of His Father in

---

3. *JD* 2:343.

Him, He is able to say, *"I AM the Father, I am the light, and the life, and the truth of the world"* (Ether 4:12; my emphasis).

Here we confront the mystery of identity. Jesus is referred to in scripture as both Father and Son. What is the nature of Jesus's identity if He is both the Son and the Father? The analogy of the water vessel helps. As the vessel with water, the Lord's body contains His spirit. The "vessel" itself has its own physical DNA, and the spirit its own eternally personal components. That is, there are fundamental principles or parts in His soul that will endure in Him in their unique form forever,[4] as there are in each of us. But it appears that as He allows His own spirit to be mixed with an additional spirit, His spirit takes on the attributes, the consciousness, and the identity of that spirit being added to His. In the scriptures, then, "Son" identifies the physical part of Him, the vessel part, with its unique components, personal history, and ministry; and "Father" identifies the predominant spirit that fills Him, making Him both the Father and the Son:

> *I am in the Father, and the Father in me, and the Father and I are one—[I am] the Father because he gave me of his fulness.* (D&C 93:3)

> *And because he dwelleth in flesh he shall be called the Son of God, and having subjected the flesh to the will of the Father, being the Father and the Son—[t]he Father, because he was conceived by the power of God; and the Son, because of the flesh; thus becoming the Father and Son.* (Mosiah 15:1–3)[5]

---

4. Joseph Smith, "There is no fundamental principle belonging to a human system that ever goes into another in this world or in the world to come; I care not what the theories of men are…. If any one supposes that any part of our bodies, that is, the *fundamental parts* thereof, ever goes into another body, he is mistaken" (*HC* 5:339).

5. Compare JST Luke 10:23—"All things are delivered to me of my Father; and no man knoweth *that the son is the Father, and the Father is the son, but him to whom the Son will reveal it."*

In the tabernacle of his body the Son voluntarily gave the predominance to His Father's spirit. Abinadi treats this difficult concept to help us understand this relationship among the Gods, because this is not only the pattern for the Gods, but also for each person, as modeled by our Savior. So we might say, as the Natural must yield to the Spiritual, so the Son yields His will to the Father's, so also must the Seeker put off his Natural Man and yield to the Son, ultimately giving the Lord the predominance in his soul (see Mosiah 3:19). As we see, this relationship of oneness between the Father and Son is not an anomaly, but a model for Man. Here we behold a great chain of linked beings, reaching into eternity.

Therefore, following this model, as a person fully yields his will to God's, he retains not only his own identity, but also takes on the identity of that Eternal Being that fills him. This person comes alive in Christ (see 2 Nephi 25:25), is empowered by Him to speak and to act in the living stream of godliness, of revelation, and heavenly empowerment, this loving current of higher Life. Elder F. Enzio Busche describes this relationship with the Savior:

> With this fulfillment of love [of our Heavenly Father] in our hearts, we will never be happy anymore just by being ourselves or living our own lives. We will not be satisfied until we have surrendered our lives into the arms of the loving Christ, and until He has become the doer of all our deeds and He has become the speaker of all our words.[6]

This is a living relationship rather than one dictated by a static list of spiritual things to do. We have seen that Man has the ability to keep the Law of God without investing himself emotionally and spiritually, his tendency being to routinize his

---

6. "Truth Is the Issue," *Ensign*, November 1993, 25.

spiritual practice so as to save himself the mental and spiritual effort of staying tuned to the Lord. So a person could be moral[7] but not alive in Christ.

The spiritual life, of course, begins with obedience to a set of commandments, a list of things to do or not to do. Indeed, the careful keeping of commandments is a necessary achievement, but as Paul implies, the commandments are not an end in themselves; rather, *"The end of the commandment is charity out of a pure heart"* (1 Timothy 1:5), that is, to be changed into a being like the Lord. Paul enlarges on this idea, speaking of the Natural Man: *"For they being ignorant of God's righteousness, and going about to establish their own righteousness, have not submitted themselves unto the righteousness of God. For Christ is the end of the law for righteousness to every one that believeth"* (Romans 10:3–4). Abinadi teaches the same principle as he chastens the apostate Nephites: *"I say unto you, that salvation doth not come by the law alone"* (Mosiah 13:28). No, Christ must be a party to it. To avoid the pitfalls of the list-approach, we must come to love Him with our might, mind, and strength. Then we sidestep dead works (see D&C 22:3), and the relationship becomes revelatory.

The Lord gives as the first commandment: *"Thou shalt love the Lord thy God with all thy heart, and with all thy soul, and with all thy mind. This is the first and great commandment"*

---

7. B.H. Roberts quotes Henry Drummond *(Natural Law in the Spiritual World)*, who writes of the "merely moral man" as opposed to the man touched by the power of God: "The end of salvation is perfection, the Christ-like mind, character and life.... Therefore the man who has within himself this great formative agent, Life, is nearer the end than the man who has morality alone. The latter can never reach perfection, the former must. For the life must develop out according to its type; and being a germ of the Christ-life, it must unfold into a Christ." He adds this quote as commentary on Joseph's words, "You have got to learn how to be Gods yourselves ... the same as all Gods have done before you" *(TPJS, 346).*

(Matthew 22:37). This commandment holds the key to the presence of Divinity itself. We must obtain this Love because it changes everything else we do, even the way we love our neighbor, even the way we do religion. This Love gives us access to perfecting grace (see Moroni 10:32). Without it we may have the form of godliness but not the power.

To possess this Love it helps to remember that the idea of the Love of God is itself Spirit, a spiritual seed to be cultivated. As we hold it in our mind throughout the details of our days, the spiritual seed sprouts in the softening heart, understanding increases, the mind begins to expand, and we taste Light (see Alma 32:28, 35). This Love for the Lord grows into the Presence Itself. Alma likens this Presence to a Tree with an ever-bearing fruit which is most precious, sweet, white, and pure and that can be feasted on forever. Without this cultivated Love, no list of commandments will suffice.

Indwelling God

This delicious Presence is not optional in the Plan of Happiness. Man was created with an eternal need for this Presence inside himself. He is specially created for the purpose of having God in him to urge him, mentor him, and enable him to increase not only in divine attributes and powers, but in the enjoyment of the Presence Itself. Without this growing Presence, Man is spiritually dead.

Brigham Young explained about God dwelling in Man and in all Creation and about the effects of aligning one's will with Heaven's:

> It is the Deity within us that causes increase.... Yes. He is in every person upon the face of the earth. The elements that every individual is made of and lives in, possess the Godhead. This

you cannot now understand, but you will hereafter. The Deity within us is the great principle that causes us to increase, and to grow in grace and truth.... Strict obedience to the requirements of heaven is necessary to obtain the end for which we were created, therefore let us commence to do the will of God in earnest from this time henceforth.... This will ... make them [those who do the will of God] as pure and holy in their sphere as God is in His. Commence with it, go through the vail into eternity with it, and still continue, and the end thereof no man on earth knoweth, nor the angels in heaven. Nothing short of the Holy Ghost [i.e., Deity in us] will do us any lasting good.[8]

Vine and Branch

In the Savior's last hours He comforted His apostles over His impending departure as He explained the principle of the indwelling God. He used the analogy of a grape vine with its branches:

Abide in me, and I in you. As the branch cannot bear fruit of itself, except it abide in the vine; no more can ye, except ye abide in me. I am the vine, ye are the branches: He that abideth in me, and I in him, the same bringeth forth much fruit: for without me ye can do nothing. (John 15:4–5)

Jesus modeled this principle over and over again in the presence of His apostles, but they couldn't have understood it very well at the time, and we today may find it elusive. But the Savior spoke repeatedly of this relationship of oneness with His Father and the principle of the indwelling God: *"The Son can do nothing of himself, but what he seeth the Father do: for what things soever he doeth, these also doeth the Son likewise ... and*

8. *JD* 1:93.

sheweth him all things that himself doeth" (John 5:19–20). Jesus had no disposition to do anything but what His Father continually showed Him—*"I do nothing of myself; but as my Father hath taught me, I speak these things. And he that sent me is with me: the Father hath not left me alone; for I do always those things that please him"* (John 8:28–29). The Lord revealed that Man also is a tabernacle, even a temple (see D&C 93:35; 1 Corinthians 3:16, 6:19), for the indwelling God.

To the Natural Mind this relationship of the complete subordination of one being's will to another is incomprehensible and smacks of authoritarianism and disempowerment. The Natural Man cannot comprehend a thoroughly benevolent and empowering Theocracy. He thinks he finds security in his individual identity and in his own will, even though he is often swayed by the opinions and fashions of others and has less freedom than he imagines. But the abandonment of his identity seems to him like falling into a fathomless void as frightening as death. And when the Savior then extends this same relationship of oneness to all believers, the Natural Mind begins to argue about the sacredness of individual identity.[9] But as Brigham said, "Jesus Christ never wanted to be different from his father: they were and are one."[10]

Bread of Life

Just before His death and just after His resurrection, the Lord prayed: *"Father, I pray unto thee for them, and also for all those who shall believe on their words, that they may believe in me, that*

---

9. The Natural Man is arguing for identity as he currently understands himself, not for that identity that expands into union with the Gods. This oneness among the Gods may exceed our finite understanding. It seems to consist of more than just a state of agreement.

10. *JD* 9:150.

I may be in them as thou, Father, art in me, that we may be one" (3 Nephi 19:23).

On other occasions, in company with nonbelievers, He taught this doctrine of divine oneness more obliquely. For example, after the miracle of the loaves and fishes, He crossed the Galilee and preached at the synagogue in Capernaum, where He revealed this sacred relationship in a discussion about manna. He said,

> *I am that bread of life.... I am the living bread.... Except ye eat the flesh of the Son of man, and drink his blood, ye have no life in you. Whoso eateth my flesh, and drinketh my blood, hath eternal life; and I will raise him up at the last day.... As the living Father hath sent me, and I live by the Father: so he that eateth me, even he shall live by me.* (John 6:48, 51, 53, 57)

These words were utterly offensive to many of the Jews present who had received from Jehovah the prohibition against eating any blood or flesh of man (e.g., see Leviticus 17:11–12). When the bystanders and miracle-seekers heard this inscrutable teaching, their interest in Jesus collapsed, and many went away. But perhaps some went away because they did understand and considered His doctrine too hard to live.

Finally, He was left with a small group who likely didn't understand either, but knew that there was no one else to go but to Jesus to whom they were now inextricably bound by love and by testimony. He explained to them that His words were to be understood spiritually (see John 6:63), but it would be some time before they understood the symbols.

At the Last Supper, He introduced the sacrament to His Apostles and instructed them in the indwelling Christ. Giving them the bread and wine, He promised, *"If ye do always remember me ye shall have my Spirit to be with you"* (3 Nephi 18:7). He

promised: *"I will not leave you comfortless: I will come to you....
If a man love me, he will keep all my words: and my Father will
love him, and we will come unto him, and make our abode with
him"* (John 14:18, 23). Again we see the power our love has with
the Gods as it draws us into union with Them. The promised
comfort was to be the divine compensation for spiritual death,
for having to be separated from the beloved Father and the Son
in the lone and dreary world.

Today we eat the same emblems, indicating our willingness
to develop the Presence of Christ in our soul, foreshadowing
that sacred relationship that the Gods have together. We covenant to subordinate our will to His and thus maintain oneness
through His Spirit by keeping His commandments and always
remembering Him. This sacramental covenant is the vow to
enter now into oneness with the Lord Jesus Christ which union
progresses to Godhood itself.

Beginningless God

Becoming aware of the manner by which a God helps a less-
developed being attain Godhood by filling him with His
presence shows us something of the way in which the Gods
themselves achieved Godhood. All the Gods were apparently
filled with power by Someone who predated them as God. They
were filled with a fulness of the same Light and Truth by which
we are filled as we progress. Elder Charles W. Penrose refers to
that Light and Truth as the "eternal spirit of intelligence," "the
great eternal God," that which makes men into Gods. He also
explains how an *infinite* Being could have had a beginning:

> The individual, the organized person, may have had a begin-
> ning, but that spirit of which and by which [he was] organized
> never had a beginning. That Priesthood which is the power of

LIGHT IN THE WILDERNESS

government in the heavens, never had a beginning, and it will never come to an end. *The works of that eternal spirit of intelligence, the great Eternal God, manifested to us in our Father and through Jesus Christ, never had a beginning.* There never was a first world or man; there will never be a last.[11]

Elder Penrose helps us to understand that even though each person who becomes a God had various "beginnings," such as his spirit organization and then his mortal birth, and so on, once a person allows a fulness of this principle of eternal intelligence and Priesthood, "the great eternal God," to occupy him, he undergoes a shift in identity from a finite being to an infinite being. His identity as a finite being ceases, and he takes on the identity of the Eternal Spirit that fills him. Truly we were created as vessels, as tabernacles, for the purpose of containing this principle of Godhood, as were all the Gods.

Brigham Young had deep insight into this issue of the Eternal Godly Principle and its relationship to Man. He says that submission is the first lesson we have to learn, and the easiest thing to learn, "one that is calculated and adapted to the capacity of the child." Then Brigham speaks of this Eternal Principle in Man and God:

> [Christ] observed to his disciples, "Except ye are one ye are not mine." "I am in my Father and ye in me, and I in you," one eternal principle governing and controlling the intelligence that dwells in the persons of the Father and the Son. I have these principles within me, Jesus has them within him, and you have them within you. I am governed and controlled by them, my elder brother, Jesus, is governed and controlled by them, and his Father is governed and controlled by them. He learned them, Jesus learned them, and we must learn them in order to receive crowns of glory, immortality, and eternal lives.

---

11. *JD* 26:27; italics added.

The principle of eternal life that sustains all intelligent beings, that governs and controls all things in eternity, the principle by which matter does exist, the principle by which it is organized, by which it is redeemed and brought into celestial glory, is the principle that is in you and me, that is in our heavenly Father.

It is life, it is the life of Christ and of every Saint; in this capacity they are in us and we in them. We must be possessed of that spirit that governs and controls the angels, we must have the same spirit within us that our Father in heaven is in possession of.

That spirit must rule you and me, it must control our actions and dictate us in life, we must cling to it and imbibe it until it becomes a second nature to us. We are accustomed to saying second nature, but in reality it is the first nature that we had, though sin has perverted it. God planted it there as the predominant principle, but our giving way to temptation has frustrated the plan and driven it from us.[12]

Brigham calls this principle of eternal life the *predominant* principle in Man and, indeed, his first nature. We were specially created and capacitated to live by revelation and the Divine Presence.

Identity

In the eternal worlds minds, even identities, can merge. The *Lectures on Faith* teach:

The Father and Son possess *the same mind*, the same wisdom, glory, power, and fulness; filling all in all—the Son being filled with the fulness of the *mind*, glory, and power, or, in other

---

12. *JD* 3:355.

words, the *spirit*, glory, and power of the Father—possessing all knowledge and glory, and the same kingdom; sitting at the right hand of power, in the express image and likeness of the Father—a Mediator for man—being filled with the fulness of the *mind* of the Father, or, in other words, the *spirit* of the Father; which spirit is shed forth upon all who believe on his name and keep his commandments; and all those who keep his commandments shall grow up from grace to grace, and become heirs of the heavenly kingdom, and joint heirs with Jesus Christ; possessing the same *mind*, being transformed into the *same image or likeness*, even the express image of him who fills all in all; being filled with the fulness of his glory; and become one in him, even as the Father, Son and Holy Spirit are one.[13]

The Gods, and all those who qualify themselves to have fellowship with Them, enter into a state of spiritual congruence, and in this state they share a perfect consciousness of things as they are, were, and will be (see D&C 93:24; Jacob 4:13).

Elder B. H. Roberts adds more to the discussion of that godly power which makes of men a brotherhood of Gods. He refers to that Great Spirit extended throughout the Cosmos, creating One God of many:

> This light then, the light of Truth and named for us men "the Light of Christ"—is also God, even the Spirit of God, or of the Gods, for it proceeds forth or vibrates or radiates from all the Gods—from all who have partaken of the One Divine Nature—hence "The God of All Other Gods" mentioned by our Prophet

---

13. *Lectures on Faith* (American Fork, Utah: Covenant, 2000), #5; emphasis added. While we cannot attribute these words directly to Joseph Smith, the lectures are a compilation of ideas presented at the School of the Prophets held in Kirtland, Ohio and later in Jackson County, Missouri, in 1833. We consider them profitable for doctrine with that proviso.

of the New Dispensation, "The God of Gods," "The Lord of Lords" proceeding forth from them, to extend the one God into all space that He might be in and through all things; bearing all the powers and attributes of God, creating power in earth and sun and stars; world-sustaining power and guiding force.

He bearing all the mind and spiritual attributes of God into the immensity of space, becoming God everywhere present—OMNIPRESENT; and everywhere present with power—OMNIPOTENT; extending everywhere the power of God; also All-Knowing, All-Seeing, All-Hearing—OMNISCIENT! Bearing forth in fact all the attributes of Deity; Knowledge, Wisdom, Judgment, Truth, Holiness, Mercy—every characteristic or quality of all Divine Intelligences—since they are one; and this Divine Essence or Spirit becoming "the light which is in all things, that giveth life to all things, which is the law by which all things are governed, even the Power of God, who sitteth upon His throne, who is the bosom of eternity, who is in the midst of all things."

United in this Divine Essence or Spirit is the mind of all Gods; and all the Gods being Incarnations of this Spirit, become God in Unity; and by the incarnation of this Spirit in Divine personages, they become the Divine Brotherhood of the Universe, the One God, though made of many.[14]

Truly it is ignorance that prompts us to choose to follow our own will instead of merging with that stream of Light and Revelation that fills and empowers the Heavenly Host. Even though we will in some way retain our identity throughout the

14. *The Last Seven Discourses of B. H. Roberts* (Salt Lake City: Deseret, 1948), 99–100. Elsewhere Roberts qualifies "omni" with the acknowledgment that God is limited by "other eternal existences which condition or limit even him," since He must obey certain eternal laws. See *Seventy's Course in Theology*, vol. 4 (Orem, Utah: Grandin Publishing Company, 1995), 69–71.

eternities, one yet wonders what is the nature of that identity? In what way could one identity differ from another if they all share the same mind, divine attributes, and powers? The Natural Mind finds this question threatening, but pondering it may lead us to let go of the accretions of the Natural Man that keep us from coming to Christ.

And so an imperfect, humble, ordinary man or woman is invited to do as all the Gods have done before and allow their inner space to be occupied by One who has this Eternal Intelligence in its fulness, the Lord Jesus Christ; in this union we effectively unite with all the Gods that have ever gone before.

This invitation to oneness appears throughout the scriptures. Many passages either issue this invitation or describe a person who has accepted it. The Lord says to Adam, for example, who has just been newly reborn in the Spirit, *"Thou art [now] after the order of him who was without beginning of days or end of years, from all eternity to all eternity. Behold, thou art one in me, a son of God; and thus may all become my sons"* (Moses 6:67–68). By his rebirth Adam's identity shifted from a finite being to one who could take his place in the order of eternal beings. Paul says, *"I am crucified with Christ: nevertheless I live; yet not I, but Christ liveth in me: and the life which I now live in the flesh I live by the faith of the Son of God, who loved me, and gave himself for me. I do not frustrate the grace of God"* (Galatians 2:20–21). Peter writes of the "day star" arising in the heart, *"We have also a more sure word of prophecy; whereunto ye do well that ye take heed, as unto a light that shineth in a dark place, until the day dawn, and the day star arise in our hearts"* (2 Peter 1:19).

We find more subtle references to the indwelling God, such as the promise the Savior gives John the Revelator: *"To him that overcometh will I give to eat of the hidden manna"* (Revelation 2:17). And Jesus says in the next chapter, *"Behold, I stand at the door, and knock: if any man hear my voice, and open the door,*

I will come in to him, and will sup with him, and he with me" (Revelation 3:20).

Pursuing Divinity

Each of us will have heard that gentle knock at the door; we may have reacted like Amulek, who says, *"I did harden my heart, for I was called many times and I would not hear; therefore I knew concerning these things, yet I would not know"* (Alma 10:6). What does it take to get us to open the door to this God who is seeking union with His children? Human flight from pursuing Divinity characterizes our mortal experience. We are the prodigal son running from the generous Father; we are Jonah heading for Tarshish.

In his poem, "The Hound of Heaven," the English poet Francis Thompson describes his flight from the pursuit of the persistent, saving God. He relates the many ways in which he has avoided the Great God, but never is he able to escape His relentless presence:

> I fled Him, down the nights and down the days;
> I fled Him, down the arches of the years...
> From those strong Feet that followed, followed after.
> But with unhurrying chase,
> And unperturbed pace,
> Deliberate speed, majestic instancy,
> They beat—and a Voice beat
> More instant than the Feet—
> 'All things betray thee, who betrayest Me.'[15]

The Lord says to him, "If you betray Me, you will find that all other things betray you." Still the poet continues in his flight

---

15. Francis Thompson (1859–1907), excerpts from *The Hound of Heaven.*

but finds that he cannot escape the Voice, but that it is round him like "a bursting sea."

At the end of the poem, the poet hears the Voice remind him that humans give love based only on another's merit, and since the poet doesn't merit any love at all ("Of all man's clotted clay the dingiest clot")—the Lord asks, "Whom wilt thou find to love ignoble thee, Save Me, save only Me?"

Finally, the poet who has suffered many losses in his flight, yields. The Lord explains Himself:

> All which I took from thee I did but take,
>   Not for thy harms,
> But just that thou might'st seek it in My arms.
>   All which thy child's mistake
> Fancies as lost, I have stored for thee at home:
>   Rise, clasp My hand, and come!

Then the poet describes his own realization that it has been the shade of the Lord's hand over him that has created the gloom in his life, as he has sought satisfaction and fulfillment everywhere but in the Lord's arms. The Lord's words conclude the poem: "Ah, fondest, blindest, weakest, / I am He Whom thou seekest! / Thou dravest love from thee, who dravest me."[16] That is to say, when we drive the Lord from us, we drive away the *experience* of pure love, and nothing else satisfies.

What would happen if we allowed this God to increase His presence in us, as did all those who became Gods before us? Would we come to know that "Someone is watching deep within" and that that Someone is joy? Doing the laundry, driving the car, paying the bills, encountering another person, teaching the class, facing the frightening prospect—His hands, His eyes, His love—Someone who loves us is there living in the

---

16. *Ibid.*

innermost part of our life, seeking increase. Our life is "flowed" by a Force that is not ourself, and were we to yield, we would find a more perceptive Love motivating our actions. Could our yielding become so complete that He would run everything we do?

Likely at some point we will realize that the Presence has done many things through us already, things for which we perhaps took credit. We learn from Moroni that all *"good"* we are able to do is done only through the power of God (see Moroni 10:25). Paul says, *"Where is boasting then?"* (Romans 3:27). With this growing awareness, life takes on a different configuration. Indeed, reality can shift.

The Nephites show us what they learned, even in the midst of persecutions and afflictions, by giving themselves entirely to the Lord:

> *Nevertheless they did fast and pray oft, and did wax stronger and stronger in their humility, and firmer and firmer in the faith of Christ, unto the filling their souls with joy and consolation, yea, even to the purifying and the sanctification of their hearts, which sanctification cometh because of their yielding their hearts unto God.* (Helaman 3:35)

Awakened awareness of a continual Presence casts a different light on circumstances. It takes the weight out of once heavy things. It detaches us from material and emotional burdens. And we find the most remarkable thing, the same thing the poet learned, that everything we thought we needed from other sources, we find in Him, and that turning our will and our all over to Him becomes a great relief, and is beautiful and full of goodness, and puts us in a new harmony. Yes, fear calls us to return to the old uneasy, self-willed mind; but with our deepening quiet, our delight in the Lord, our growing awareness, our steady intention, and our patience with the way of things, at some point beyond our control, Divine Powers touch the dead stones, and they shine.

CHAPTER TWELVE

THE POWER OF FAITH AND BELIEF: APPRENTICES TO GOD

Who cannot see, that if God framed the worlds by faith ... that faith is the principle of power? And if the principle of power, it must be so in man as well as in the Deity?

Lectures on Faith #1

ຕ

He that believeth on me, the works that I do shall he do also; and greater works than these shall he do.

John 14:12

ຕ

"Jesus said unto him, If thou canst believe, all things are possible to him that believeth" (Mark 9:23). Faith in Jesus Christ is the first principle of the gospel. If we don't believe, He has no power to help us. Faith gives us access to all the powers of God.

Elder Lynn A. Mickelsen[1]

---

1. Mission Presidents' Seminar, Provo, Utah, MTC, June 1996.

As the earth rolled away from the place of its first creation, Man found himself in a labyrinth of dilemmas that exceeded his own ability to resolve.[2] Soon he realized that earth life required solutions that he could not supply but that might be sought from the other world. Thus, he was led to discover in his being the power of Faith.

A Believing Response

In this world of illusion, many essential Truths are not apparent, but Man has within him a divine instinct to exercise Faith, and he will do so, with or without true information. In order, then, to keep him from placing his Faith in powerless things, the Lord prepares the way for Man to have true Faith by revealing to him, directly by the Spirit or through messengers or scripture, the Lord Jesus Christ and His gospel:

> *Wherefore, by the ministering of angels, and by every word which proceeded forth out of the mouth of God, men began to exercise faith in Christ; and thus by faith, they did lay hold upon every good thing; . . . And by so doing, the Lord God prepareth the way that . . . men may have faith in Christ, that the Holy Ghost may have place in their hearts, according to the power thereof.* (Moroni 7:25, 32)[3]

---

2. Brigham Young: "When the earth was framed and brought into existence and man was placed upon it, it was near the throne of our Father in heaven. And when man fell . . . the earth fell into space, and took up its abode in this planetary system, and the sun became our light. . . . This is the glory the earth came from, and when it is glorified it will return again unto the presence of the Father, and it will dwell there, and these intelligent beings that I am looking at, if they live worthy of it, will dwell upon this earth" (*JD* 17:143).

3. "Faith comes by hearing the word of God through the testimony of the Servants of God[;] that Testimony is always attended by the Spirit of prophecy & revelation" (*WJS*, 3).

Immediately the message of Truth creates a crisis for a person and puts him on trial, because in his soul is the power to recognize saving Truth (see 2 Nephi 2:5). As the Lord reaches after him, he cannot avoid choosing: *"If ye give place that a seed may be planted in your heart ... if ye do not cast it out by your unbelief, that ye will resist the Spirit of the Lord, behold, it will begin to swell"* (Alma 32:28).

If he accepts the seed and cultivates it, the Holy Spirit begins to gather spiritual energy in him, accompanied by an expanding inner vision of things as they really are. This divine activity in his soul continues growing with the person's acceptance and obedience. Faith, then, at its primary level, is a *believing response* to the Spirit which initiates a dynamic and reciprocal relationship with the Lord.

Unbelief, on the other hand, is resistance to the Truth sown in the heart by the Spirit. The vision closes down, and the person is left in his Natural condition. He may find, in fact, that he is in worse condition spiritually than he was before the message of Truth came to him. Elder F. Enzio Busche tells his own experience as the covenant of baptism was offered to him. He prayed about it; he reports, "I was startled to learn that if I did not make that covenant, I would lose my right and privilege to pray and the ability to communicate with my Heavenly Father that I had already developed."[4] One's relationship with the Lord is never the same after he has in some way been penetrated by the Spirit of Truth. He has to choose.

But once one summons the courage to believe and obey, many fruits of Faith begin to appear, such as repentance, remission of sins, revelation, testimony, additional gifts of the Spirit, Priesthood power, and sanctification. The *Lectures on Faith* add: "For where faith is, there will the knowledge of God be also, with all things which pertain thereto—revelations, visions, and

---

4. *Yearning for the Living God,* 87.

dreams, as well as every other necessary thing in order that the possessors of faith may be perfected and obtain salvation" (*Lecture #7*). All these are miraculous and originate in the eternal world, lying beyond Man's ability to obtain, or even to find out about on his own. These signs and miracles always appear in one form or another when a person accepts unconditionally the revelation of the Lord Jesus Christ.

It is important to notice, then, that Faith is not the power of positive thinking or a great exertion of emotion; it is, rather, a divine power that comes into the person who acts on revealed Truth as the Spirit of Revelation moves upon his soul, as, for example, in the account of the stripling sons: *"They did obey and observe to perform every word of command with exactness; yea, and even according to their faith it was done unto them"* (Alma 57:21).

Elder Richard G. Scott expands on the idea of strengthening obedience in order to increase divine help:

> The Lord is asking for a total commitment to serve. Learning from the Lord is not a linear equation where you keep a commandment and you learn more. He expects us to live as fully as we can, and the closer we get to perfection in that, then there is a sudden, powerful increase in his ability to communicate to us, inspire us to know what to do, and to give us the power or capacity to do it.[5]

Faith and righteousness are inextricably linked: "Faith is a gift of God bestowed as a reward for personal righteousness. It is always given when righteousness is present, and the greater the measure of obedience to God's laws the greater will be the endowment of faith."[6]

---

5. Devotional at the Provo, Utah, MTC, June 13, 1995.

6. Elder Bruce R. McConkie, *Mormon Doctrine* (Salt Lake City: Bookcraft, 1966), 264.

Faith as a Principle of Power

Earth life has been configured in such a way as to present each person with the dilemmas he particularly needs in order to grow in the power of Faith. The Lord has set out to perfect us and, since we don't develop in a vacuum, He provides a laboratory with problems to work on. Through the solving of problems with the Lord's help, a person takes on the powers and attributes of God Himself: "When men begin to live by faith they begin to draw near to God; and when faith is perfected, they are like him" (*Lecture #7*). His and our shared goal is "not only [to] commune with him and behold his glory, but [become] partakers of his power and stand in his presence" (*Lecture #2*).

But, as important as belief and obedience are, they do not suffice alone for a person to perfect his Faith, because it is possible for Man to believe and obey without being changed or perfected. He must, with an increasing tenderness for the Lord, continually search after communion with Him and a knowledge of what the Lord would have him do. A statement generally attributed to Brigham Young clarifies this additional element of Faith:

> Some have supposed that it would make but little difference with them whether they learned much or little, whether they attained to all the intelligence within their reach or not while they tarry in this world, believing that if they paid their tithing, went to meetings, said their prayers and performed those duties which were especially commanded, that it would be well with them and that as soon as they lay off this mortal body all would be well with them. But this is a mistaken idea and will cause every soul to mourn who embraces and practices upon it. When they arrive in the [spirit] world ... they will realize, to their sorrow, that

God required of them in this world not only obedience to His revealed will, but searching after His purposes and plans.[7]

In searching after the Lord's will they become persons experienced in using Faith as a power, for "faith is not only the principle of action, but of power also, in all intelligent beings, whether in heaven or on earth" (*Lecture* #1).

> What situation must [a person] be in, in order to be saved?... They must be persons who can work by faith ... and they must have faith to enable them to act in the presence of the Lord, otherwise they cannot be saved. And what constitutes the real difference between a saved person and one not saved—is the difference in the degree of their faith—one's faith has become perfect enough to lay hold upon eternal life, and the other's has not. (*Lecture* #7)

What does it mean to perfect one's Faith and to be able to work by Faith? *"All men... "* the Lord says, *"must... [have] perfect faith in the Holy One of Israel, or they cannot be saved in the kingdom of God"* (2 Nephi 9:23). Perfect Faith implies that a person has set out to become perfectly obedient in the intents of his heart to the Lord Jesus Christ, but also that he looks at every problem with the eyes of Faith. Elder Bruce R. McConkie explains how Faith develops miraculously over time, from a lower degree to a greater, as a person works to meet his needs in life through exercising the power of Faith:

> We grow in faith; we go step by step from a lower degree to a higher degree. We add grace to grace until eventually we get to a state where we have perfected our faith.... Don't go out now and try to cast sycamine trees [see Luke 17:6] into the sea.

---

7. Unsigned statement from the *Deseret News,* 7 February 1852.

Don't go out and try to move mountains, but go out and start in a small degree to do the things that you need to do in your life to get what you ought to have temporally and spiritually. "Faith without works is dead" (James 2:20). Work on the projects ahead, and when you have taken one step in the acquiring of faith, it will give you the assurance in your soul that you can go forward and take the next step, and by degrees your power or influence will increase until eventually, in this world or the next, you will say to the Mt. Zerins [see Ether 12:30] in your life, "Be thou removed." You will say to whatever encumbers your course of eternal progress, "Depart," and it will be so.[8]

The Seeker who believes, obeys, and has desires in the Lord is invited to step up to the next level and learn to work with Faith as a principle of power, to "work by Faith" to affect material and spiritual circumstances.

Working by Faith

For God also works by Faith. Throughout Christian history, the apostle Paul has been misunderstood in his teaching that: *"Through faith we understand that the worlds were framed by the word of God, so that things which are seen were not made of things which do appear"* (Hebrews 11:3). Many have understood these words to mean that it is by our Faith that we believe that God created the worlds. But the *Lectures* teach that it is *God* who had the Faith and Man who can learn to work as God does:

> [Faith] is the principle by which Jehovah works, and through which he exercises power over all temporal as well as eternal things.... Who cannot see, that if God framed the worlds

8. "Lord, Increase Our Faith," *BYU Speeches of the Year,* 31 October 1967, 9, 11.

249

by faith, that it is by faith that he exercises power over them, and that faith is the principle of power? And if the principle of power, it must be so in man as well as in Deity?... It was by faith that the worlds were framed. God spake, chaos heard, and worlds came into order by reason of the faith there was in him. So with man also. (*Lecture #1*)

As faith, then, is the principle by which the heavenly hosts perform their works, and by which they enjoy all their felicity, we might expect to find it set forth in a revelation from God as the principle upon which his creatures here below must act in order to obtain the felicities enjoyed by the saints in the eternal world; and that... God... would teach them the necessity of living by faith. (*Lecture #7*)

We would perhaps think that Faith was for Man only and might ask why God would need Faith if He already knows everything. This aspect of Faith as a characteristic of Deity begins to open our mind to the spiritual dynamics among the Gods and the possibilities for Man. For both God and Man, Faith as a principle of power has to do with bringing to pass something yet unrealized, whether in the temporal or spiritual realm.

It appears that the principle works this way: God takes into His heart something that He will do—which does not yet exist; for example, He undertakes to create a world. His desire reaches into the not-yet-realized, uncreated realm where only potential lies. Reaching with power into the unknown is the essence of Faith: it is the knowing that that which does not yet exist can be brought into existence. Let us say, then, that God has a desire to create a world; He has seen it in His mind, has seen how it must be, but the tangible realization of it does not yet exist. *"There is nothing that the Lord thy God shall take in his heart to do but what he will do it"* (Abraham 3:17).

The Lord says that His creations were accomplished by the word of His power, *"which is mine Only Begotten Son.... And worlds without number have I created;... and by the Son I created them"* (Moses 1:32–33). The Son, to whom the creative act was delegated, says that He brought to pass *"all things whatsoever I have created by the word of my power, which is the power of my Spirit. For by the power of my Spirit created I them; yea, all things both spiritual and temporal"* (D&C 29:30–31). I'm taking these two scriptures together to mean that the Father commissioned the Son to bring to pass the creation by the word of power, which is the power to command holy spirit.

Perhaps one reason Christ is referred to as the Word (see John 1:1; also Alma 34:5–6) is that He is able to speak the word of power, and the holy spirit embedded throughout the Cosmos obeys, bringing all into the arrangement the Lord requires, whether the desired thing lies out in the great macrocosm of space or within the microcosm of the human body or mind. To say that Christ is the Word is to say that He is the Creator, and indeed that He is God. We considered in Chapter Three the proposal that God can be defined as one who has full authority to command holy spirit. Holy spirit is the tool of the Gods' Faith.

The creation account from Abraham adds: *"And the Gods watched those things which they had ordered until they obeyed"* (Abraham 4:18). Considering the use of the mind in the process of bringing things to pass, the *Lectures* say that in both God and Man, Faith is exercised by mental exertion as well as by the spoken word:

> We ask, then, what are we to understand by a man's [or a God's] working by faith? We answer—we understand that when a man works by faith, he works by mental exertion instead of physical force. It is by words, instead of exerting his physical

powers, with which every being works when he works by faith. God said, "Let there be light:" and there was light, Joshua spake, and the great lights which God had created stood still. Elijah commanded, and the heavens were stayed for the space of three years and six months, so that it did not rain: he again commanded and the heavens gave forth rain. All this was done by faith. (*Lecture #7*)

In summary, the process of creating or "bringing to pass" by Faith, whether in God or Man, begins with an inspired desire, a plan or a detailed idea of what is wanted, a spoken creative word, and the power of mind to see the plan to its realization. By this understanding, Faith could be defined as divine energy set in motion by the focused, purified mind. It is the mind that is first fully aligned with Truth, thereby developing the power to reach out into the uncreated quantum soup and cause both things and events to materialize.

Power Aspect of Faith in Man

Elder Boyd K. Packer discusses Faith as a power to cause things to happen:

> There are two kinds of faith. One of them functions ordinarily in the life of every soul. It is the kind of faith born by experience; it gives us certainty that a new day will dawn, that spring will come.... There is another kind of faith, rare indeed. This is the kind of faith that *causes* things to happen. It is the kind of faith that is worthy and prepared and unyielding, and it calls forth things that otherwise would not be. It is the kind of faith that moves people. It is the kind of faith that sometimes moves things. Few men possess it. It comes by gradual growth. It is a marvelous, even a transcendent, power, a power

as real and as invisible as electricity. Directed and channeled, it has great effect....In a world filled with skepticism and doubt, the expression "seeing is believing" promotes the attitude, "You show me, and I will believe." We want all of the proof and all of the evidence first.... When will we learn that in spiritual things it works the other way about—that believing is seeing? Spiritual belief precedes spiritual knowledge.[9]

Again we see the kinds of attributes that characterize a person who has power in Faith: "worthy, prepared, unyielding," making possible those things that would have remained only in the realm of the potential. "Directed and channeled" reveals the strength of focus that allows Faith to have "great effect."

President J. Reuben Clark, Jr., describes Faith as an intelligent force and urges us to use Faith as a tool:

As I think about faith, this principle of power, I am obliged to believe that it is an intelligent force. Of what kind, I do not know. But it is superior to and overrules all other forces of which we know....You brethren, we brethren, have had this great power given unto us, this power of faith. What are we doing about it? Can you, can we, do the mighty things that the Savior did? Yes. They have been done by the members of the Church who had the Faith and the righteousness so to do. Think of what is within your power if you but live the Gospel, if you but live so that you may invoke the power which is within you.[10]

I remember hearing President Thomas S. Monson in a Regional Conference relate an experience he had had in a sacrament meeting where one of the priests was blessing the

9. "What Is Faith?" in *Faith* (Salt Lake City: Deseret Book, 1993), 42–43. Italics in the original.

10. *Conference Report of The Church of Jesus Christ of Latter-day Saints,* April 1960, 21.

sacrament and just couldn't seem to get the prayer right. The prayer was repeated a couple of times, and still it wasn't right. President Monson spoke of then fixing his mind in love on the young man as the prayer was begun yet again, focusing the power of his Faith on the boy, upon which the boy was able to complete the prayer accurately. The focused mind of developed Faith can be used continually to bless others.

All three of these Brethren remind us that the full nature of Faith eludes definition, but that this intelligent force in a spiritually developed being can be channeled to bring things to pass. We might consider that Faith is the power to set holy spirit in motion.

God Apprentices Man to Himself

We see that God intends to apprentice Man to Himself and teach him about the heavenly powers as he lives by line and precept according to what God reveals to him. All the basic equipment to work by power is already in him. Elder Gene R. Cook explains that this potential in Man must remain latent until he responds to the Spirit and initiates its use:

> Faith is spiritual; it comes from the Lord. But it is actuated by you.... When the Brother of Jared saw the Lord, was it because the Lord said, "Well, he is a pretty good man. I guess I will just show myself to him"? No, the brother of Jared learned a law and obeyed it.... I think often the Lord says, "Don't ask me to do it—you do it."... If you were dependent on the Lord to do all of the work, which is what Satan wanted and still wants, you would be a puppet on a string. But because of the great love of the Lord, he says, "I will give you some of my power until you learn to act independently, just as I do, if you will do my will. And if you will, I will eventually give you all my power."...

[Quoting Elder James E. Talmage:] "Somehow the Latter-day Saints have the mistaken notion that in the end, when the day comes that the Lord will make them gods or goddesses, when someone lays their hands on their heads and, as it were, says to them, You have now all that you need to be a God—go ahead—this is not true. All that you need to be a God is in you right now. Your job is to take those crude elements within you and refine them."... In other words, the Lord is saying, "Take the reins. Take charge under the direction of my Spirit. Don't wait for someone to tell you everything to do."... You prevail over people, things, and situations by your faith.[11]

Elder Cook's counsel here could easily be misconstrued to mean that in taking the reins, we have free-rein. Sometimes the passage, "Men should... do many things of their own free will... for they are agents unto themselves" (D&C 58:27–28) is likewise taken to mean that we can come up with any idea we want. But this interpretation may be a misreading of this scripture and not in harmony with the context of this passage as well as other scriptures on the subject. The Lord's main concern in D&C 58 seems to be the slothfulness of the Saints (see verses 26 and 29) in failing to use their agency even to keep the commandments already given or to work out the details in doing so. They're waiting for someone to tell them personally what to do when the avenues for revelation are open and much counsel has already been given. What the Lord seems to be advocating is a proactive attitude toward obedience and a diligent seeking to counsel with Him. As He says in verse 25, *"Wherefore, let them bring their families to this land, as they shall counsel between themselves and me."* He's looking for initiative and He promises to give both power and direction.

11. *Living by the Power of Faith* (Salt Lake City: Deseret Book, 1991), 89–92.

The Lectures record: "According as [Man's] faith was, so were his blessings and privileges; and nothing was withheld from him when his faith was sufficient to receive it" (*Lecture #7*). But again, lest we mistake, Faith implies revelation. A Priesthood holder may ask whether the Lord would support him in granting whatever blessing he pronounced on a person's head. The Lord answers:

> *He that is ordained of God and sent forth, the same is appointed to be the greatest, notwithstanding he is the least and the servant of all. Wherefore, he is possessor of all things; for all things are subject unto him, both in heaven and on the earth, the life and the light, the Spirit and the power, sent forth by the will of the Father through Jesus Christ, his Son.*
>
> *But no man is possessor of all things except he be purified and cleansed from all sin. And if ye are purified and cleansed from all sin, ye shall ask whatsoever you will in the name of Jesus and it shall be done.*
>
> *But know this, it shall be given you what you shall ask.* (D&C 50:26–30)

This last line answers the question: it will be given what the person should ask for. Two scriptures express the Lord's way of working with us: (1) *"Counsel with the Lord in all thy doings, and he will direct thee for good"* (Alma 37:37), and (2) *"Seek not to counsel the Lord, but to take counsel from his hand"* (Jacob 4:10). The apprentice learns that everything in Heaven and Earth takes place under the direction of the One Perfect Will.

One of the main reasons that God apprentices Man to Himself is that He may lead him along in the development of divine attributes, like the power to bring something to pass. The development of these attributes in Man is an example of reaching into the unrealized realm of possibilities to bring forth the miracle of a fully developed God-Man: a true act of creation and likely the greatest.

Obviously, then, the Plan of Salvation itself is a "system of faith—it begins with faith and continues by faith" (*Lecture #7*). To produce salvation, Faith develops from its slender beginnings as belief, progresses through obedience, and becomes an actual power to shape people and events. Faith's primary role is to produce a person who can be exalted and take his place among the Gods.

Retraining the Mind

As we consider the way the Gods work and see that power in Faith is connected to the powers of the mind, we realize that we must train our mind. We have to think with purpose along fruitful lines because the Lord responds to focus and persistence. He grants the inspired desires of the Brother of Jared, saying: *"And thus I will do unto thee because this long time ye have cried unto me"* (Ether 1:43). Two apostles, Elders Orson Hyde and Orson Pratt, spoke in tandem on this subject in a general conference, the one inspiring the testimony of the other on the power of the focused mind:

> Let the mind be concentrated, and it possesses almighty power. It is the agent of the Almighty clothed with mortal tabernacles, and we must learn to discipline it, bring it to bear on one point, and not allow the Devil to interfere and confuse it, nor divert it from the great object we have in view.[12]

> If a person trains his mind to walk in the spirit, and brings his whole mind to bear upon its operations, and upon the

---

12. Orson Hyde, *JD* 7:153.

principles of faith which are calculated to put him in possession of the power of God, how much greater will be his faculties for attaining knowledge.[13]

The focused mind infused with Spirit can have power over things and events. But this focus takes practice. Perhaps tedious and difficult at first, it becomes increasingly rewarding. Hugh Nibley describes the retraining of the mind and the temptation to give up, even in the midst of the presence of the Heavenly Gift:

> I am reminded here of the marvelous book of Fourth Nephi, which describes the model society and how it disintegrated.... But why did they lose it all? Because it was too strenuous; it required great mental exertion: they spent their time constantly in meetings and prayer and fasting—in concentrating on things (see 4 Nephi 1:12). The exercise of mind was simply too exhausting. It was less wearying just to give up and let things drift, to go back to the old ways. They had to work hard to preserve that marvelous order of things....
>
> The one thing that all the experimenters in psychokinesis, telepathy, and ESP, and all the borderline probings into the workings of the mind ... agree on is that whenever the task is set, successful performance is directly related to the power of concentration, to the will, to the desire, to total interest and involvement. The person has to be excited; then he can do amazing things. But if the interest and concentration are not kept at a high level, nothing much goes on. When the level is high, the mind actually has a direct effect on things. The mind can do astonishing things just by thought. It is a matter of concentrating and ordering it.[14]

13. Orson Pratt, *JD* 7:155–56.

14. *Temple and Cosmos,* in *The Collected Works of Hugh Nibley,* ed. Don Norton (Salt Lake City: Deseret Book, 1992), 13–14.

The *Lectures on Faith* show how one can bring might, mind, and strength together to open the Heavens:

> *How do men obtain a knowledge of the glory of God, his per-fections, and attributes?* By devoting themselves to his service through prayer and supplication, incessantly strengthening their faith in him, until, like Enoch, the brother of Jared, and Moses, they obtain a manifestation of God to themselves. (*Lecture #2*)

Facilitating Faith

Exercising Faith is a holistic endeavor and depends on the condition of Man's mind and heart. To facilitate the power of Faith, the mind and heart must be cleansed in order to remove obstacles and bring his system into harmony with divine ener-gies and powers. We could multiply examples of the efficacy of specific practices such as scripture study, fasting, prayer, and temple; or personal attributes such as humility—*"Save they shall … consider themselves fools before God, and come down in the depths of humility, he will not open unto them"* (2 Nephi 9:42–43); or desires—*"I am called by his Holy Spirit … and a portion of that Spirit dwelleth in me, which giveth me knowledge, and also power according to my faith and desires which are in God"* (Alma 18:34–35); or personal purity—*"And if ye are puri-fied and cleansed from all sin, ye shall ask whatsoever you will in the name of Jesus and it shall be done"* (D&C 50:29). We will consider two examples here to show how the cleansing of the mind gives place to new powers.

President Henry B. Eyring tells of a time when he needed revelation and was required to exercise his Faith to receive it.

> I have prayed, as you have, to know what to do when choices that I faced would have eternal consequences. Over many years I have seen a recurring pattern in the times when the answers to

such a prayer have come most clearly.

Once, for instance, I prayed through the night to know what I was to choose to do in the morning. I knew that no other choice could have had a greater effect on the lives of others and on my own. I knew what choice looked most comfortable to me. I knew what outcome I wanted. But I could not see the future. I could not see which choice would lead to which outcome. So the risk of being wrong seemed too great to me.

I prayed, but for hours there seemed to be no answer. Just before dawn, a feeling came over me. More than at any time since I had been a child, I felt like one. My heart and my mind seemed to grow very quiet. There was a peace in that inner stillness.

Somewhat to my surprise, I found myself praying, "Heavenly Father, it doesn't matter what I want. I don't care anymore what I want. I only want that Thy will be done. That is all that I want. Please tell me what to do."

In that moment I felt as quiet inside as I had ever felt. And the message came, and I was sure who it was from. It was clear what I was to do. I received no promise of the outcome. There was only the assurance that I was a child who had been told what path led to whatever He wanted for me.[15]

Obtaining power in Faith requires getting down under all our mortal programming, personal preferences, opinions, so-called knowledge, resistance, and fear. To get us to this depth, the Lord requires us to humble ourselves and to realize that we comprehend spiritual realities as one looking at the universe through a straw. We must plumb the depths of humility, or He will not open us (see 2 Nephi 9:42). This humility does not come easily to the Natural Man, so we press ourselves out of

---

15. "As a Child," *Ensign*, May 2006, 14–17.

our comfort zone to experience humility's depths. We contemplate Nephi's low valley and plain road (see 2 Nephi 4:32) and that rest promised those who achieve meekness and lowliness of heart (see Alma 37:34). We wrestle with the question, "Could ye say, if ye were called to die at this time, within yourselves, that ye have been sufficiently humble?" (Alma 5:27). We find to our great consolation that the depths of humility are continuous with the presence of the Lord Himself.

A second example of the efficacy of the cleansing effort concerns the experience of a much respected acquaintance of mine, Hershel Pedersen. He describes how he used temple, fasting, prayer, and scripture to release the power in his Faith and Priesthood:

> I went to the hospital to minister [to a member dying of cancer] about 3:00 on Sunday afternoon. Another elders quorum president from Lehi who worked with us at Geneva was walking out and said, "You'll never heal that one." I said, "I didn't come to heal him. I came to administer to him. I didn't think about healing him." As I walked down the hall the thought came to me, Why don't we heal people? So I administered to him. That night about 10:00 the wife called, asking me to speak at the funeral. The brother had passed away.
>
> I became possessed with the thought about healing with the priesthood so I started going to the Temple regularly, fasting and praying. I spent two years reading and studying all the scriptures and everything I could about developing power in the priesthood. I knew we belonged to the true church; that we were given the priesthood; that our faith had to increase, our righteousness had to increase; we had to find credibility with the Lord.

About two years after he administered to his friend, Brother Pedersen's wife went to the hospital to have a baby, and the doctor said that the baby was in distress. When the child was born Brother Pedersen was told to go home because the child needed some tests. About 1:00 a.m. the doctors called and told him that if he wanted to give the baby a blessing and a name, he'd better come right to the hospital because they didn't think the child would make it until morning. He reports:

> I knelt and prayed and quoted all the scriptures I could re-member about healing the sick to the Lord. I called my coun-selor, and we went to the hospital. I told the Lord if the child was to die, I knew it would die unto the Lord; if it lived, it would live unto the Lord, but it would be hard for my wife if the child died. As we put our hands through the isolette and gave the baby a blessing and a name, I stepped back and looked at the child for a long time. I just stared. I said to the doctor, "The child is all right." A few days later we took the child home and had no difficulties.

The doctor told them that he had not seen a child with this problem live in over three years. Brother Pedersen said, "We receive power by fasting and praying and reading the scriptures. We gain a certain amount of strength, and God acknowledges that."[16]

The purpose of the cleansing process is that it brings us to that point where we are finally able to pray in the Spirit, which then guides us as to what we should ask for (see 3 Nephi 19:24, *"for it was given unto them what they should pray, and they were filled with desire")*. Obtaining the Spirit then makes it possible to exercise perfect Faith in that thing: *"He that asketh in the Spirit asketh according to the will of God; wherefore it is done even as he asketh"* (D&C 46:30).

---

16. "Blessings of the Temple," CD available from Covenant Communica-tions, Inc.

It is helpful to know that our desires may indeed have been planted by the Lord to indicate a path we are to take in bringing something to pass. When I can sense that this is so, it greatly strengthens the power of my Faith to know that what I want, wants me.

Power of Belief[17]

God repeatedly invites us to ask, since there are many blessings that He cannot grant until we do. Jesus asks the Twelve, *"What is it that ye desire of me?"* (3 Nephi 28:1). Scattered abundantly throughout the scriptures is the promise that if we ask according to certain principles, we will receive. Here are a few examples to refresh the reader's mind about the promises and the conditions:

1. *If thou canst believe, all things are possible to him that believeth.... Lord, I believe; help thou mine unbelief.* (Mark 9:23–24)

2. *What things soever ye desire, when ye pray, believe that ye receive them, and ye shall have them [RSV:[18]* **believe that you have received it***, and it will be yours].* (Mark 11:24; emphasis added)

3. *Ask the Father in my name, in faith believing that you shall receive, and you shall have the Holy Ghost, which manifesteth all things which are expedient unto the children of men.* (D&C 18:18)

A word recurs here that draws our attention—"believe." Elder Packer said, "spiritual belief precedes spiritual knowledge"; that is, we must believe before we can receive. The Lord

---

17. In the Greek New Testament, one word, *pisteuo*, underlies the translation of both *faith* and *belief* and no distinction is made between the two. In this section of the chapter, "faith" and "belief" will overlap in meaning.

18. RSV refers to a translation of the Bible known as the Revised Standard Version.

responds to the person who believes that the answer in some form is on its way. Additional scriptures stress the importance of *believing* as a prerequisite for receiving:

> *The reason why he ceaseth to do miracles among the children of men is … that they dwindle in unbelief, and depart from the right way, and know not the God in whom they should trust. Behold … whoso believeth in Christ, doubting nothing, whatsoever he shall ask the Father in the name of Christ it shall be granted him; and this promise is unto all, even unto the ends of the earth.* (Mormon 9:20–21)
>
> *But hearken unto the words of the Lord, and ask the Father in the name of Jesus for what things soever ye shall stand in need. Doubt not, but be believing, and begin as in times of old, and come unto the Lord with all your heart.* (Mormon 9:27–28)

Unbelief is a state of spiritual weakness and has no power to bring things to pass. The channel is not cleansed and the spiritual energy level is not high enough.

Energizing Belief through the Eye of Faith

After cleansing the channel, Man has the innate power to deepen his belief through profound acceptance of all the Lord's revelations, casting away all conflict and doubt and acting accordingly. Then a person can strengthen his belief through a faculty related to imagination. This inherent power is the *eye of faith* that the prophets refer to, is related to the focus of mind that we have explored, and is the rudimentary organ of Faith and Creation in Man. To exercise the eye of Faith is to engage fully the imagination and senses under the influence of the Spirit.

Notice the reference in these passages to looking, hearing, and feeling in the exercising of Faith:

1. *Do you **look** forward with **an eye of faith and view** [yourself] ... before God? Can you **imagine** to yourselves that ye **hear** the voice of the Lord, saying unto you, in that day: Come unto me ye blessed? ... How will any of you **feel**, if ye shall stand before the bar of God?* (Alma 5:15–16, 22)

2. *If ye will not nourish the word, **looking forward** with an **eye of faith** to the fruit thereof, ye can never pluck of the fruit of the tree of life. But if ye will nourish the word, yea ... by your faith with great diligence, and ... **looking forward** to the fruit thereof, it shall take root.* (Alma 32:40–41)

3. *And there were many whose faith was so exceedingly strong, even before Christ came, who could not be kept from within the veil, but truly saw with their eyes the things which they had **beheld with an eye of Faith,** and they were glad.* (Ether 12:19)

In the apostle Paul's great discourse on Faith, he teaches that we must live and endure as *"seeing him who is invisible"* (Hebrews 11:27). Employing the sensory imagination can be a great help in energizing belief as we construct in our mind's eye the vision of the reality that we cannot see with the natural eyes. Our mental environment must conform to the Lord's description of things as they really are in order for us to have power in Faith. This power to visualize is part of Man's divine nature. It is the power in one's mind to enter into the visualized fulfillment of one's desires: to see, to hear, to feel, to imagine how it would be to have this blessing—believing *"that you **have** received it"* as Mark 11:24 says above—what you would do, what you would say. This kind of believing can cause the tumblers to fall into place to unlock the realization of the blessing.

This principle is used by many people to bring their desires to pass: athletes who want to improve their tennis game, actors who want to portray their characters authentically, people who want to overcome fear, and Saints who need a blessing from the

Lord. Some have used as part of their therapy a deep reading and visualizing of the scriptures, such that, when they arrived at the Savior's appearance to the Nephites and His healing them, they have imagined the sensation of His hands on their head and thereby received the healing blessing they needed. Others use it to keep themselves at the spiritual energy level that produces what they want in life. And yet others use this principle to see themselves as if they were already what they want to become.

Steve DeVore tells about his struggle learning to walk after a life-threatening bout with paralytic polio. His mother told him during his therapy sessions that since he had walked before his polio, the memory of walking was already within him. She had him focus on watching his two older brothers walk, run, and play; then she would have him close his eyes and replay in his imagination the images of his brothers at play, pretending he was running and playing along with them. To the doctors' surprise, he regained his ability to walk, run, and play and became a good athlete because, he said, of the intense physical and mental therapy he went through. He later developed a line of role-model-based training videos in golf, tennis, skiing, bowling, and racquetball. In these videos, all the poor performances were edited out and only the really good ones were left. In this way, watching the successful performances over and over again, a person had imprinted on his inner eye the vision of himself succeeding, which repetition then produced higher levels of performance. Brother DeVore has seen significant success in making these principles available to athletes all over the world.[19]

Bookstores and libraries are full of books and videos that draw a connection between what the mind focuses on and

19. Steve DeVore in "The Power of Positive Images: Visualizing Your Way to Success," Meridian Magazine (online), August 2, 2001. See www.sybervision.com.

what shows up in one's life. Thousands of personal stories show that believing power begins with a clear desire, a strong specific inner vision, and a focused intention. These stories may or may not have a spiritual component. But we know that this faculty of visualization and the potential for firmness of mind are placed in Man to help him develop the powers and attributes of God. Helaman reports, *"Now this was the faith of these of whom I have spoken;... their minds are firm, and they do put their trust in God continually"* (Alma 57:27).

Of course there have been times when we have not received what we've exercised our Faith for. But if we do not obtain our desire, we may still know with certainty that the prayer has been heard and our honest efforts have been noted. Note this unequivocal promise: *"For every one that asketh, receiveth; and he that seeketh, findeth; and to him that knocketh, it shall be opened"* (3 Nephi 14:8). It may be that He has to prepare us or try us or take us down another path, and so things may not always appear on the schedule we want: *"Nevertheless the Lord seeth fit to chasten his people; yea, he trieth their patience and their faith. Nevertheless—whosoever putteth his trust in him the same shall be lifted up at the last day"* (Mosiah 23:21). The answer will come in its own time and way.

But when it does not seem to have arrived, we do not lose Faith in the Lord Jesus Christ; rather we redouble our trust and Faith in the Lord in the profound gratitude that He will bring the greatest blessing possible and will also teach us how to ask and receive. For all our effort, we remember that we do not place our Faith solely in the thing that we want, but in the Lord Jesus Christ Himself who knows how to give good gifts and will never forsake us.

Faith and Miracles: *"The Just Shall Live by Faith"*

For the Seeker, Faith becomes a way of life, both in the believing aspect and the power aspect. For example, considering miracles, just how many of them could a person expect, day to day? Are miracles something that are rationed out—each person only gets so many now and again? Or does the Lord have a different expectation? We learn that the Nephites had *"power given them to do all things by faith"* (2 Nephi 1:10). We read in another example that when the Lord's people exercised their faith, diligence, and heed according to what the pointers in the ball showed, they had many miracles *"wrought by the power of God, day by day."* But when they got lazy and forgot to exercise their faith and diligence, *"then those marvelous works ceased, and they did not progress in their journey,"* but they got hungry and thirsty and lost (see Alma 37:40–42). The prophet urges, *"Do not let us be slothful because of the easiness of the way"* (Alma 37:46), because it seems that there really is no limit to the miracles we might participate in.

The Book of Mormon describes two ways of going about life: doing things in one's natural strength (as in Helaman 4:13, *"And because...their boastings in their own strength, they were left in their own strength"*), or continually seeking the strength of the Lord.[20] Ammon says, for example, that in the strength of the Lord he can do all things (see Alma 22:12). This realization of the availability of the power in Faith might make us wonder whether the Lord would indeed have us ask for Grace in all that we do, would have us live by our Faith in Him, and thereby mix into our lives that continual miraculous element. Alma taught the people that they should humble themselves and continue *"in the supplicating of his grace,"* that they could be

---

20. See 1 Nephi 4:31; 1 Nephi 21:5; Mosiah 9:17, Helaman 4:13; 3 Nephi 3:12; etc.

"blameless before him" (Alma 7:3). Exercising Faith to obtain the miracle of Grace is the only way to walk blameless before the Lord because, otherwise, the strength is not in us. By Faith we obtain both the inner and outer miracles that we need to finish our work on the earth. The Lord says, *"For behold, I am God; and I am a God of miracles; and I . . . work not among the children of men save it be according to their faith"* (2 Nephi 27:23).

Moroni describes the miracle of Faith in the perfecting of Man:

> *Yea, come unto Christ, and be perfected in him, and deny your-selves of all ungodliness; and if ye shall deny yourselves of all ungod-liness, and love God with all your might, mind and strength, then is his grace sufficient for you, that by his grace ye may be perfect in Christ; and if by the grace of God ye are perfect in Christ, ye can in nowise deny the power of God.* (Moroni 10:32)

We have seen here that Faith is first, a principle of revela-tion, and second, a principle of creation, both in Man's interior as well as his exterior; and that the restored Church of Jesus Christ has put these enhanced powers into the hands of the Saints as tools for exaltation. If our life is focused on the greater purposes of the Lord, and we understand the nature of the laboratory we find ourselves in, we may experience miracles in both the great issues and also in the small details of life—embracing all that is *"expedient for man to receive"* (1 Nephi 17:30)—which is likely more than we have yet dreamed to ask for. That means that we can get up in the morning, call on the name of the Lord, contemplate Him in the depths of our hu-mility, and expect to participate in miracles through the course of our day. We can do life, expecting miracles. This is the Great Plan of Happiness.

Chapter Thirteen

Faith: The Key to Knowledge

As well might man stretch forth his puny arm to stop the Missouri river in its decreed course, or to turn it upstream, as to hinder the Almighty from pouring down knowledge from heaven upon the heads of the Latter-day Saints.

D&C 121:33

❧

If thou wilt inquire, thou shalt know mysteries which are great and marvelous; therefore thou shalt exercise thy gift, that thou mayest find out mysteries, that thou mayest bring many to the knowledge of the truth.

D&C 6:11

❧

I advise all to go on to perfection and search deeper and deeper into the mysteries of Godliness.... [As for myself] it has always been my province to dig up hidden mysteries, new things, for my hearers.

Joseph Smith[1]

---

1. *WJS*, 366.

Behind the scrim on the Wilderness stage lie the gems of glittering Truth. Special effects of sound and light and delusion play on the scrim, dazzling the Natural Man. But the Seeker, not satisfied with the appearance of things, discerns rustlings behind the scrim and tries to draw near to the vast spiritual realities veiled from his view. Immersed in his scriptures, he can't help but notice how frequently the Lord offers the revelation of these gems—as though they were the best reward, next to eternal life, that He could give out of His Treasure House.[2] In fact, the Seeker learns, eternal life cannot be separated from a body of knowledge that the Lord has promised to reveal: *"If thou shalt ask, thou shalt receive revelation upon revelation, knowledge upon knowledge, that thou mayest know the mysteries and peaceable things—that which bringeth joy, that which bringeth life eternal"* (D&C 42:61). The scriptures refer to this knowledge by various names, such as, "the greater things," "the mysteries of godliness," "great treasures of knowledge," to be accessed by "the key of knowledge" and "the keys of asking and receiving." This chapter is written to encourage the Spiritual Seeker who wants to know and experience more, but isn't sure that it is appropriate to ask.

Elder Parley P. Pratt likened a hungry seeker to a man famished for the foods to which his fathers had had access. This man has in his possession a book on the history of feasting. In the book he finds that his forefathers enjoyed a feast of delicious meats and a rich variety of delicacies spread on a plenteous board. He reads of the joys of those who feasted there. "O that I too might partake of the feast." Just then a messenger comes and tells him that he does not need the food his fathers did, and, since the canon is complete and the record full, he does not need to eat as they did nor drink as they did—just reading the

---

2. For example: 1 Nephi 10:19, Alma 26:22, D&C 6:7 (11:7), D&C 63:23, D&C 76:7.

history of their feasting and believing in it and rejoicing in it would answer the same purpose. The messenger adds that it was wicked, even presumptuous, to desire or even ask for any food other than that which the reading of the record afforded him. He must be content.

The man tries to restrain his appetite, condemning himself a hundred times for feeling hungry and thirsty. But he keeps reading the history of feasting over and over again, committing it to memory, pressing it with fervor to his heart, kissing it with reverence—but he does not find relief. Then he notices a sentence that he had overlooked which informs him that he must indeed partake of the food for himself, as they did for themselves, or starve to death. Just then another messenger arrives with food and drink, and kindly invites him to eat. But the starving man quotes his first instructor who had told him that the history of feasting was all he needed and that he shouldn't ask for more. The kind messenger tells him that the previous messenger was a deceiver and that he should indeed eat. The poor starving man comes at last to his senses and is prevailed upon to eat and drink and live: "His spirit is then renewed, his soul is satisfied, and he looks with astonishment and wonder upon his former absurdity and ... is surprised to think that such foolish ideas should have ever entered the human mind."[3] Elder Pratt finishes his little allegory with these impassioned words:

> O ye hungry, famishing souls who have thus been deceived, rouse from your slumbers, break off the shackles of your minds, burst through the thick darkness and gloom of ages with which you are surrounded, and emerge forth into the light and liberty of the gospel, that you may enjoy those great and glorious privileges which have been hid from ages and generations; but which

---

3. *Writings of Parley Parker Pratt* (Salt Lake City: Deseret New Press, 1952), 23–24.

are again made manifest in these last days for the restoration of all things spoken by the prophets.[4]

Elder Pratt wrote his story to reach people who did not know about the Restoration of the Gospel. But the Latter-day Saints themselves sometimes need the same encouragement.

Some among us feel that searching after "the mysteries" is inappropriate, even dangerous, yet the Lord repeatedly issues the invitation to ask. He even gives instructions on the most effective way to ask and to receive; He has in fact revealed ordinances to make asking and receiving more potent. Yes, the pursuit of Truth can be dangerous, but not seeking it results in the yet greater danger of losing one's exaltation. Elder Orson Pratt responded to the objection about seeking spiritual knowledge:

> We should not get into that old sectarian notion, that we have no right to know anything about this, that or the other, and that we must not pry into this, that or the other. That is an old sectarian notion, which we have fought against all the day long, and we do not want it to creep into the Church of Jesus Christ of Latter-day Saints. It is the privilege of its members to let their minds expand, and to ponder upon the things of God, and to enquire of him, and by and by, when we have prepared ourselves by getting all the knowledge we possibly can from that which is written, God will give us more.[5]

Notice that the unwritten knowledge is given after the written knowledge has been well gleaned.

It will inspire the reader to review a selection of scriptures in which the Lord encourages us to look into the mysteries:

---

4. *Ibid.*, 24.

5. *JD* 16:354.

1. *Unto him that keepeth my commandments I will give the mysteries of my kingdom, and the same shall be in him a well of living water, springing up unto everlasting life.* (D&C 63:23)

2. *And to them [who serve me] will I reveal all mysteries, yea, all the hidden mysteries of my kingdom from days of old... yea, even the wonders of eternity.... For by my Spirit will I enlighten them, and by my power will I make known unto them the secrets of my will—yea, even those things which eye has not seen, nor ear heard, nor yet entered into the heart of man.... Neither is man capable to make them known, for they are only to be seen and understood by the power of the Holy Spirit, which God bestows on those who love him, and purify themselves before him; to whom he grants this privilege of seeing and knowing for themselves: That through the power and manifestation of the Spirit, while in the flesh, they may be able to bear his presence in the world of glory.* (D&C 76:7–8, 10, 116–118)

3. *And all saints who remember to keep and do these sayings, walking in obedience ... shall find wisdom and great treasures of knowledge, even hidden treasures; ... and ... the destroying angel shall pass by them.* (D&C 89:18–19, 21)

4. *Yea, he that repenteth and exerciseth faith, and bringeth forth good works, and prayeth continually without ceasing—unto such it is given to know the mysteries of God; yea, unto such it shall be given to reveal things which never have been revealed; yea, and it shall be given unto such to bring thousands of souls to repentance.* (Alma 26:22)

5. *Come unto me, O ye Gentiles, and I will show unto you the greater things, the knowledge which is hid up because of unbelief.... Behold, when ye shall rend that veil of unbelief which doth cause you to remain in your awful state of wickedness, and hardness of heart, and blindness of mind, then shall the great and marvelous things which have been hid up from the foundation of the world [come unto you].* (Ether 4:13, 15)

Let us pause here and define *mystery:* a mystery is an unseen Truth, the substance of which lies beyond Man's senses and rational faculties, and therefore must be revealed by God in order for it to be known by Man; Man cannot find it out with the limited resources he has unless God uncovers it for him. As Alma says, *"There are many mysteries which are kept, that no one knoweth them save God himself. But I show unto you one thing which I have inquired diligently of God that I might know...."* (Alma 40:3). Alma wasn't afraid to ask the Lord a question because he already knew that the whole body of gospel doctrine consists of mysteries—saving Truths that could never have been known had God not revealed them. Examples of these are the origin and destiny of Man, the existence and workings of the Holy Ghost, priesthood power, baptism by authority, sanctification, temple ordinances, resurrection, and the three degrees of glory.

Ultimately all godly mysteries that pertain to life and salvation will be known and understood, but there are conditions which must be met so that the knowledge is acquired safely so as not to impede, or even destroy, the aspirant. The Lord told the brethren through the prophet Joseph that the world *"cannot bear meat now, but milk they must receive; wherefore, they must not know these things, lest they perish"* (D&C 19:22). Alma remarked that there are many who know the mysteries of God, but *"they are laid under a strict command that they shall not impart only according to the portion of his word which he doth grant unto the children of men, according to the heed and diligence which they give unto him"* (Alma 12:9). The scriptures urge us to qualify spiritually so as to be able to receive increasing instruction. So much awaits us that we must keep reaching beyond our present understanding, carefully laying the foundation of obedience upon which greater and greater knowledge can be added. The Savior told the Nephites that when the Saints in the latter days received the Book of Mormon as we have it today (i.e., "the lesser part"), they would be put to a test:

> *And when they shall have received this [lesser part], which is expedient that they should have first, to try their faith, and if it shall so be that they shall believe these things then shall the greater things be made manifest unto them. And if it so be that they will not believe these things, then shall the greater things be withheld from them, unto their condemnation.... I will try the faith of my people.*
> (3 Nephi 26:9–11)

Mormon wrote similarly, *"And whoso receiveth this record, and shall not condemn it because of the imperfections which are in it, the same shall know of greater things than these"* (Mormon 8:12). The "lesser part" is designed to provoke questions about the "greater part." The Lord says that He will try our faith before He gives more knowledge.

Joseph Fielding Smith said that the Lord is in fact withholding knowledge from the Saints because of our unworthiness[6] and unbelief as reflected in Ether 4:13, 15 cited above; and, in our day, the Lord speaks sternly to His covenant people:

> *Your minds... have been darkened because of unbelief, and because you have treated lightly the things you have received—which vanity and unbelief have brought the whole church under condemnation.... The children of Zion shall remain under this condemnation until they repent and remember... the Book of Mormon and the former commandments which I have given them, not only to say, but to do according to that which I have written.* (D&C 84:54–57)

The Faith to collect and observe the "to-do's" in scripture leads to rending the veil of unbelief and to increasing readiness

---

6. *DS* 2:304.

for revelation. Only obedience—that is, coming into line with Truth received—can prepare the spirit of Man to receive more. As Elder Bruce R. McConkie writes, "Finally, in obtaining or increasing faith, the great governing principle is personal righteousness. A man's faith cannot exceed his righteousness and obedience. The greater the adherence to the truth, the greater is the faith of an individual."[7]

"Knowledge," the prophet Joseph said, "is Revelation. Hear all ye brethren, this grand Key: Knowledge is the power of God unto Salvation."[8] We can't be saved any faster than we gain knowledge: *"It is impossible for a man to be saved in ignorance"* (D&C 131:6). Brigham Young, a great advocate of education, talked to the Saints about gaining knowledge from Heaven:

> As Saints in the last days we have much to learn; there is an eternity of knowledge before us; at most we receive but very little in this stage of our progression. There is a vast store of information that exists for the faithful Saints. It cannot be understandingly exhibited by any individual, not even by an angel, to the people any further than they are able to receive and comprehend it.... This principle is inherent in the organization of all intelligent beings, so that we are capable of receiving, and receiving, and receiving from the inexhaustible fountain of knowledge and truth.[9]

Just before His crucifixion, the Lord said to his apostles: *"I have many things to say unto you, but ye cannot bear them now. Howbeit when he, the Spirit of truth, is come, he will guide you into all truth: for he shall not speak of himself; but whatsoever he*

---

7. *Doctrinal New Testament Commentary* (Salt Lake City: Bookcraft, 1974), 1:525.

8. *WJS*, 207.

9. *JD* 3:354.

shall hear, that shall he speak" (John 16:12–13). Shortly after that scene, He said to His people in the New World, *"I perceive that ye are weak, that ye cannot understand all my words.... Therefore, go ye unto your homes, and ponder upon the things which I have said, and ask of the Father, in my name, that ye may understand, and prepare your minds for the morrow, and I come unto you again"* (3 Nephi 17:2–3). In our day He has said, *"Behold, ye are little children and ye cannot bear all things now; ye must grow in grace and in the knowledge of the truth"* (D&C 50:40); and again, *"Ye are little children, and ye have not as yet understood how great blessings the Father hath in his own hands and prepared for you; And ye cannot bear all things now; nevertheless, be of good cheer, for I will lead you along"* (D&C 78:17–18). Our Father is very kind; He understands our slowness. He does not impose too great a burden but continually presses us to move on to that "perfect day" (see D&C 50:24).

The *Lectures on Faith* reveal the pattern by which a person who has obtained Faith uses it to get closer to the scrim and finally to penetrate it. We note here that in the scriptures and in the *Lectures, knowledge* of God signifies, not just knowing about Him, but coming to know Him through personal experience, until He fully reveals Himself. The fulness of this personal knowledge generally comes through particular ordinances, about which we will speak further on. But once that personal knowledge of God is obtained, one has qualified to enter into the Treasure House. The *Lectures* show the pattern, referring to the *knowledge* of God as the key to all knowledge:

> And if the question is asked, how were they to obtain the knowledge of God?... The answer is given—through faith they were to obtain this knowledge; and having power by faith to obtain the knowledge of God, they could with it obtain all other things which pertain to life and godliness.... It was by obtaining

a knowledge of God that men got all the knowledge of all things which pertain to life and godliness; and this knowledge was the effect of faith, so that all things which pertain to life and godliness are the effects of faith. (*Lecture #7*)

For where faith is, there will the knowledge of God be also, with all things which pertain thereto—revelations, visions, and dreams, as well as every necessary thing, in order that the possessors of faith may be perfected, and obtain salvation.... And he who possesses it will through it, obtain all necessary knowledge and wisdom, until he shall know God and the Lord Jesus Christ whom he has sent, whom to know is eternal life. (*Lecture #7*)

And how is it that Faith leads to knowledge of God? We refer again to the answer from the *Lectures on Faith:*

How do men obtain a knowledge of the glory of God, his perfections and attributes? By devoting themselves to his service through prayer and supplication, incessantly strengthening their faith in him, until like Enoch, the brother of Jared, and Moses, they shall obtain a manifestation of God to themselves. (*Lecture #2*)

This *Lecture* suggests a complete immersion in spiritual matters. Those who want to know must become thoroughly permeated with the things of the Lord, thus fulfilling a law that requires Faith, obedience, and saturation with the Lord's things to reach a sort of critical-mass point before Faith can become "perfect" knowledge. Faith is not perfect knowledge, but is designed to become that. In scripture, to have a perfect knowledge of something is to have seen and even touched it.[10]

---

10. Joseph Smith observes, "Men at the present time testify of Heaven & of hell, & have never *seen* either—& I will say that no man *knows* these

The *Lecture* just cited mentions the brother of Jared as an example of one who used his Faith to get a perfect knowledge. First he proved his Faith by doing all things the Lord required of him; his Faith was strengthened as the Lord kept responding to his obedience. Suddenly, the law of Faith-to-Knowledge was fulfilled. As the brother of Jared brought the sixteen small stones before the Lord, persisting with Him by expressing his testimony over and over to Him, saying that he knew that the Lord had all power and could show forth great power and whatsoever He wished He could do *"for the benefit of man"* (Ether 3:4), the Lord then drew aside the veil, and the brother of Jared saw and knew; his Faith in the Lord became perfect knowledge: *"He had faith no longer, for he knew, nothing doubting. Wherefore, having this perfect knowledge of God, he could not be kept from within the veil"* (Ether 3:19–20).

Having made the transition from Faith in to Knowledge of the Lord, he could now be shown all things. Faith in the Lord Jesus Christ leads in one direction and that is into the order of the Son of God and into the Lord's presence. The brother of Jared's experience seems to illustrate the model.

---

things without this" (*WJS*, 10; emphasis added). A small sampling of several pertinent scriptures will show that the Lord often uses the word *know* with the word *see* when describing "perfect knowledge": 1 Nephi 5:4, *"If I had not seen the things of God in a vision I should not have known the goodness of God"*; Alma 36:26, *"Many have been born of God, and have tasted as I have tasted, and have seen eye to eye as I have seen; therefore they do know of these things … as I do know"*; D&C 45:46, *"You now behold me and know that I am"*; 3 Nephi 11:15, *"The multitude … did see with their eyes and did feel with their hands, and did know of a surety"*; D&C 50:45, *"And the day cometh that you shall hear my voice and see me, and know that I am"*; D&C 93:1, *"Every soul who forsaketh his sins and cometh unto me, and calleth on my name, and obeyeth my voice, and keepeth my commandments, shall see my face and know that I am."*

Nature of Priesthood

Seeking spiritual knowledge, we soon arrive at the doorstep of Priesthood. Let us revisit here a statement of Elder Penrose to help us penetrate more deeply the nature of Priesthood. He links Priesthood and the "eternal spirit of intelligence":

> The individual, the organized person may have had a beginning, but that spirit of which and by which [he was] organized never had a beginning. That Priesthood which is the power of government in the heavens, never had a beginning, and it will never come to an end. The works of that eternal spirit of intelligence, the great Eternal God, manifested to us in our Father and through Jesus Christ, never had a beginning.[11]

The power of Priesthood is conveyed in an eternally flowing stream. The Gods set up a channel by which this power can be conferred on one who qualifies. It flows down this channel from generations of Gods, through *"the fathers; it came down from the fathers... even from the beginning, or before the foundation of the earth, to the present time"* (Abraham 1:3). This power takes up residence in a qualified man, conferred by one who already has the authority, and connects him in its stream with all the Gods that have ever been. It manifests itself incrementally in those who commence in the lower degrees of Priesthood, progresses through the various covenants and obligations of the Priesthood, and arrives finally at its full expression in Godhood itself. This is the order of the Priesthood. "It is a perfect system of government," Brigham says, "a kingdom of Gods and angels and all beings who will submit themselves to that government."[12]

---

11. *JD* 26:27.

12. *JD* 7:142.

For all the imperfections in those who occupy Priesthood offices on earth, those who step out of the chain of true authority, to follow their own will, run the risk of stepping out of the stream of eternal Priesthood power and revelation. The Lord honors the channel He has established as those ordained to this power honor the oath and covenant with which it is conferred (see D&C 84:35, 37–41, 44).[13]

By this oath and covenant, a man learns to be governed by Heaven and begins to ascend by degrees toward the order of the Son of God and may, as his Faith becomes sufficient, enjoy the power that the Gods themselves use. Melchizedek is an example of such a man:

> *[Melchizedek] was ordained an high priest after the order of the covenant which God made with Enoch, it being after the order*

---

13. Nevertheless, it is the responsibility of each of us to perfect our lives to such a degree that we can discern the inspiration of our leaders. Two prophets, Brigham Young and J. Reuben Clark, comment on this responsibility: "I am more afraid that this people have so much confidence in their leaders that they will not inquire for themselves of God whether they are led by Him. I am fearful they settle down in a state of blind self-security, trusting their eternal destiny in the hands of their leaders with a reckless confidence that in itself would thwart the purposes of God in their salvation, and weaken that influence they could give to their leaders, did they know for themselves, by the revelations of Jesus, that they are led in the right way. Let every man and woman know, by the whispering of the Spirit of God to themselves, whether their leaders are walking in the path the Lord dictates, or not" (Brigham Young, JD 9:150).

"The question is, how shall we know when the things they have spoken were said as they were 'moved upon by the Holy Ghost'? ... We can tell when the speakers are 'moved upon by the Holy Ghost' and when we, ourselves, are 'moved upon by the Holy Ghost.' In a way, this completely shifts the responsibility from them to us to determine when they so speak" (J. Reuben Clark, Jr., "When Are the Writings or Sermons of Church Leaders Entitled to the Claim of Scripture?" Speech given at Brigham Young University, July 7, 1954).

of the Son of God.... For God having sworn unto Enoch and unto his seed with an oath by himself that every one being ordained after this order and calling should have power, by faith, to break mountains, to divide the seas, to dry up waters, to turn them out of their course; to put at defiance the armies of nations, to divide the earth, to break every band, to stand in the presence of God; to do all things according to his command, subdue principalities and powers. (JST Genesis 14:27–28, 30, 31)

In this passage, we see the close relationship between Faith and Priesthood power. It is first the ordination, then the focused consecration of a man's mind and spirit, that is, his Faith, which gives him access to this power. If he is not sufficiently permeated with the things of God, if his will is fragmented and scattered in other directions, he will not experience this power.

Since holy spirit is the essence of Priesthood power, and we understand that this spirit has a particular set of qualities, we would expect that these qualities would have to operate in the man who was seeking power in his Priesthood. This is a familiar list of qualities, but it bears looking at again, as we realize that this list underlies the very efficacy of Priesthood power and the nature of Godhood itself: *"The rights of the priesthood are inseparably connected with the powers of heaven, and ... cannot be controlled nor handled only upon the principles of righteousness"* (D&C 121:36). The man who possesses the attributes of godliness given in this section does not care for the honors of the world; does not cover his sins, or gratify his pride, or vain ambition, or exercise control or dominion or compulsion upon any soul unrighteously; his Priesthood functions only by persuasion, long-suffering, gentleness and meekness, and by love unfeigned; he exercises it by kindness and pure knowledge; he is not tainted with hypocrisy or guile; he is able to reprove by the power of the

Holy Ghost but in the same moment to show forth love; he is full of charity towards all men, and his thoughts continually entertain virtue. As a result, this person's confidence waxes strong in the presence of God, because he is oriented the way God is. The doctrine of the powers of the Priesthood distill upon his soul providing a deep-structure understanding he would be denied were he not cultivating divine attributes and powers. The Holy Ghost becomes his constant companion, and his Priesthood grows into his eternal Godhood, flowing to him without restriction, forever (see D&C 121:35, 37–46). The Lord understands how carefully protected must be the channel of the Priesthood in which flow all the blessings that can come to a child of God. He comprehends how consonant a man's nature must be with godly intentions in order to manage these powers.

But, before we explore the issue of Priesthood and knowledge further, let us consider how women fit in a discussion on the powers of Priesthood.

Woman Is Not Left Behind

Woman was created spiritually equal to Man. The Lord has chosen for now to withhold more detailed information on the spiritual blessings and powers of the Priesthood in a woman, and this perhaps due to the sacredness of the Woman, and perhaps also to strengthen her Faith and other divine attributes. But from what the Lord has said and what we have experienced, every woman who has received Melchizedek Priesthood ordinances, and been faithful to the associated covenants, has this predominant power of godliness flowing in her as well. And though she may not in this life use specific keys, power is released in her for full spiritual development, for the exercising of spiritual gifts, for the blessing of others, and for the obtaining of knowledge and eternal life.

Her Priesthood ordinances have power for her in and of themselves. One indication of this truth lies in the practice of the Church with respect to temple cancellation of sealings. This cancellation is not granted to a woman who has been divorced until she is ready to be sealed in the temple again to a new companion. The reason for this is that the possession of that ordinance, even without a companion, holds a blessing for her, and having once received the ordinance of sealing, she would not want to be without it. This practice shows that there is Priesthood power in the ordinance itself which is for her personal blessing. Of course the blessings of the Priesthood in their fullest expression include a man and woman united for eternity in Godhood. But even though that union may not yet exist in the temporal probation, the woman may know that her Priesthood ordinances empower her.

Elder James E. Talmage teaches that even though it is not given to woman to exercise the authority of the Priesthood independently from her husband, nevertheless,

> in the sacred endowments associated with the ordinances pertaining to the House of the Lord, woman shares with man the blessings of the Priesthood. When the frailties and imperfections of mortality are left behind, in the glorified state of the blessed hereafter, husband and wife will administer in their respective stations, seeing and understanding alike, and cooperating to the full in the government of their family kingdom. Then shall woman be recompensed in rich measure for all the injustice that womanhood has endured in mortality. Then shall woman reign by Divine right, a queen in the resplendent realm of her glorified state, even as exalted man shall stand, priest and king unto the Most High God. Mortal eye cannot see nor mind comprehend the beauty, glory, and majesty of a righteous woman made perfect in the celestial kingdom of God.[14]

---

14. "The Eternity of Sex," *Young Women's Journal*, 25 [October 1914]: 602–3.

And Elder Joseph Fielding Smith wrote with respect to a future estate: *"Women do not hold the priesthood, but if they are faithful and true, they will become priestesses and queens in the kingdom of God, and that implies that they will be given authority."* [15] It appears that some things are held in reserve, according to the Lord's loving purposes.

Elder Franklin D. Richards asked some Priesthood brethren a pointed question about the Priesthood power of their wives:

> I ask any and everybody present who have received their endowments, whether he be a brother Apostle, Bishop, High Priest, Elder, or whatever office he may hold in the Church, "What blessings did you receive, what ordinance, what power, intelligence, sanctification or grace did you receive that your wife did not partake of with you?" I will answer, that there was one thing that our wives were not made special partakers of, and that was the ordination to the various orders of the priesthood which were conferred upon us. Aside from that, our sisters share with us any and all of the ordinances of the holy anointing, endowments, sealings, sanctifications and blessings that we have been made partakers of.
>
> Now, I ask you: Is it possible that we have the holy priesthood and our wives have none of it? Do you not see, by what I have read, that Joseph desired to confer these keys of power upon them in connection with their husbands? I hold that a faithful wife has certain blessings, powers and rights, and is made partaker of certain gifts and blessings and promises with her husband, which she cannot be deprived of, *except by transgression* of the holy order of God. They shall enjoy what God said they should. And these signs shall follow them if they believe. [16]

---

15. *DS* 3:178; italics in original.

16. *Collected Discourses*, vol. 5, July 19, 1888. Italics in original.

The scriptures, for the Lord's purposes, refer only to men being received into the holy order of God, but it becomes obvious that women too can be received into that order.

Except, then, for specific performances, such as ordination to the Priesthood and the authority to preside and to perform ordinances, all the blessings of the Priesthood belong to the endowed and faithful woman; and all that is said in this chapter and in this book pertains fully to the spiritually seeking woman. That these powers are not fully defined in her case does not diminish the fact that, by these ordinances, she has greater access to knowledge and to God than she would have without them. However, the manner in which she will partake of these powers and blessings is a matter that she can take up with the Lord.

Priesthood and the Key of Knowledge

Joseph said, "We are called to hold the keys of the mysteries of those things that have been kept hid from the foundation of the world until now."[17] He explained that the acquiring of this knowledge comes through the Priesthood, which is "the channel through which all knowledge, doctrine, the plan of salvation and every important matter is revealed from heaven.... It is the channel through which the Almighty commenced revealing his glory at the beginning of the creation of this earth and through which he has continued to reveal himself to the children of men to the present time and through which he will make known his purposes to the end of time."[18]

The Lord revealed on several occasions the power of the Melchizedek Priesthood in gaining knowledge:

---

17. *TPJS*, 137.

18. *WJS*, 38–39.

1. *And this greater priesthood administereth the gospel and holdeth the key of the mysteries of the kingdom, even the key of the knowledge of God.* (D&C 84:19–20)

2. *The power and authority of the higher, or Melchizedek Priesthood, is to hold the keys of all the spiritual blessings of the church—To have the privilege of receiving the mysteries of the kingdom of heaven, to have the heavens opened unto them, to commune with the general assembly and church of the Firstborn, and to enjoy the communion and presence of God the Father, and Jesus the mediator of the new covenant.* (D&C 107:18, 19)

3. *Now the great and grand secret of the whole matter, and the* summum bonum *of the whole subject that is lying before us, consists in obtaining the powers of the Holy Priesthood. For him to whom these keys are given there is no difficulty in obtaining knowledge of facts in relation to the salvation of the children of men, both as well for the dead as for the living.... This, therefore, is the sealing and binding power, and in one sense of the word, the keys of the kingdom, which consist in the key of knowledge.* (D&C 128:11, 14)

We learn from these passages that the Melchizedek Priesthood holds the keys of access to God, to a personal knowledge of Him, and to all other knowledge pertaining to life and salvation. In the last passage cited, the Lord links the obtaining of this knowledge to the sealing power, which immediately connects the whole subject to the temple:

> *For therein [in the temple] are the keys of the holy priesthood ordained, that you may receive honor and glory.... Joseph...shall show unto him the keys whereby he may ask and receive.... Let my servant...receive the keys by which he may ask and receive blessings.* (D&C 124:34, 95, 97)

We understand from these verses that it is in the temple that we are endowed with the means of greater access to God and greater power to ask and receive. President Ezra Taft Benson taught: "When you attend the temple and perform the ordinances that pertain to the House of the Lord, certain blessings will come to you.... You will receive the key of the knowledge of God. (See D&C 84:19.) You will learn how you can be like Him. Even the power of godliness will be manifest to you. (See D&C 84:20)."[19]

The temple is the place designated for obtaining access to certain kinds of essential knowledge.

Temple Worship

Some may wonder how to claim those blessings if they struggle to find meaning in the temple. Let us consider here a few ideas that might be helpful.

The temple operates on a spiritual dynamic. Everything else operates on a spiritual dynamic too, but we don't perceive it because our everyday world is so sensorily rich and intellectually engaging that we are often not conscious of the presence of a spiritual dimension there. But in the temple the Lord seems to have deliberately reduced the sensory and intellectual stimulation to the point that it is soon exhausted on a superficial level. We find sooner or later that we have to tune into another dimension to pick up the subtle energies of the Spirit; we have to yield to the spiritual-feeling-perceiving part of ourself if we are going to gain access to what is really going on there. And we find that maybe we can't just turn that perception on in the temple if we're not working with temple covenants outside the temple.

The key seems to be to make the temple covenants the focus of our daily walk, growing in consecration. When our spirit knows that we are arranging our own agenda to

19. "What I Hope You Will Teach Your Children about the Temple," *Ensign*, August 1985, 6.

consecrate ourself to the Lord, putting the Lord's things first, then the personal relationship becomes real and spiritual perception begins to open inside.

Instead, we may try to access things in the temple with our every-day mind without really having taken the temple covenants to heart. But if the temple is really as sacred as we are taught, then we would not be surprised to know that it is operating on a dynamic that is only accessible to those who prepare themselves through sacrifice to penetrate that spiritually perceived world. Perhaps, indeed, the temple is designed to be a sort of structure or model for daily life as the journey to greater Truth and Godliness is outlined for us there.

But if one sits in the temple and essentially blocks out what his spirit knows the temple is requiring of him, the sins of his casualness with the things of God will hang in the air like a veil. He may try to analyze the symbols, but even so may have a hard time staying focused. In that state of mind he can come in and go out of the temple without being much changed by what is going on there. So, he may wonder, what is the point?

Not entirely accessible to the intellect, the object of temple worship is to enter this other dimension and experience the presence of God and the revelatory world, the timeless world, the world of spirit. The Lord promises that that world is there and even perceivable: *"And inasmuch as my people build a house unto me in the name of the Lord, and do not suffer any unclean thing to come into it, that it be not defiled, my glory shall rest upon it; Yea, and my presence shall be there, for I will come into it, and all the pure in heart that shall come into it shall see God"* (D&C 97:15–16). It is as though there is a dimension of activity going on there that the every-day mind simply will not perceive. The problem is, we get used to indulgence in things that are not of the Spirit and can get into the habit of treating the Lord's things lightly, and then He will not open to us. But when He sees that we are taking Him seriously, then He takes us seriously. So, the solutions to benefiting from temple worship become more obvious. This is the question that presents itself to our spirit as we contemplate attending the temple: Do you want to enter the Lord's presence in the temple—or not?

But the specifics of how temple blessings are to be sought must be taken up personally with the Lord. There is, after all, horizontally communicated information in spiritual matters and then there is information that is communicated largely vertically, that is, from the Lord directly to a person. Some spiritual information is not to be written and is unlawful even to be uttered by man:

> Great and marvelous are the works of the Lord, and the mysteries of his kingdom which he showed unto us, which surpass all understanding in glory... which he commanded us we should not write while we were yet in the Spirit, and are not lawful for man to utter; neither is man capable to make them known, for they are only to be seen and understood by the power of the Holy Spirit, which God bestows on those who love him, and purify themselves before him; to whom he grants this privilege of seeing and knowing for themselves; that through the power and manifestation of the Spirit, while in the flesh, they may be able to bear his presence in the world of glory. (D&C 76:114–18)

The Lord may continually test our trustworthiness in being able to keep certain things to ourselves. Joseph, upon whom the visions of eternity rolled, had to say, "There are some things in my own bosom that must remain there."[20] And Brigham observed, "The Lord has no confidence in those who reveal secrets, for he cannot safely reveal himself to such persons."[21] But about the priority of inquiry, Brigham was unequivocal:

---

20. WJS, 207.

21. Discourses of Brigham Young, ed. John A. Widtsoe (Salt Lake City: Deseret Book, 1978), 41.

Take a course to open and keep open a communication with your ... Savior. Were I to draw a distinction in all the duties that are required of the children of men, ... I would place first and foremost the duty of seeking unto the Lord our God until we open the path of communication from heaven to earth—from God to our own souls. Keep every avenue of your hearts clean and pure before him.... To get this revelation it is necessary that the people live so that their spirits are as pure and clean as a piece of blank paper that lies on the desk ... ready to receive any mark the writer may make upon it.[22]

Inspired inquiry begins to open a beautiful vision of what the Lord is inviting us to. He tells us the conditions upon which we may proceed, with the absolute certainty that our desires for more Truth will be heeded:

> *Therefore, sanctify yourselves that your minds become single to God, and the days will come that you shall see him; for he will unveil his face unto you, and it shall be in his own time, and in his own way, and according to his own will. Remember the great and last promise which I have made unto you: cast away your idle thoughts and your excess of laughter far from you.* (D&C 88:68–69)

Opening our own revelatory channel becomes a necessity to us. As we grow and have increasing experience with the Lord personally, we want to know less of others' opinions and more for ourselves, realizing that until we each experience spiritual realities for ourselves, there will be some distortion in our perception of things as they really are. As Joseph said, "Reading the experience of others, or the revelation given to *them*, can never give *us* a comprehensive view of our condition and true relation to God. Knowledge of these things can only be obtained

---

22. *Ibid.*

by experience through the ordinances of God set forth for that purpose."[23] He invited the Saints to find out for themselves:

> God hath not revealed anything to Joseph but what He will make known unto the Twelve, and even the least Saint may know all things as fast as he is able to bear them, for the day must come when no man need say to his neighbor, Know ye the Lord; for all shall know Him (who remain) from the least to the greatest. How is this to be done? It is to be done by this sealing power, and the other Comforter spoken of, which will be manifest by revelation.[24]

We have considered in this chapter some compelling ideas that may raise questions, and we want to be aware that when we begin to explore topics such as the ones touched on here and in the next chapter, we move into a realm where deception is a real peril. Some have left the Church on doctrinal issues that led them into apostasy. The reason is that the Adversary awaits every opportunity to deceive. Deception can be presented in spiritually irresistible guises to the unwary. For example, implicit in Man's nature is the desire for holiness; therefore, when the serpent whispered to Eve, *"Your eyes shall be opened, and ye shall be as gods, knowing good and evil,"* and when Eve saw that the tree was *"to be desired to make her wise"* (Moses 4:11–12), she ate the fruit. The desire for that higher knowledge that leads to greater holiness is fraught with pitfalls, not only opening the way to revelation and exaltation, but also driving many an

---

23. *TPJS*, 324; italics in the original.

24. *TPJS*, 149. Those who would like to examine responsible, scholarly material on such issues as the keys for asking and receiving, as well as statements by the prophet Joseph and by early brethren and sisters close to him, may consult the *Words of Joseph Smith* by Andrew Ehat and Lyndon Cook.

apostate movement; hence the great importance of building a strong spiritual practice established in the security of the Priesthood channel.

Brigham Young observed that the Adversary is not our only trial; the Lord Himself does considerable testing:

> God never bestows upon his people, or upon an individual, superior blessings without a severe trial to prove them, to prove that individual, or that people, to see whether they will keep their covenants with him, and keep in remembrance what he has shown them. Then the greater the vision, the greater the display of the power of the enemy.... You will be tempted in proportion to the visions, revelation, or manifestation you have received.[25]

But we sing the hymn "Yes, say, what is truth? 'Tis the brightest prize to which mortals or Gods can aspire. Go search in the depths where it glittering lies, or ascend in pursuit to the loftiest skies: 'Tis an aim for the noblest desire."[26]

Despite the hazards, we see that we have no option. We must press on to the prize.

25. *Discourses of Brigham Young*, 338.

26. "Oh, Say What Is Truth," *Hymns of the Church of Jesus Christ of Latter-day Saints* (Salt Lake City: Church of Jesus Christ of Latter-day Saints, 1992), No. 272.

Chapter Fourteen

The End of the Wilderness Journey:
Perfection and Election

In spiritual things you have a heavenly power lifting you beyond where you are now. You can set your expectations for yourself a little higher and then a little higher, with confidence that a loving Heavenly Father and His Beloved Son will send you the Holy Ghost and lift you higher and higher, toward them.

President Henry B. Eyring[1]

☙

Make no small plans; they have no magic to stir men's souls.

President Spencer W. Kimball[2]

☙

I advise all to go on to perfection, and to search deeper and deeper into the mysteries of Godliness.... I am going on in my progress for eternal life.... Oh! I beseech you to go forward, go forward and make your calling and your election sure.

Joseph Smith[3]

---

1. "Seek Higher Ground," BYU-Idaho Devotional, 26 January 2005.

2. *Regional Representatives Seminar,* 1979, quoting Daniel Burnham.

3. *TPJS,* 364, 366.

We return now to events in the premortal world where we were permitted to view the unfolding vision of the path we now travel in the Wilderness.[4] There we contemplated the ends to be achieved in the journey to come. We received our "first lessons" and *were prepared to come forth in the due time of the Lord to labor in his vineyard for the salvation of the souls of men* (D&C 138:56). Called and set apart, heads bowed under Priesthood hands, we received foreordinations to a personal ministry, to tasks and callings that would unfold unto exaltation and conform us *to the image of [God's] Son* (Romans 8:29). We listened as the Gods took counsel together: *"We will make an earth whereon these may dwell; and we will prove them herewith, to see if they will do all things whatsoever the Lord their God shall command them"* (Abraham 3:24–25). We knew that the purposes of our earth's journey would not be fulfilled until we had conformed to that premortal mandate.

Now that same foreordination, that same calling and election, that same invitation to holiness and to the likeness of Christ, may lie unquietly in our breast—and with them, an ancient memory: *"He hath chosen us in him before the foundation of the world, that we should be holy and without blame before him in love"* (Ephesians 1:4). The election, already in place there, must be made sure here. The premortal Voice speaks into the recesses of the heart: *"I am the Lord your God: ye shall therefore sanctify yourselves, and ye shall be holy; for I am holy"* (Leviticus 11:44).

---

4. See President Joseph F. Smith, *Gospel Doctrine* (Salt Lake City: Deseret Book, 1978), 13–14. He says that the Savior possessed a foreknowledge of all the vicissitudes through which He would have to pass in the mortal tabernacle. Then he says, "If Christ knew before hand, so did we. But in coming here, we forgot all, that our agency might be free indeed."

CHAPTER FOURTEEN

Evolving and Lifting Power

Holiness and election might be daunting concepts, but scriptural voices from every dispensation urge us on: *"Wherefore ... brethren, give diligence to make your calling and election sure"* (2 Peter 1:10); *"Ye should be perfect even as I, or your Father who is in heaven is perfect"* (3 Nephi 12:48); *"Sanctify yourselves; yea, purify your hearts, and cleanse your hands and your feet before me, that I may make you clean"* (D&C 88:74).

We take courage as we consider the *"exceeding great and precious promises: that by these [we] might be partakers of the divine nature"* (2 Peter 1:4). Elder George Q. Cannon describes the forces at work in our behalf.

> God is doing a great work among us, much greater than many of us imagine. We do not see Him, but He is nevertheless in our midst.... God is working to get this people to the perfection that He desires them to attain.... God demands of us a holiness of life that we cannot conceive of at the present time.... There are also angels around us ... continually inviting us and pleading with us to do that which is right.[5]

The Heavens continually mingle themselves in our affairs. Many subtle supports are mediated to us through unseen angelic messengers.[6]

In this life we will never fully penetrate the mystery of life or the powers at work that support and enlarge and transform it, but the endless evolvings in Nature are a type and shadow

---

5. *Gospel Truth* (Salt Lake City: Deseret Book, 1957), 84.

6. See, e.g., Omni 1:25; Moroni 7:25, 29; and D&C 43:25 on angelic ministration. The prophet Joseph said, "And now, I ask, how righteousness and truth are to sweep the earth as with a flood? I will answer. Men and angels are to be co-workers in bringing to pass this great work" (HC 2:260).

of the unseen forces at work in Man as well. Deepak Chopra observes a cocoon outside his study window and reflects on the mysterious processes that turn the caterpillar into a butterfly: "What goes on invisibly inside the chrysalis remains deeply mysterious—the caterpillar's organs and tissues dissolve into an amorphous, soup-like state, only to reconstitute into the structure of a butterfly's body that bears no resemblance to a caterpillar at all."[7] As Nature unfolds flowers and ripens fruit, so holy forces carry on operations in us often beyond our conscious awareness, lovingly supporting our development toward fruition.

Let us put no limitations on the premortal promises of grace carrying us through our transformations. More goes forward in our behalf than we can know, but what we can know is that as we yield to spiritual things, our relationship with Divinity shifts and more transforming processes become available. With Faith in the possibility of all things, we can take on the identity of a person called and elected and can expand into the divine.

Life-Quest

This sense of a life-quest, the searching for significance in one's life, is deeply planted in the human spirit from the life before. Literature from diverse times and places describes people who embark on a journey to find some sort of pearl of great price and, in the process, find themselves changed and purified by their quest.

The mythology expert, Joseph Campbell, found in his extensive research that an integral part of all world cultures is the tale of the hero who sets out to accomplish an objective and is

---

7. Deepak Chopra, *The Book of Secrets: Unlocking the Hidden Dimensions of Your Life* (New York: Random House, 2004), 23; referring to Eric Carle's *The Very Hungry Caterpillar* (New York: Philomel, 1994).

profoundly changed by his adventures. He challenges everyone to see the presence of a heroic journey in his or her own life. In a television series on the Power of Myth, Campbell and Bill Moyers engage this theme:

> *Campbell:* "There is a typical hero sequence of actions which can be detected in stories from all over the world and from the many, many periods of history. It is essentially the one deed done by many, many different people. The hero or heroine is someone who has given his life to something bigger than himself or other than himself.... Losing yourself, giving yourself to another, that's a trial in itself, is it not? There is a big transformation of consciousness that's concerned. And what all the myths have to deal with is the transformation of consciousness—that you're thinking in *this* way, and you have now to think in *that* way."
>
> *Moyers:* "Well, how is the consciousness transformed?"
>
> *Campbell:* "By trials."
>
> *Moyers:* "The tests that the hero undergoes?"
>
> *Campbell:* "Tests or certain illuminating revelations. Trials and revelations are what it's all about."[8]

This primeval impulse reminds us that we are not here to live randomly. Called and elected in the premortal world, all the Lord's covenant people have a built-in impetus for accomplishing the purposes of their being. In the deepest part of our soul, we know who we are and what we are here to do. The world in its restless search for meaning and fulfillment thrashes about trying to find out what to do. But it is the restored gospel of Jesus Christ that helps us to identify the mysterious energies inside that simply will have their expression and fulfillment. We begin to think along new lines. Assuring one's calling and

---

8. *The Power of Myth*, Program 1: The Hero's Adventure, Joseph Campbell with Bill Moyers. Public Broadcasting System series, 1988.

election has to do with taking on a new identity and thinking and acting with inspired purpose. As Seekers, we will not be satisfied with anything in our lives until we know that we are walking the path that leads to our destiny.

We occasionally have well-meaning people come among us who, on seeing the spiritual dismay in some members, tell us not to be concerned about perfection in this life. They mean to help; they mean to dissuade us from an anxious perfectionism on the one hand or despairing discouragement on the other; they want us to reexamine our expectations. But we would not want their remarks to cause us to abandon the quest. No, of greater help is the counsel that clarifies the path, strengthens our faith, quickens our understanding of the holy purposes of this stage in the eternal journey, inspires us to embrace a spiritual practice, and to immerse ourselves more deeply in the grace of the Lord Jesus Christ. A sense of fulfillment will elude us until we know Jesus Christ in the perfecting process and accept that Infinite Intelligence that acts through us, loving us, caring for us, "rescuing all that is finest down deep inside of [us], and bringing to flower and fruitage the latent richness of the spirit."[9]

Remission of Sins and a Perfecting Brightness of Hope

But if we have not yet made the commitment to the path marked out to divinity, we will find ourselves in a sort of spiritual twilight; we will feel the hopelessness of accomplishing our spiritual ends; we will be filled with doubt and also guilt. This semi-light condition often develops from carelessness in our relationship with the Lord, and with each other; then the former

---

9. J. Reuben Clark, Jr., cited in *A Leader's Guide to Welfare: Providing in the Lord's Way* (Salt Lake City: The Church of Jesus Christ of Latter-day Saints, 1990), title page.

sins all seem to return (see D&C 82:7), wrecking our spiritual confidence. In this state our prayers become superficial because we are not responding to the Spirit's promptings to come clean. On honest reflection, we confess that we have been living in denial, taking care not to face too squarely the little lies that we are living. We find ourselves vacant of a vibrant hope.

Alma identifies two states for Man: *"joy or remorse of conscience"* (Alma 29:5). Perhaps mankind exists only in one or the other state, a degree of remorse underlying much of the emotional experience of most people, until they come to the Lord and obtain a remission of sins. Alma learned the difference between the two states from his own experience; he speaks of *"sore repentance"* (Mosiah 23:9) and *"wading through much tribulation, repenting nigh unto death"* (Mosiah 27:28). He learned: *"Now, there was a punishment affixed, and a just law given, which brought remorse of conscience unto man"* (Alma 42:18). Sin makes remorse inescapable: *"Every man must repent or suffer"* (D&C 19:4). And in some degree, it is always *now,* as well as later.

We may only vaguely sense that a remission of sins could clear everything up, strengthen the inner man, and renew our incentive; but the prospect can seem too daunting. It is so easy to become *"entangled again in the vanities of the world"* (D&C 20:5). Then sin causes us to smite ourselves, although we often try to offload this discomfort by smiting others—creating a yet greater distress. This smiting of ourselves and others can go on for many years in an unconscious reaction to buried and unrepented sins. These are the major cause of emotional damage in the soul.

Remorse of conscience manifests itself in varying forms in the soul, but they are all negative. Elder F. Enzio Busche speaks with penetrating insight about the effects of losing the battle between good and evil in the soul:

As our mind is opened through our study of the plan of salvation, each of us comes to see that ... the "real me," or "the spiritual child of God," created in innocence and beauty, is engaged in a fight for life or death with the elements of the earth, the "flesh," which, in its present unredeemed state, is enticed and influenced by the enemy of God....

This war is a war that has to be fought by all of Heavenly Father's children, whether they know about it or not. But without a keen knowledge of the plan of salvation, and without the influence of the divine Light of Christ to bring us awareness, this war is being fought subconsciously, and therefore its battlefronts are not even known to us, and we have no chance to win. Wars in the inner self that are fought subconsciously, with unknown battlefronts, lead to defeats which also hurt us subconsciously. These defeats are reflected in our conscious life as expressions of misery, such as a lack of self-confidence, lack of happiness and joy, lack of faith and testimony, or as overreactions of our subconscious self, which we see then as pride, arrogance, or in other forms of misbehavior—even as acts of cruelty and indecency.

No! There is no salvation without Christ, and Christ cannot be with us unless we pay the price of the constant fight for self-honesty.[10]

Perhaps we do not realize that our life is worth investigating with penetrating self-honesty. Yes, innumerable tiny decisions closed up the well, but it takes only a moment to open it again: *"Yea, I would that ye would come forth and harden not your hearts any longer; for behold, now is the time and the day of your salvation; and therefore, if ye will repent and harden not your hearts, immediately shall the great plan of redemption be brought about unto you"* (Alma 34:31). The key word in this passage is "immediately" as it describes the relief available.

---

10. "Truth Is the Issue," *Ensign*, November 1993, 24.

This relief comes as we identify what we have to do and covenant with the Lord to do it. If we have disobeyed, we will now obey and take whatever steps necessary or make whatever adjustments required. Immediately we feel what Amulek means, for in the very moment of recommitment, the Spirit returns, and with it comes a reawakened hope, even joy filling the heart, even so much that utterance ceases, so exceedingly great can that joy be (see Mosiah 4:20). So, when we want to come to Christ but feel too laden with the past, we come anyway and feel the Lord in His mercy turn His judgments away from us, because of the Son (see Alma 33:11). We can feel the Atonement at work. Then we're able to get on with the journey and again respond to the restored "lifting power," the pull, to be better than we had hoped we could be.

One benefit of learning to retain a remission of sins is that it allows greater levels of goodness to be understood. Fine shades of righteousness are not obvious to the person who has indulged over time in overt sins of flesh or ego, or more subtle ones like resisting others or seeking validation. Only gradually is he privileged to see what "clean" is and to escape the polluting effects of sin. Yes, there is hope for becoming innocent in mind and heart even after a lifetime of self-seeking. Thus we can *always rejoice, and be filled with the love of God, and always retain a remission of sins*" by which we *"grow in the knowledge of the glory"* of the Lord *"or in the knowledge of that which is just and true"* (Mosiah 4:12).

Sin precludes spiritual hope, but remission always restores it. Nephi links steadfastness in Christ, a perfect brightness of hope, and a love of God and men with eternal life (see 2 Nephi 31:20). We see that more than the vague sort of hope that we experience in everyday life—that someone or something will come—scriptural Hope is the light of eternal life kindled in the soul by the Spirit of the Lord. This light is the precursor to the actual witness that ultimately seals a person up. Everyone can have this *"hope of his glory"* (Jacob 4:4). Paul teaches that *"only he who hath the light and the hope of immortality dwelling in him"* can expect to see the Lord (JST 1 Timothy 6:16).

Resuming the Quest

President Spencer Kimball urges us to enter the perfecting process. He describes the lifting power that Man himself must exert:

> In each of us is the potentiality to become a god—pure, holy, influential, true and independent of all these earth forces. We learn from the scriptures that each of us has an eternal existence, that we were in the beginning with God. And understanding this gives to us a unique sense of man's dignity.
>
> I would emphasize that the teachings of Christ that we should become perfect were not mere rhetoric. He meant literally that it is the right of mankind to become like the Father and like the Son, having overcome human weaknesses and developed attributes of divinity.
>
> [Even though] many individuals do not fully use the capacity that is in them, [that] does nothing to negate the truth that they have the power to become Christlike. It is the man and woman who use the power who prove its existence; neglect cannot prove its absence....[11]
>
> Man can transform himself and he must. Man has in himself the seeds of godhood, which can germinate and grow and develop. As the acorn becomes the oak, the mortal man becomes a god. It is within his power to lift himself by his very bootstraps from the plane on which he finds himself to the plane on which

---

11. *Teachings of Spencer W. Kimball,* ed. Edward L. Kimball (Salt Lake City: Bookcraft, 1982), 26.

he should be. It may be a long, hard lift with many obstacles, but it is a real possibility....[12]

Man alone, of all creatures of earth, can change his thought pattern and become the architect of his destiny.[13]

Again we see that all our progress begins with discerning our thought patterns and learning to focus, as we contemplate a new identity: "pure, holy, influential, true and independent of all these earth forces"—a very compelling prospect. The roots of perfection flower in the mind. This transformation likely will not happen until we come to center our mind on that which develops Spirit. We can develop confidence in our mind as an instrument of transformation, taking hold of our consciousness and storing up power for change.

What finally dawns on us as we seek deeper into the Lord's things is that, while daily life has to go forward with its duties on many fronts, still, even in the midst of all life's demands, we can become imbued with the Light of Eternal Life, the sense that we are His and He is ours. This way of traveling with quickened Hope is beautiful and makes possible our dealing both fearlessly and gently with what life brings.

Nature of the Perfection We Seek

President Kimball speaks on another occasion to the subject of Man's perfectibility, helping us to understand just what sort of perfection is required:

> He is talking to every soul.... To every man, woman, youth and child. "Be ye perfect." ... Let it sink deep in our hearts [with] a realization of it. We don't need to become sober-faced to the

---

12. *Ibid.*, 28.

13. *Ibid.*, 27.

point that we are pious without natural and proper living. The Lord has arranged so that we can live a very normal life with joy and laughter and peace and happiness and associations of family, fatherhood, motherhood, childhood—family life. All these things are a part of this gaining perfection. The Lord has required it of us. Now we have to start by forsaking our sins—forsaking the temptations.[14]

It appears that the perfection the Lord is requiring of us is not about never making a mistake. Terry Warner observes, "The point of it all … is not to polish ourselves to a non-human perfection, but to stand self-forgetfully and conscience-free in the light and to recover our balance quickly if we start to fall."[15] Perfection is more about intent than it is about polish. The perfecting process is designed to liberate us from an anxious self-absorption. Our joys should deepen. But if our stress gets heavier and our death-wish stronger, we can remind ourselves that our mandate is centered in our loving relationship with our Heavenly Father and the welfare of His children.

Intent is the purifying issue. Elder Boyd K. Packer speaks of his personal decision to perfect his intention: "Is there any reason why every one of us without exception, every single solitary soul cannot be perfect in his desire to do that which is right? Then it can be said one day when you're standing to be judged … that your desire was right…. Beginning at a certain point in my life, any mistake I made I could truthfully say I didn't want to."[16]

With purified intent and steadfastness in Christ, it may be that we can reach that point at which we live largely

---

14. Fireside given by President Kimball, president of the Quorum of the Twelve, Santa Monica Stake, November 18, 1973.

15. C. Terry Warner, *Bonds that Make Us Free* (Salt Lake City: Deseret Book, 2001), 265.

16. *That All May Be Edified* (Salt Lake City: Bookcraft, 1982), 271.

without sin—not without mistakes, errors in judgment, etc.—but without the impure motives which create sin:

> [Jesus] descended in suffering below that which man can suffer; or, in other words, suffered greater sufferings, and was exposed to more powerful contradictions than any man can be. But notwithstanding all this, he kept the law of God, and remained without sin, *showing thereby that it is in the power of man to keep the law and remain also without sin* ... and have no excuse for [his] sins. (*Lecture #5*; my emphasis)

Brigham Young discusses the way in which, with right intent, a degree of salvation can become a present-moment experience:

> Our work is a work of the present. The salvation we are seeking is for the present, and, sought correctly, it can be obtained, and be continually enjoyed.... If we are saved, we are happy, we are filled with light, glory, intelligence, and we pursue a course to enjoy the blessings that the Lord has in store for us. If we continue to pursue that course, it produces just the thing we want, that is, to be saved at this present moment. And this will lay the foundation to be saved for ever and for ever, which will amount to an *eternal salvation*.... Some will inquire, "Do you suppose we shall finish this Temple, brother Brigham?" I have had such questions put to me already. My answer is, I do not know, and I do not care any more about it than I should if my body was dead and in the grave, and my spirit in Paradise. I never have cared but for one thing, and that is, simply to know that I am now *right* before my *Father in Heaven.* If I am this *moment,* this *day,* doing the things *God requires of my hands,* and precisely where my *Father in Heaven wanted me to be,* I care no more about tomorrow than though it never would come.[17]

---

17. *JD* 1:131–32; italics in the original.

Wisdom says that we can control only our intent. We cannot control the past or the future, and we cannot control the consequences of what we do. The results of our best efforts always lie in the Lord's hands. How much stress might recede if we gave up feeling that we had to control anything beyond our own preparations and intentions. Our happiness would be greater as we humbly accepted what finally plays out. The Savior said a comforting thing to Martha: *"Thou art careful and troubled about many things; but one thing is needful"* (Luke 10:41–42). Life is ever only about one thing, this present moment, the Presence within, and the present thing to do.

Were I to distill the various aspects of the perfection we seek to one central approach, it would be the ceaseless striving to harness my restless and unfocused mind, guiding my thoughts and feelings to embrace that which produces spiritual fruit. This achievement lies within our power, even though at a distance, as we work patiently and persistently in the Lord. My experience thus far teaches me that progress in this aspect of perfection benefits from a deepening awareness of the motions of the mind through close observation and also practice in meditation. It is not immediately apparent at the outset of training the mind just what is entailed. I hope to make these themes the subject of a future book.

Sacrifice: "The Favorites of Heaven"

Brigham's phrase, "doing the things God requires of my hands," points to the deeper issues of the perfecting process and how it is that we expand into the divine. Obviously, this process must answer the task which the Gods set for Man before the foundations of the earth: *"We will prove them herewith, to see if they will do all things whatsoever the Lord their God shall command them"* (Abraham 3:25). There is really only one basic question to answer in life: Will you do it? Will you do whatever is required? Once the answer is an unequivocal *yes*, the process is underway.

The details of the sacrifice required of each of us vary, but the question is the same for each. One person will be asked to sacrifice time, energy, comfort, even health, to a degree that another will not. Yet another will be required to lay down "his character and reputation, his honor and applause, his good name among men, his houses, his lands, his brothers and sisters, his wife and children, and even his own life also—Counting all things but filth and dross for the excellency of the knowledge of Christ Jesus (Philippians 3:8)" (*Lecture #6*). But whatever is asked, all who answer the Lord's question can come to know that they are "the favorites of heaven" through "their having embraced that order of things which God has established for the redemption of man," enabling "them to exercise that confidence in him necessary for them to overcome the world and obtain that crown of glory which is laid up for them that fear God" (*Lecture #6*). In each person's life is plenty and to spare of the Natural Man to lay on the altar. The imperatives in each of our lives are sufficient to produce the broken heart and contrite spirit.

The prophet Joseph describes the main elements of the offering:

> After a person has faith in Christ, repents of his sins, and is baptized for the remission of his sins and receives the Holy Ghost, (by the laying on of hands), which is the first Comforter, then let him continue to humble himself before God, ... and the Lord will soon say unto him, Son, thou shalt be exalted. When the Lord has thoroughly proved him, and finds that the man is determined to serve Him at all hazards, then the man will find his calling and his election made sure.[18]

---

18. *TPJS*, 150.

He then adds his voice to those holy prophets who have preceded him: "I would exhort you to go on and continue to call upon God, until you make your calling and election sure for yourselves by obtaining this more sure word of prophecy, and wait patiently for the promise until you obtain it."[19]

Circles of Commitment

As Joseph describes above, there are two main stages in the life of a member. These might be illustrated as one large circle with a smaller concentric circle. At the very center of the circles is the Lord Jesus Christ Himself. The outer circle pertains to the preparatory Church which helps the children of God to understand their potential, to move toward their high destiny, and to provide the means by which they enter the inner circle. In fact, the earth was created and the Church established to make possible their entrance into that holy, inner circle.

With baptism we enter into the first circle, the preparatory one. In this phase we undertake the probation of Church membership. The Hosts of Heaven watch quietly as we choose our way. What is the intent of the heart? According to plan, we move forward toward the inner circle, albeit unevenly, increasing our ability to obey and keep covenant with the Lord, demonstrating our intention to "serve Him at all hazards," entering more deeply into the promises of the Lord. Here we make continuing adjustments in our life as we order it before Him.

Within this outer, preparatory circle we find two groups. It is to the teaching and conversion of these two groups that the greater ministry of the Church is directed: (1) those who have just entered this outer circle by baptism and are beginning their probation and (2) those who have gotten stuck in selective

---

19. *TPJS*, 299; see D&C 131:5 and 2 Peter 1:19.

commandment keeping and casual intent. This latter group of members may not see, for example, the value of a full tithe and generous fast offering, of temple ordinances, of regular attendance at meetings, of supporting their leaders, of scriptures, of cultivating the voice of the Spirit. They have "partial and indistinct views of religion" and may flounder in mixed motives.[20] They may be easily offended, have trouble accepting counsel, be selective about what callings they will accept, and find many things wrong with other members and leaders. They may be impatient with contradictory behavior in the Church and consider going inactive, failing to understand the Church's preparatory ministry. These members do not realize that they cannot be exalted from this outer circle in their stalled condition. They have not finished their preparations. They've lost the vision of the kingdom of God in their midst and have failed to enter in (see John 3:3–5).

---

20. Cardinal John Henry Newman comments on the characteristics of those not fully converted: "Perhaps, however, others may say, 'We know something of the power of religion—we love it in a measure—we have many right thoughts—we come to church to pray; this is a proof that we are prepared for heaven: we are safe, and what has been said does not apply to us.' But be not you, my brethren, in the number of these. One principal test of our being true servants of God is our wishing to serve Him better; and be quite sure that a man who is contented with his own proficiency in Christian holiness, is at best in a dark state, or rather in great peril. If we are really imbued with the grace of holiness, we shall abhor sin as something base, irrational, and polluting. Many men, it is true, are contented with partial and indistinct views of religion, and mixed motives. Be you content with nothing short of perfection; exert yourselves day by day to grow in knowledge and grace; that, if so be, you may at length attain to the presence of Almighty God.... We are the instruments, but we are only the instruments, of our own salvation. Let no one say that I discourage him, and propose to him a task beyond his strength.... We form mean ideas of the difficulty, and in consequence never enter into the greatness of the gifts given us to meet it." (*Selected Sermons, Prayers, and Devotions*, "Holiness Necessary for Blessedness," ed. John F. Thornton and Susan B. Varenne [New York: Random House, 1999], 11.)

One way to resume progress toward the goal is to recover the power in "Yes, I will do it—all" and to become involved again with the honest intent to come to full obedience in the Spirit. Elder George Q. Cannon urges casual members to move out of the periphery:

> How many of you are seeking for these gifts that God has promised to bestow? How many of you, when you bow before your Heavenly Father in your family circle or in your secret places, contend for these gifts to be bestowed upon you? How many of you ask the Father in the name of Jesus to manifest Himself to you through these powers and these gifts? Or do you go along day by day like a door turning on its hinges, without having any feeling upon the subject, without exercising any faith whatever, content to be baptized and be members of the Church and to rest there, thinking that your salvation is secure because you have done this? I say unto you, in the name of the Lord, as one of His servants, that you have need to repent of this. You have need to repent of your hardness of heart, of your indifference and of your carelessness. There is not that diligence, there is not that faith, there is not that seeking for the power of God that there should be among a people who have received the precious promises that we have.... If any of us are imperfect, it is our duty to pray for the gift that will make us perfect. Have I imperfections? I am full of them. What is my duty? To pray to God to give me the gifts that will correct these imperfections.... They [spiritual gifts] are intended for this purpose.... That is the design of God concerning His children. He wants His Saints to be perfected in the truth.... Every defect in the human character can be corrected through the exercise of faith and pleading with the Lord for the gifts that He has said He will give unto those who believe and obey His commandments.[21]

---

21. *Gospel Truth*, 195–96.

We can lift our sights and stir our soul with a larger vision. We could secure in this life the assurance of eternal life. Elder Marion G. Romney frequently counseled the Saints on the topic of calling and election. The price, he says, must necessarily be very exacting, but is within the reach of us all.

> What is required is wholehearted devotion to the gospel and unreserved allegiance to the Church of Jesus Christ of Latter-day Saints.... A half-hearted performance is not enough. We cannot obtain these blessings and be like the rich young man who protested that he had kept the commandments from his youth up but who went away sorrowful when, in answer to the question, "What lack I yet?" Jesus said unto him, "If thou wilt be perfect, go and sell that thou, hast, and give to the poor . . . and come and follow me" (Matthew 19:21). Evidently he could live everything but the welfare program.
>
> There can be no such reservation. We must be willing to sacrifice everything. Through self-discipline and devotion we must demonstrate to the Lord that we are willing to serve him under all circumstances. When we have done this, we shall receive an assurance that we shall have eternal life in the world to come. Then we shall have peace in this world....
>
> Let us each day in solemn honesty confront ourselves with the rich man's question, "What lack I yet?" And thus, with utter frankness, discovering our own limitations, let us conquer them one by one until we obtain peace in this world through an assurance that we shall have eternal life in the world to come.[22]

The price may seem great, but the goal is obtained by putting one foot in front of the other, day after day, beginning and then beginning again, with a grateful heart for the marking of

---

22. *Conference Report of The Church of Jesus Christ of Latter-day Saints,* October 1949, 39–45.

the path. We learn the value of making small changes in the things we do everyday, adding, subtracting. The Lord focuses our mind: *"Seek the face of the Lord always, that in patience ye may possess your souls, and ye shall have eternal life"* (D&C 101:38); and, *"Continue in patience until ye are perfected. Let not your minds turn back"* (D&C 67:13). This patient focus on His face helps us maintain communion.

Section 76 describes the characteristics of those who obtain the inner circle as it traces the trajectory from baptism, through the probationary period, to the assurance of eternal life: first, having faith in Jesus Christ, they receive baptism and the Holy Ghost, are cleansed by keeping the commandments, *"overcome by faith"* (the probationary period), and *"are sealed by the Holy Spirit of promise, which the Father sheds forth upon all those who are just and true. They are they who are the church of the First-born"* (D&C 76:53–54). Here the Lord identifies entrance into the inner circle as the receiving of the seal of the Spirit and admission into the Church of the Firstborn.[23] These members simply do what they have covenanted to do, and when the Lord has proved them through an extended time, they are admitted into a new relationship with Him.

Well acquainted with repentance, but nevertheless un-daunted, they continue to develop commitment power. The intent of their heart becomes fixed, even in the midst of their own continuing imperfection. These are ordinary people who become less ordinary as they exercise themselves to take the Lord seriously. The Lord describes these Saints:

> *All among them who know their hearts are honest, and are broken, and their spirits contrite, and are willing to observe their covenants by sacrifice—yea, every sacrifice which I, the Lord, shall command—they are accepted of me.* (D&C 97:8)

---

23. Not to be confused with an apostate group that has taken that name.

They understand that by taking the Lord seriously, He will deepen His testing of them for their blessing. As these ordeals come upon them, they continue to serve the true and living God. They may even give thanks.

These members see more deeply into the temple as they practice obedience, sacrifice, and deepening consecration. They seek to partake of the power of godliness (see D&C 84:19–22) available in those ordinances. Their experience differs in height and depth and richness from the experience of the people stalled in the first circle, even though they may rub shoulders in the same chapel. Of course they are aware of the problems and contradictions in the Church; nevertheless, they keep their grip on the rod. They realize that it may be in the Church itself that they will encounter some of their most disconcerting trials. But they are in the Church to serve the Lord "at all hazards"; as a result, they either will receive, or have already received, the seal of the Holy Spirit of Promise. The prophet Joseph explained about the sealing up to eternal life: *"The more sure word of prophecy means a man's knowing that he is sealed up unto eternal life, by revelation and the spirit of prophecy, through the power of the Holy Priesthood"* (D&C 131:5).[24]

---

24. Elder McConkie testifies of additional possibilities deeper into the circle as he defines spiritual maturity: "After the true saints receive and enjoy the gift of the Holy Ghost; after they know how to attune themselves to the voice of the Spirit; after they mature spiritually so that they see visions, work miracles, and entertain angels; after they make their calling and election sure and prove themselves worthy of every trust—after all this and more—it becomes their right and privilege to see the Lord and commune with him face to face. Revelations, visions, angelic visitations, the rending of the heavens, and appearances among men of the Lord himself—all these things are for all of the faithful. They are not reserved for apostles and prophets only. God is no respecter of persons. They are not reserved for one age only, or for a select lineage or people. We are all our Father's children. All men are welcome... (2 Nephi 26:33) The fact is that the day of personal visitations from the Lord to faithful men on earth has

It was mid-morning in the Area Offices in Buenos Aires. Elder Jeffrey R. Holland and his wife were due to arrive, but had been delayed by an emergency in a distant place. With little sleep and little time to refresh themselves, they entered our seminar room. After Elder Holland greeted each of us personally, he stood in the semicircle formed by some thirteen mission presidents and their wives and said, "We are not yet the Church of Jesus Christ." His context was "the real way to do missionary work," but the larger meaning of his principles went down into our hearts. "I testify that we are preparing for something, and there is a big gap between what we are and what we must become. I don't know when the Savior will come, but the work is going very fast—faster than you think."

"Why isn't it easier?" he asked. "Because," he answered, "we don't believe in *cheap* salvation or *cheap* grace. We have to be pushed to the limit, back to the wall. *Then* the angels come and God speaks: 'Be patient, I'll give you success. The only way out is through.' We have to drink the bitter cup, even though we're wanting, wishing for, another way. The Savior is the model: 'I'll drink the bitter cup to its dregs.' The last words he said in the Old World were, 'I will finish.' The first words in the New World were, 'I did finish.' He suffered the will of the Father. This is required of all of us too. We bow our head and say, 'Yes.' *That's* when all the miracles happen. We must be stretched as we can be, and *then* God will step in with His power."

Then this: "If there are no miracles, it's because we don't want them. The majority don't have miracles because they don't live where miracles happen. When we become as obedient as Christ, we will have miracles." He paraphrased the little French

---

no more ceased than has the day of miracles. God is an unchangeable Being; otherwise he would not be God. The sole issue is finding people who have faith and who work righteousness" (*Promised Messiah: First Coming of Christ* [Salt Lake City: Deseret Book, 1995], 575–76).

poem about our having to risk coming to the edge in order
to experience the miraculous: "God says to us: 'Come to the
edge.' 'No, I'll fall.' 'Come to the edge.' 'No, I'll fall.' Come to
the edge.' So, I came to the edge, He pushed me, and I flew."[25]

Then he paused and said, "I love Jesus Christ and have a relationship I cannot really share. He is the most compelling theme
in my life—a very rewarding obsession. I have often borne witness; now I AM a witness. I am a witness of the Resurrection in
the same sense as Peter, James, John, Brigham, and Wilford."
His witness is the fruit of unconditional commitment.

Finally, the same sacrifice is asked of us that was required
of the Savior; it is only a matter of degree. President Joseph F.
Smith's vision of the redemption of the dead allowed him to see
an innumerable company of the just in the spirit world who
were awaiting the visit of the Lord. These had been *"faithful
in the testimony of Jesus while they lived in mortality"* and had
*"offered sacrifice in the similitude of the great sacrifice of the Son
of God, and had suffered tribulation in their Redeemer's name"*
(D&C 138:12–13). Each person gets to offer a sacrifice "in similitude," which is, simply, everything that is asked.

We would be doing ourselves a disservice if we did not acknowledge the challenge that the pursuit of perfection presents us. Referring to 1 Peter 4:18, Brigham Young describes the
strength of effort required:

> Recollect the saying of one of the Apostles, when speaking
> about getting into the kingdom of heaven, that "if the righteous
> scarcely be saved, where shall the ungodly and the sinner ap-
> pear?" The best man that ever lived on this earth only just made
> out to save himself through the grace of God.... It requires all
> the atonement of Christ, the mercy of the Father, the pity of

25. Based on my notes from the Mission Presidents Seminar, Buenos Aires,
October 1997.

angels and the grace of the Lord Jesus Christ to be with us always, then to do the very best we possibly can, to get rid of this sin within us, so that we may escape from this world into the celestial kingdom.[26]

This issue of measuring up deeply moved the prophet Joseph while prophetic visions rolled upon his soul in Liberty Jail. As he consulted his sensitive heart, he was led to exclaim:

When I contemplate the rapidity with which the great and glorious day of the coming of the Son of Man advances, when he shall come to receive his saints unto himself where they shall dwell in his presence and be crowned with glory & immortality; when I consider that soon the heavens are to be shaken, and the earth tremble and reel to and fro; and that the heavens are to be unfolded as a scroll when it is rolled up, that every mountain and island are to flee away—I cry out in my heart, What manner of person ought I to be in all holy conversation and godliness! [27]

And he said:

How vain and trifling have been our spirits, our conferences, our councils, our meetings, our private as well as public conversations—too low, too mean, too vulgar, too condescending for the dignified characters of the called and chosen of God,

---

26. *JD* 11:301.

27. *Personal Writings of Joseph Smith*, ed. Dean C. Jessee (Salt Lake City: Deseret Book, 1984), 304. The Prophet's reference is to Peter's exhortation: "*Seeing then that all these things shall be dissolved, what manner of persons ought ye to be in all holy conversation and godliness.... Nevertheless we, according to his promise, look for new heavens and a new earth, wherein dwelleth righteousness. Wherefore, beloved, seeing that ye look for such things, be diligent that ye may be found of him in peace, without spot, and blameless*" (2 Peter 3:11, 13–14).

according to the purposes of His will, from before the foundation of the world! We are called to hold the keys of the mysteries of those things that have been kept hid from the foundation of the world until now.... [Let us] exhort one another to a reformation with one and all, both old and young, teachers and taught, both high and low, rich and poor, bond and free, male and female; let honesty, and sobriety, and candor, and solemnity, and virtue, and pureness, and meekness, and simplicity crown our heads in every place; and in fine, become as little children, without malice, guile or hypocrisy.[28]

Let us then encourage and humbly help one another to obtain the witness of the acceptability of our reformation to the Lord.

And then, one day, we will from a distant vantage point look back upon the hazardous waters that we navigated and the rocky Wilderness that we trod, and upon that moment when we came to view each thing that crossed our path as an opportunity to demonstrate that, hard or easy, safe or dangerous, whatever the hazard, we would serve the Lord in the Spirit. There we will see the point at which we realized the load of the Natural Self had lightened. We will see that it eventually became almost transparent as Something higher took hold of us and began to carry us. We will reflect on that hour when we knew that a new day was dawning and that the Day Star was arising in our heart (see 2 Peter 1:19). And we will contemplate the moment when we heard the much-worshipped Voice say, *"Well done, thou good and faithful servant: thou hast been faithful over a few things, I will make thee ruler over many things: enter thou into the joy of thy lord"* (Matthew 25:21). Then, like our Jaredite brethren, will we bow down and humble ourselves before the Lord, with our loved ones and fellow-laborers, and

---

28. *TPJS*, 137–38.

shed tears of joy before Him, *"because of the multitude of his tender mercies"* shed upon us in the precious moments of our Wilderness journey.

Abbreviations of Titles Used

DS   Joseph Fielding Smith. *Doctrines of Salvation.* Comp. Bruce R. McConkie. 3 vols. Salt Lake City: Bookcraft, 1954–56.

HC   Joseph Smith. *History of the Church of Jesus Christ of Latter-day Saints.* Salt Lake City: Deseret News, 1904.

JD   *Journal of Discourses. 26 vols. Liverpool: F. D. Richards, 1854–1886.*

TPJS   *Teachings of the Prophet Joseph Smith,* ed. Joseph Fielding Smith. Salt Lake City: Deseret Book, 1976.

WJS   *Words of Joseph Smith,* ed. Andrew F. Ehat and Lyndon B. Cook. Provo, Utah: Religious Studies Center, 1980.

Afterword

A Spiritual Odyssey:
My Life as a Seeker

I understood her reply to mean that for certain kinds of knowledge you have to undertake a journey. It isn't like pouring water into a bucket— a process by which neither water nor bucket is much changed. And before setting out, I couldn't predict what that change would be.

John Tarrant[1]

✧

There are more things in heaven and earth than are dreamt of in your philosophy, Horatio.

Hamlet, Act 1

✧

We sat down to lunch the other day in an Italian restaurant in Santa Cruz de Tenerife. Our guest, born in Barcelona, told us the story of his conversion to the Church. He had been a serious student of parapsychology and read everything he could find

---

1. *Bring Me the Rhinoceros* (Chatsworth: Harmony Publishing, 2004), 15.

on it. One day the missionaries knocked on his door. When he saw through the peephole who they were, he tiptoed back to bed. But later, he went to his neighbor's house, and there were the missionaries! Our guest told the missionaries he was not interested in their religion, but that he was very interested in parapsychology. One of the missionaries piped up, "Why, I know all about parapsychology. Why don't we get together and talk?" Our friend allowed the missionaries to come. When they sat down the missionaries opened with prayer, began to teach, and gave him a Book of Mormon. Our friend began to read the Book of Mormon every day as he made the forty-five-minute train trip to and from work. Finally, waiting on one of the benches for the train, he finished the book. He clasped it to his bosom and began to cry. People passed by looking at him, but he just cried and cried, overcome by the sheer weight of witness. Later he reminded the missionary that they had never gotten around to discussing parapsychology. The missionary said, "Oh, I don't know anything about parapsychology." A prevaricating missionary had gotten him into the Church, but the parapsychology had been his first conscious contact with a world beyond this one.

Our friend's story reveals a pattern, perhaps especially apparent in the life of a convert. The pattern looks something like this: a child is born into spiritual death with foreordinations on his head. He is driven to find a link between the visible and invisible worlds. He searches in many, often strange, places, becoming entangled perhaps in things like stones, divining rods, magic, and money-digging. During a certain stage in the journey, these may be the signs of a true seeker. This is, in fact, Joseph the prophet;[2] this is Adam cast out of the Garden,

2. Richard L. Bushman writes about Joseph's money-digging: "By the fall of 1827, Joseph Smith stood on the line dividing visionary supernaturalism from rational Christianity—one of the many boundaries between the

wandering in the Wilderness, offered tainted gifts from the dark side. The Enemy knows us from the life before, but we do not yet know him. He offers us a link. Some of us may experiment with those tainted things because they seem to hold promise. The real test comes when the Light is finally presented; then the true Seeker is revealed.

Life provides the searching child with conflict and pain. The divinity driving the child from the inside and the turmoil of life roiling on the outside make the search for resolution and consolation paramount. It may be, indeed, that pain is among the greatest motivators for spiritual growth. It can be cherished for the revelations and resolutions it ultimately provokes.

My father, Elroy John Center, was born in Hibbing, a small, iron-ore mining town in northern Minnesota, the oldest of three children. When he was twelve years old he built a chemistry set in his basement and began to distill his own alcohol—which he drank. His mother would put a New Testament in his back pocket as he went out of the brownstone house to the school down the street, but the drinking continued. A tall, sensitive, slender, black-haired, brown-eyed boy, he knew more than many of his teachers. He did so well on the first of a series of high-school math tests that his teacher accused him of cheating. Later, having saved some money from his work in the mines, he went off to Ann Arbor, Michigan to school and later became a chemical engineer in qualitative chemistry at the Battelle Memorial Institute in Columbus, Ohio.

---

traditional and modern world in early-nineteenth-century America. He was difficult to place in relation to that line because he faced in both directions. Joseph looked backward toward folk beliefs in divine power communicated through stones, visions, dreams, and angels. At the same time, he turned away from the money-diggers' passion for treasure and reached for higher, spiritual ends. The gold plates and angels scandalized rational Christians, while the religious impulse confused the money-diggers" (*Rough Stone Rolling* [New York: Alfred A. Knopf, 2005], 57).

But one morning, before Ohio, he and some friends went down to meet the train to take a look at the new school teachers coming to work in Hibbing. A group of young women got off the train, and my father spotted a vivacious twenty-four year old with curly brown hair. Her name was Nelda Mae Spencer.

A naïve, sheltered girl, daughter of the town newspaper editor and pillar of the Methodist Church, Nelda was born in the back bedroom in the house on Grant Street and raised in the dry, western town of Fort Morgan, Colorado. Her mother, Carrie Alice, sickly and bored, was forty when Nelda was born. An intelligent woman, she was not allowed by her community-minded husband to work outside the tidy white-frame house with the porch that went nearly all around the house; but many friends and visitors would come to get her insights and counsel. Nelda was Carrie's youngest of five children and certain that she was not wanted in the family. True or not, hers was a life-long search for love.

But this morning she stepped off the train as a recent graduate of the Music Conservatory of Oberlin College. It had been obvious early on that she was exceptionally gifted musically. Her sister Alice, exactly ten years older than she, to the day, was an accomplished concert pianist. Nelda was often taken out of her school classes to play for something or other in the school. This brought her the attention she so much longed for, but led her to feel under par. In school, whenever she raised her hand to answer questions, she was laughed at; her answers always seemed to be wrong. Of course, she thought she was stupid. But she did love walking down the isle of the local theatre to take her place at the organ in front of the stage where the silent movies were shown. The organ had gadgets and whistles, and drums. Everyone would whisper as she came in, and she felt very important. She was given a cue sheet that would say something like: "play 1 ½ minutes of music like 'The Men Came over the Mountain'"—but she couldn't read very fast yet, so she made up the music as she went along. She had a good ear and could also play from memory. In 1934 Nelda followed Alice to Oberlin. Her grades ordinarily wouldn't have admitted her, but she was, after all, Alice's sister. As it turns out, Nelda finished her senior year at Oberlin playing one of the top three of all fifty recitals that year.

Standing on the train platform that morning in 1940, my father had an irresistible air of mystery and charisma about him. Their marriage was inevitable, even though the night before the marriage, my father's mother told Nelda she could back out if she wanted to. But, uncertain, she married him on a snowy February day in 1941, and they set off for Columbus.

I was born in June 1942, the firstborn of John and Nelda. They brought me home to their apartment on King Avenue in Columbus on a sweltering July day, while the world struggled in developing chaos. Roosevelt and Churchill had agreed six months earlier to establish a Combined Chiefs of Staff and to make defeating Germany their first priority. The day I came into the world, the U.S. Army Corps of Engineers initiated the Manhattan Project to develop an atomic bomb. My father would later work at Oak Ridge on that project. He never talked about it.

I was baptized in my grandmother's Presbyterian Church in Hibbing. A year and a half later back in Columbus my sister Barbara was born. Life was not easy for her. I was so dismayed by her arrival in the family that, as she grew a little older and could stand on the back of my trike, I put a scarf on her head and rode her downtown intending to leave her. Once I took her to the community swimming pool and came home alone. Because of interfering neighbors, none of these ploys worked. Allowed to grow up, she became a charming and responsible person. Later Nancy and John were born, but I was used to displacement by then.

Music was part of the home I grew up in. Mother had the university's classical music station playing as she worked—when she wasn't playing the piano. She gave untold numbers of piano lessons all throughout my growing up to supplement the family income. I came home from school from time to time to find the wintery house cold—not enough money to buy the fuel—until the next couple of piano lessons. It was a problem if the students didn't pay the day they had their lesson. Anyway, I somehow learned to read music even though she didn't actually sit down to teach me piano. I didn't have much interest in fingering or counting. Things came quickly and easily to me, and I was often uninterested in the particulars. As I play today I hear her calling from the kitchen, "Cathy, COUNT that!"

I often wandered through whatever large Protestant church she was currently playing Sunday services for. I'd go with her during the week as she practiced for the coming Sunday. The organ music made everything vibrate and lent a marvelous, mystical atmosphere to the empty church, the daylight filtering through the stained glass windows, casting pools of colored light into the dim rooms. I grew up on the organ bench next to my mother or in the choir as she played in this church or that. It was often my job to turn pages for her when the music was especially demanding. Once, during a performance of *Messiah* for which she was the sole accompanist, we got into the Hallelujah Chorus. At one point I turned more than one page. We panicked, but she never missed a note. Sitting on the organ bench, amidst the music, I also heard a lot of dreary sermons. I rejected organized religion.

In 1958 my precious Dad was finding life increasingly painful. Dreams and memories from his childhood recurred and robbed him of peace. He began drinking heavily. We hated the weekends—they were the worst. We hated the holidays—someone always brought him a case of whisky. He never hurt

us children, but life was full of turmoil and strife and confusion. My first grade teacher was concerned that I was "too serious. She doesn't know how to play." The proverbial elephant
sat in the living room, and we didn't know how strange our
lives were. About the time I was twelve I said to my Aunt Mary
Charlotte, Dad's sister, "I don't think I've been affected much
by Daddy's drinking." She turned and looked at me, "You will
see that you have been." She was right, of course. His drinking
persisted over many years, even after I'd left home and had a
family of my own. But I will leave the sorrows and distresses of
those years in silence, commenting only that they had a formative effect on my fearful relationship to life, an effect that I have
been blessed to spend much of my adult life resolving.[3]

There were of course things that saved us from a worse fate.
My mother cared for us in a consistent way. We could count
on meals, and clothes from second-hand shops, and trips down
to the drugstore on Sunday afternoons where we each got to
spend a dime on a comic book and come home with some
Necco wafers. Then we'd spend the rest of the day reading
and swapping. She often sacrificed for us, buying me once
a new formal for a big dance. She felt that somehow the money would always work out and, amazingly, it did. I remember
her in depressive moods. But on good days she also had a sense
of humor and a ready laugh. I remember one hot summer
afternoon while she was ironing in the living room, I brought
in *Cheaper by the Dozen,* lay down on the couch, and read
it out loud. We laughed and laughed 'til we cried. We also loved
to play piano duets together, which often ended soon after
beginning as one of us would start to play our part way too
fast or some such silly thing and then we'd break up laughing

---

3. For a little more detail, see my "Love and Fear," among other related
chapters, in the reprinted *Selected Writings* (Provo: Amalphi Publishing,
2007), 179.

too much to go on. And she loved words and insisted we use them correctly.

I would not have chosen another situation to grow up in. I feel only gratitude for those years and their fruitful experiences. It seems, doesn't it, as though there are always two of us traveling in the same skin—the one of us struggling with the current situation in daily life and the other, deeper down, in which a brightness of hope, even a joy, seems to cast its light up through the shadows of the soul. Sometimes the shadows won, but for the most part the indefatigable light prevailed.

But the idea of two traveling together suggests a passage from T.S. Eliot who, in a dialogue with himself, sees yet a third:

> Who is the third who walks always beside you?
> When I count, there are only you and I together
> But when I look ahead up the white road
> There is always another one walking beside you
> Gliding wrapt in a brown mantle, hooded
> I do not know whether a man or a woman
> —But who is that on the other side of you?[4]

I felt I understood my Dad's spirit. He wanted to be wise and good, but alcohol was defeating him. He began to see the signs of the times in twisted telephone poles. He left Battelle and was committed to a sanitarium. My mother bought her first New Testament and began to study with Jehovah's Witnesses; we were searching, searching.

We talked often of Jesus Christ. Who was He? Had He suffered when He was on the cross as some said? Or as others said, was He too much God to have suffered? Then what was the meaning of His life? I had no doubt of His reality. I talked

---

4. *The Waste Land* 5.359–65.

to Him; but how to bring Him closer? I checked out books from the library on the human mind, on parapsychology, and especially on the occult. I remember finding a multi-volume set of some ancient teachings of Jesus, but none of these supplied a link. As I looked for some conduit to the "other world," my researches led me into some strange paths.

When I was about fourteen, Battelle was engaged in a massive project of investigating UFOs, about which my father spoke little, except for the day when he took a picture of a domed disk up in the sky over the dam on the Scioto River. Another day my father brought home an FBI man who was also involved in these investigations. He stood by the fireplace in the living room in our little house on Maize Road, which was set way back from the road with chickens and turkeys and ducks around back, and began to unfold the research. All this was the first I had heard of flying saucers, and I was captivated. Dad had said earlier to my mother, "I don't know if we should tell Cathy about this—she won't be able to leave it alone." He was right; it became the air I breathed. Some time later I went with some friends to hear Donald Keyhoe of Project Bluebook speak in a large auditorium in downtown Columbus. He spoke of "cover-ups." We were thrilled and spent a good deal of time out on starry nights hoping to catch a glimpse. I never did, but continued to believe. This association with young people who were serious students and at the same time interested in UFOs led me into my first contact with the other world.

A friend of mine told me in confidence that he had met one of the men from a flying saucer and that he was in constant telepathic contact with him; the alien's instructions to my friend were that we should prepare to recruit people in order to go into the saucer to be transported to some better place—I wasn't clear what place that was. Certain activities were also suggested that I did not want to engage in. I never did see this man from outer space, but the conflict that much of this developed in me led me to yet another contact.

A school friend of mine, Doug, had a mother who had recently become a medium. Her specialty was automatic handwriting, which she engaged in when her spirit-friend, Mark, on the other side, was invoked. As he spoke to Doug's mother, she would write in a notebook that I brought to our sessions. These were words of encouragement and of love for my father and for me. They had a healing influence. He told me that the "man from outer space" was a disembodied spirit and was dangerous. He advised me not to see my former friend anymore. I was very relieved to hear all that. I believe today that that was likely a correct assessment of my friend's "space-man." My friend's mother wrote pages and pages for me in my notebook, and they carried me along during the tumultuous years of my father's drinking and the general unsteadiness of life. I was also introduced to other mediums who showed me how to use a Ouija board, but also how to protect myself by calling on the white light of Christ. I didn't care for them and did not return to visit them, but kept my board, even though it had never worked for me. Mark told me one day that there were several spirits near him who were interested in me, but he didn't know why.

I was sixteen the summer a great spiritualism conference was to be held a couple of hundred miles away. A young married woman in my neighborhood suggested we go together and check it out. My mother gave permission. That night I dreamed that I was in a terrible car wreck. I woke up and was about to get out of bed to tell my mother, but then I couldn't see any reason to do that, so fell asleep again. In the morning I did not remember the dream. We got into my friend's old green Studebaker and set off for Indiana. Late into the night, driving on back country roads, my companion got a little sleepy, and her right foot got a little heavy. As we approached a sharp curve, she was unable to navigate it; the car left the road, hitting the ditch nose first. Her head went through the windshield, and I flew out the door onto the dewy, herby grass, bouncing once on each hip. Soon there were car lights and voices and then police. Kind strangers drove us to the local hospital. Suddenly my dream came back. I felt a wave of nausea as I realized I had seen all this the night before. My friend had broken her arm; I was only quite bruised, but also traumatized.

When I was back home, I immediately demanded of Mark, "Why did you let this happen to me?" Doug's mother wrote, "You see that you were really not hurt. But had you made it to the spiritualism conference, you would not have been so lucky. Be grateful that you were protected from something worse." I was silenced, but disappointed, as I'd been hoping to find some answers at the conference.

When I finished my junior year in high school, my father, having left Battelle, was hired by an adhesives company up north in Hudson, Ohio. I was reluctant to leave Mark, but eager to start a fresh life. I took my Ouija board with me. One day in our new home in Hudson, I invited my sister Nancy to come sit by me and to use the Ouija board. I thought she might be able to contact Mark for me. As she sat next to me and put her hand on the board, she looked at me suddenly and said, "This is not good. I'm not doing this anymore. It's creepy." I was disappointed, but honored her impression. I put the board away.

That year I was in the homecoming queen court in Hudson High and got a scholarship to Oberlin College. Oberlin's history boasted a hotbed of abolitionists who had run an underground railway for fugitive slaves; the college took credit for starting the Civil War. It was also the place where Lorenzo Snow, of whom I had never heard in those days, spent his last year of college. Off I went to this intellectual mecca and signed

335

up for a New Testament course which, through the course of the semester, sapped the Bible of miracles. I also took a philosophy class in which the first assignment was to write a paper proving that I existed. The paper came back with an A, as I had written that we cannot prove that we exist. I proclaimed myself an agnostic. It was a low point in my spiritual researches.

I made friends with some students there who wanted to seek their fortune in California. Did I want to come? I finished that year of school, and off we went. I packed my Ouija board and settled in Menlo Park, where I first worked in an electronics firm—tedious work in a smoky setting. In a searching mode I went to get my teeth worked on, and the dentist said he knew of another dentist who was looking for a receptionist. That is how I met Dr. Ernie Webb, who interviewed me for the job. He didn't want to hire me because I didn't know anything about dentistry and would likely get married and leave just after he had trained me. But the Spirit whispered to this stake missionary that he could baptize me.

One afternoon, a few days later, a Mormon patient asked me what I knew about the Church. Nothing, except maybe Brigham Young and the Tabernacle Choir. He asked me if I'd like to know more. I warily said yes. Dr. Webb stepped in and thanked the patient and said that we would talk about it. Soon after, he invited me into his office at lunch time and told me the First Vision and showed me a Book of Mormon. I felt these swelling motions in my chest and was embarrassed to find myself crying in front of my employer. He seemed to be happy and showed me where to begin reading and how to pray. Each day as I would come to work, he would put the stereo earphones on his non-Mormon patients, and as I worked chairside with him, he would teach me. One evening he invited me to a "cottage meeting" where a young man was being interviewed for baptism. As I listened to the interview questions, I realized that I was answering them all in my heart with faith. Nobody had yet asked me if I wanted to be baptized. Dr. Webb was being wisely reticent. As we gathered in the little dining room for refreshments, during a lull in the small talk, I asked if I could be baptized. I was unprepared for the happy reaction from my friends. As I drove my little Volkswagen through the dark streets, I cried all the way home as I contemplated what I had found. I couldn't believe the indescribable happiness I felt. I hadn't ever felt it before.

But first, I had to find Mark. One Saturday morning about a week before my baptism date, I sat on my sofa in the living room, put the Ouija board on my lap, called on the white light of Christ and then called to Mark. What did Mark think about the Mormon church? He must know if it is true. I don't know why I was even trying this because there was no evidence that I had any psychic ability, except for the dream, and the board had never worked for me. I'd just carried the board from place to place as some sort of unrealized link with the other world. But as I sat there wondering if the planchette would move under my hand, a nauseating and chilling feeling came over me. In a moment some power surged through my right arm causing the planchette to fly off and hit the wall and the board to fall to the floor. And I heard the words, "This is dangerous. Have nothing more to do with it. Go forward and be baptized." I was stunned and also thrilled. I picked up the board, went outside behind the apartment, dumped it in the incinerator, and set it on fire. I was never to touch one again or have anything to do with spiritualism. I now had a testimony of both the dark and the light sides. And who was Mark?[5] I do not know, but whoever he was, he had blessed my life.

---

5. Brigham Young said at a funeral: "There are millions and millions of spirits in these valleys, both good and evil. We are surrounded with more evil spirits than good ones, because more wicked than good men have died here.... The spirits of the just and unjust are here" (JD 4:133).

As I've reflected on that event, I have realized that it was an exceptional gift of grace that with the warning to abandon spiritualism would come also a confirmation of the Church. In my ignorance, I was strangely protected from the dangers the board represented, but had I continued with it, I'm sure I'd have fallen into dangerous waters. Like Alma, I felt snatched, and look back with shivers at what I was blessed to avoid.

A few days later on March 10, 1962, about three weeks after I began to learn about the Church, I was baptized in Menlo Park, California, by Dr. Webb. His wife Joyce sang, "Open the Gates of the Temple." In recent days I had begun to cry—a thing that I had not allowed myself for many years. And though I had prayed that I wouldn't cry at my baptism, it was an unanswered prayer. It seemed as though with the washing of my body in the water, my soul opened up to cry out all the confusion and sorrow and pain and sins and darkness of the previous years. I was being purged inside and out. What exquisite joy! I had found what I'd been searching for all my life.

Like Lehi, my next thought was of my family. How to proceed? By then Dr. Webb had sent me to the local LDS institute director, Leon Roundy Hartshorn, a man sent from God to open the Heavens for me. I took every class he offered in his humble home with his beautiful family. I read and read, I listened, I drank it all in. I couldn't get enough. He, so connected himself, helped me make a connection with Heaven.

I had tried to teach my family the gospel just after I was baptized, but they had not been receptive. They had trouble listening to me because I was always so "intense" when I was taken by any new idea. Discouraged I went back to California. Then my sister Nancy came to visit with me in California for several weeks one summer. I talked and talked, but the light just wouldn't go on. She assented to it, but the fire was not kindled. Then, in one of Brother Hartshorn's classes we learned about the power of faith. That night I went home, knelt down, and prayed. Nancy was leaving soon, I said, and could carry the gospel back into the family. I asked Him with urgency to give her a dream or SOMETHING. The next morning when we got up, she said to me, "I had the strongest dream last night. I dreamed that the Lord Jesus Christ was coming to the earth and that He needed my help to get people ready." The fire had been kindled. Nevertheless, more was needed.

I was eager to go back to school and was accepted at San Jose State. But a few weeks into the semester, too late to get my money back, I came to know that I had to go home to Ohio to teach my family. That November I took a Greyhound from Menlo Park to Cleveland. But before I went, I visited with Brother Hartshorn and told him I needed a blessing for sharing the gospel with my family. He put his hands on my head and told me that three of the family would believe, but that two would not be ready yet. He told me that the Spirit would go before me to prepare the way and that I would find that they were more receptive, that their time had come. I was not conscious of the long ride home; I felt I was flying in my spirit. My sister Nancy, my brother John, and my mother were baptized the following February. My father, who had been in Alcoholics Anonymous for a time, was baptized later. Barbie has not yet been baptized.

Three months after my baptism I went for my patriarchal blessing. I will share a relevant part of it. I was told that my ancestors knew I had been baptized and were waiting for me to do the work in the temple for them. I wondered if those ancestors were the spirit people around Mark who had expressed interest in me. Who can say? I went to work in their behalf, sensing somehow that I was fulfilling a promise I had made long before this life. I found it engrossing, even thrilling, work.

About two years later I decided to leave California and go to BYU. First I had to get a blessing from Brother Hartshorn. I told him I needed a job that would pay enough and also would be something compelling. He laid his hands on my head and told me I would be interviewed for several jobs and that I should not take the first job but should continue to be interviewed until I found the one that I knew was right. He said he had some friends in Provo who would help me find a place to live with other students. I had an address. I put all my stuff in my little red Volkswagen bug with a sunroof and set off for Zion. When I arrived that warm summer afternoon, I realized that I knew nothing about the town and didn't know where to go. I drove around for awhile, praying. Soon I came to a residential area where a woman was standing on the grass with a hose in her hand. I pulled up to the curb and reached for the address. She said, "You must be Cathy. You've come to the right place." Then she looked at my address and said, "Good thing you didn't go to this address; one of the girls is having some problems, and the whole house is in turmoil. No, I have a better place." We drove a couple of streets away to a little house with three pleasant girls. In that experience, I felt the love of the Lord very directly.

I soon began lining up job interviews. I thought it might be good to be a receptionist since I'd had a little dental office experience in California. I went to my first interview. I was not interested. I went to another, and it didn't seem quite right. Then I went to the medical complex in north Provo, the office of Howard Francis, obstetrician and gynecologist. I walked into the office and was struck by the Magleby painting of a vibrant fall scene hung above cobalt-blue upholstery in the waiting room. This was where I wanted to be. The receptionist/ nurse took me back to his office. He asked for my experience. I had none in his specialty, but I had been an avid reader and was interested in medical things. Just then his nurse opened the door and informed him of a procedure to be done on one of his patients. When she closed the door I said, "Dr. Francis, I can tell you what she was talking about." I explained what I knew and told him I would be a good learner. He was very kind and agreed to give it a try. I was ecstatic. He would, many years later, deliver me of our sixth baby, Anne.

I learned a lot, but it wasn't long before I really wanted to go back to school. How to do that I didn't know. I was always rather poor and also felt I owed more time to Dr. Francis. Not long after, a notice came to the doctors in the area saying that they needed to let their uncertified personnel go since liability was a problem. He was sorry, Dr. Francis said, but he had to let me go. I went into an examining room at lunch time and knelt down and thanked the Lord but told Him I needed some money. I called my Mom. She called her brother, my uncle Bob, at the newspaper in Fort Morgan. She called back and told me that Bob could let me have a few hundred dollars. He never let me pay it back. I entered BYU and moved into an apartment on University Avenue.

My mother tried to send me money from time to time, but she couldn't do that very often. Good thing I loved peanut butter and grape jelly sandwiches. But I was able to earn a little here and there, and some kind friends would unexpectedly invite me to dinner and, on one occasion, even make a loan to me.

About that time Brother Hartshorn, still in California, accepted the first chairmanship in the Religion Department at Church College of Hawaii (now BYU–H). He invited me to come to Hawaii to be with his family and to work at the college while I pursued my studies. I found the idea electrifying. I finished that year and went home to work through the summer. About July I received a letter from Brother Hartshorn announcing that he and his family were coming to BYU (Provo) and why didn't I just plan to stay in BYU, and he could help me make some financial arrangements. I started to fast and pray. It became clear in there that for some inexplicable reason I was to go to Hawaii even without the Hartshorns. I finished the summer of work and went to Provo in preparation to meet a girl friend who was going on with me to Hawaii. It was wonderful to be back on campus again, and there seemed every reason to stay there. Finally on the morning of the day that my friend was coming, I knelt down again and asked the Lord if I should really go to Hawaii. A certain witness washed over me like warm water, and I heard something like, "I told you before and I tell you again, go to Hawaii."

I settled in at CCH. I was twenty-three years old. Why was I in Hawaii? My bishop called me to be Relief Society President. Maybe that was the reason. But I wanted to get married. I looked over the student body—too young and mostly of different ethnic origins. I heard about this young single English professor on campus. I promptly signed up for his Modern British Literature class. I was also working in the bookstore, so I came up with some pretext or other to meet him and went to his office. He says that when I came in the door, he was "immediately smitten." I found him attractive and very intelligent. He had, however, taken a vow not to date students on campus—too small a community. But about eight weeks later, while I was working in his writing lab, where we had become a little acquainted, the other bishop on campus came to him and told him he should take me out. He said, "I have this vow." His friend said, "I'm not talking as your friend; I'm talking as a bishop." Gordon thought, "Well, you're not my bishop." A few days later my bishop came to him and said, "You should take this Cathy Center out." He said, "I have this vow." "I'm not talking to you as a friend; I'm speaking as a bishop." Gordon thought, "Yes, but you're not my bishop." I'm not sure just what it means that it took two bishops to get him to ask me out, but finally he did by asking me if I'd like to see a little of the island. I allowed as how I probably had time. We got in his red Dodge Dart convertible, with the top down, and we headed for Hanauma Bay, where we sat on the beach. It was quite awkward. What was I supposed to call him?—"Professor," "Brother,"—certainly not "Gordon." The date didn't last long; he had to get me back early because I was being crowned Miss Na Hoa Pono that night at a dance, and he wasn't my date.

Our next date came the following weekend when he offered to show me the other side of the island. I was glad because I didn't think I was ever going to see him again, except in class. This time things were different. We drove around looking at the beautiful island, and then he took me to the Crouching Lion restaurant, which sat at the top of a green hill sloping down to the ocean. This old stone building had a veranda with a candle on the table. As the dusk deepened, someone came out and lighted the candle and we talked and talked. Indescribably romantic.

The following week, November 19, we went into Honolulu to the University of Hawaii's production of Oliver Goldsmith's *She Stoops to Conquer.* Driving out of Laie in a steady rain, he asked me if I would marry him. Of course this was only the third date in two weeks, but—when you know, you know. I of course said yes. He took me directly into the Ala Moana Shopping Center and bought a ring, saying he wanted to make sure I didn't change my mind. Then we went to dinner in the revolving restaurant up on top of the Ala Moana building. Neither of us could eat the filet mignon we'd splurged on. At the theatre we sat in a trance, and neither of us could remember a thing about the production.

I turned in my roundtrip ticket to the mainland, finished the semester with a hard-earned A, and married my English literature professor in the Hawaii temple in January, nine weeks after we were engaged. Now I was pretty sure I knew why I'd come to Hawaii. Next to being baptized, it was the best thing I ever did. He has been a steadying, healing influence in my life. Three children came to us, one daughter, Laura Marie, born in New Orleans, where my husband received his Ph.D. from Tulane. We went back to Laie and another daughter, Jennifer Lynne, was born in Honolulu. I was three-months pregnant with our Christopher Lee when I finished my BA in English at CCH and spoke as valedictorian at commencement. Elder Gordon B. Hinckley also spoke that night.

By way of a rapid denouement, we went to Colombia for four months and Buenos Aires for six months, where my husband taught on two Fulbright lectureships. I began to pick up a little Spanish. And there, in the Little Company of Mary Hospital, our Amy Elizabeth was born by the Lamaze method of natural childbirth and the assistance of a fine Anglo-Argentine doctor, the "Father of Lamaze" in Argentina. He challenged me to get off the delivery table and walk out of the delivery room—which I did. We took our little Argentine home to Laie thirteen days later on Christmas Day.

From Laie we went to Flagstaff for a couple of years, in the midst of which we passed a summer in Odessa, Texas, in the Permian Basin, where our Jefferson Kent was born. While we were there, an invitation to join the English faculty at BYU brought my husband and our family to Provo. The house we built on Stadium Avenue sat right down under the street that led to the Marriott Center. Our sixth child, Anne Catherine, was born to us there. When she was old enough to enter a playschool in the neighborhood my mind began to turn again to school. One day, while everyone was in school, I sat at the piano in our living room on Stadium Avenue and as I played in an unfocused way, the thought came to me, call Ellis

Rasmussen and see if he'll hire you to teach part time in the Religion Department. Soon I was teaching a class, and then a couple of classes. I loved it. I knew what I wanted to do. Through generous support from mentors in the Religion Department and an act of faith on the history faculty's part, I was admitted to a Ph.D. program in the History Department—having no Master's and having had no history. The dissertation, entitled "The Influence of Asceticism on the Rise of Christian Text, Doctrine, and Practice in the First Two Centuries," was a miracle of grace and even won an award for best dissertation that year. I finished the degree in 1989 and was hired for the following September in the Religion Department, the first woman hired in Ancient Scripture. During one period, my office was just down the hall from Leon Roundy Hartshorn. Not in my wildest dreams.

Through all this, I have had first-hand experience with grace—more grace than I likely yet recognize. During the seven or so years that it took to get the doctorate, I taught part time, stayed active in the Church, served as a visiting teacher, fed the family, cleaned the house (a little), and got good support from everyone—and did all of it very imperfectly with a few family lapses of one kind or another. Our children can tell stories of deprivation. But the grace is especially apparent in these six children, who have turned out so well in spite of everything. I'd have been a more relaxed mother had I known how wonderful each of them was destined to become. Indeed, "I cannot say the smallest part which I feel" (Alma 26:16).

Those years at BYU also included our serving as faculty on three London Study Abroad programs and two in Jerusalem. About 4 a.m. on January 18, 1991, in the first of our studies-abroad in Jerusalem, I heard gunfire in the Palestinian village below the BYU Center. I went out in the dark on the balcony and looked at the scene below where men were shooting off guns and burning bonfires. I wondered out loud, "What's go-ing on?" A voice from a security guard on the balcony in the dark above me said, "Don't you know? The U.S. has declared war on Iraq." Because of the imminence of the war, no students had come that semester, but we had made the decision while we were in London finishing a study-abroad, to go to Jerusalem anyway. This was a rich experience with wartime feelings, with taped safe-rooms, gas masks in cardboard boxes swinging from black straps on everyone's shoulder, and joltings-awake in the middle of the night as we were summoned many times to the bomb shelter in the Center. The sirens would go off in the vil-lage below, and then in the Center, and then there would be a pounding on the door of our apartment. We'd jump up and pick up our prepared baskets by the front door and trail other sleepy faculty and family up the stairs to the shelter.

We had our young Jeff and Anne with us and after awhile, as other families made the decision to return to the States, I wondered if we were being irresponsible in our decision to stay. Our director, George Horton, boldly declared that he wasn't going to abandon the building until he saw Arab tanks come over the Judean hills. He knew, and we knew, that the First Presidency were praying for us—for more than one reason. I would lie dressed, on my bed at night, my little radio on my chest, listening to the outside world's reports on what was hap-pening in Israel. We had no idea who was winning. Down be-low the Center we could see the lights burning all night in the old King David Hotel. Most of the Jews had left, but the world's reporters had taken up residence there. We prayed about what we should do. Independently, Gordon and I learned that we were safe and that life would go on after our time in Jerusalem and that we should relax and enjoy the experience. And we did. It was in Jerusalem that I learned that our life is in the Lord's hands. "Either a bullet has your name on it or it doesn't." This experience reconfigured my understanding of the Lord's complete control over birth and death on this planet.

These were marvelous experiences, but I found in these and other opportunities, such as my time as a faculty member at BYU, that life was pretty tense. I always felt so inadequate—I didn't know enough, I wasn't good enough, I didn't belong in those hallowed halls. Those and similar feelings made my hands sweaty and kept my stomach in turmoil and made every opportunity harder than it needed to be.

Nevertheless, I loved those years of association with the religion faculty and students. "Fair seed-time had my soul."[6] It was a time of germination. I had always been aware that thoughts came to me that illuminated life and gospel. Now I had an outlet for them. My writing began as I felt the need to explain some gospel principle or other to my students in the form of hand-outs. I was always coming at a particular understanding in a way that needed context. They seemed to like them. Then requests came in the normal course of faculty life to write for this or that. I would sit at my computer and put down thoughts for symposiums, for articles, for a chapter in somebody's book, and for talks. Even though I believed in what I was writing, I was always surprised when it was accepted and that people wanted to read it.

One day, after a fireside, my long-time friend, Jackie, came up on the stand and said, "Why don't you put some of those things into a book?" So I did, and the result was *Spiritual Lightening*. Some years later, Deseret Book invited me to collect my scattered pieces into *Selected Writings*. On Pearl Harbor Day in December 1995 I gave the BYU devotional, entitled "The Doer of Our Deeds." Its premise that the self-esteem issue be

---

6. Wordsworth, *The Prelude* 1.301. The two lines read: "Fair seed-time had my soul, and I grew up / Fostered alike by beauty and by fear."

replaced with faith in the Lord Jesus Christ brought relief in some quarters, but raised hackles in others.

In 1996, my husband was called to preside over the Argentina Mendoza Mission. I'd been very busy at BYU—too busy. The mission was the answer but it took some adjusting to as my busyness suddenly plummeted; nevertheless, there was a completely new set of challenges. I remember the plane trip from Buenos Aires across the country to Mendoza. The closer we got, the harder my heart beat. I had no idea what a mission president's wife did and I knew I didn't know enough Spanish. Our very capable *asistentes* met us at the airport and shepherded us through the many challenging events of the first days and weeks of the mission. It was there that I learned that in challenging circumstances which the Lord requires you to confront, the secret is just to show up. Just show up to do the thing that needs to be done, and the Lord meets you there to expand what little you have to give. We loved that mission as we got acclimated. We love missionaries, and our hearts always leap up now as we see a black nametag on a white shirt or blouse. We learned how missionary work goes forward by faith and miracles. We saw many miracles of conversion, angelic ministration, and the power of Divine Love as some of the most spiritually battered of Heavenly Father's children came up out of the waters of baptism. Just witnessing all that changed me, and I learned that there is no person the Lord doesn't both love and have a plan to save.

We returned on a spiritual high to Provo in 1999 and six months later found ourselves across the Andes in Santiago serving as Chile Area Welfare Agent. I had thought I wouldn't be interested in welfare work, but this mission turned out to be an unexpected revelation of the Lord's temporal and spiritual dealings with His children. A couple of years after that we served in the Mexico North Area as Area Welfare Agent again but were transferred into the South Area to serve as executive secretary to the Area President. At this writing, we are serving our fourth mission together, this time as proselyting missionaries in the Canary Islands. Our mandate is to help these wonderful Saints turn their district into a stake.

And in the course of the years of our missionary work, we acquired sixteen outstanding grandchildren. Our testimony is that the Lord has blessed our family for our missionary service, as imperfect as that service has been.

The foregoing is, of course, an expurgated version of my life. I have omitted most of the foolishness and vanity and self-ishness and sins—but there were plenty of those. My fervent hope is that through my repentance, the Lord will judge the sanitized version.

But the memory of sins can be bothersome. The prophet Joseph wrote of a time when he was detained away from his home and family and had time on his hands; he wrote to Emma,

> My situation is a very unpleasant one although I will endeavor to be contented, the Lord assisting me. I have visited a grove which is just back of the town almost every day where I can be secluded from the eyes of any mortal and there give vent to all the feelings of my heart in meditation and prayer. I have called to mind all the past moments of my life and am left to mourn and shed tears of sorrow for my folly in suffering the adversary of my soul to have so much power over me as he has had in times past but God is merciful and has forgiven my sins.[7]

In recalling my own past moments, I too have shed tears. But I have contemplated how we can change our history so that

---

7. *Personal Writings of Joseph Smith*, ed. Dean Jessee (Salt Lake City: Deseret Book, 1984), 238; spelling and punctuation regularized for readability.

we don't have to weep over it. My friend, Cindy, whose life has been full of daunting challenges from her birth, recently wrote me, "Those things that I remember, and the way I remember them are entirely a reflection of the spin I put on the past. If I choose to focus on the blessings and love, my memory of my past, at least in my mind, HAS CHANGED. If I also remember that the Lord arranges everything for our personal growth, then the only emotion that past events can evoke is gratitude—which means I've had the most marvelous life of anyone ever put on earth. Actually, I HAVE had the most marvelous life history possible for me, as have you, and all of God's children who've had the blessing of repentance. So, by seeing and understanding 'things as they really are,' I not only change my present life, I also change, that is, truly *recognize*, my past."

Like my friend, I've recast certain parts of my past, forgiving my life with gratitude for all that I have learned, knowing that God had put in place many compensations for the lapses He knew I'd suffer; I have come to accept what cannot be changed as somehow right. I have also come to recognize that in the Lord's ecosystem, everything, noble and ignoble, serves a purpose. And even though I have especially deeply regretted those times that I did not act with kindness, I am grateful for every little kindness I have been able to express. I now know that with the Atonement, things really are all right and that everything in the past can take its proper place. President Spencer W. Kimball wrote:

> I am positive in my mind that the Lord has planned our destiny. Sometime we'll understand fully, and when we see back from the vantage point of the future, we shall be satisfied with many of the happenings of this life that are so difficult for us to comprehend.[8]

---

8. "Death: Tragedy or Destiny?" in *Faith Precedes the Miracle* (Salt Lake City: Deseret Book, 1972), 105.

My testimony and my experience are that there is a plan for each person and that that plan is always operating, relentlessly unfolding toward his or her exaltation, even with all its bumps and scrapes and wipeouts on the journey. And thus we plumb the depths of the bittersweet in the light and shadows of our adventure in the Wilderness.

Topical Index

Note: (fn) = footnote

resistance, and acceptance, 30
responding to others, 160, 161
restoration, the blessings of, 221
retraining the mind, 257
revelation, and the light of Christ,
    xi; and the natural man, 88;
    and faith, 256, 259, 260
Richards, Franklin D., on women
    and priesthood authority, 287
righteousness, and faith, 246
Roberts, B.H., on one divine
    nature, 236, 237
roles played by others for us, 164
Romney, Marion G., on calling
    and election, 315
Ruiz, Don Miguel, on love as a
    way of being, 110
sacramental covenant, 233
sacrifice, 25, 26; and perfection,
    309, 310
salvation, and spiritual activity, 45
Salzberg, Sharon, on the true
    nature of thoughts, 79, 80; on
    opposition in all things, 195
Scott, Richard G., teachings: trials,
    4; the endurance of burdens,
    31; the power of Christ to
    heal, 193, 194; obedience, 246
scriptures, as important for spiri-
    tual energy, 105
Second Coming, and the safety of
    Zion, 142
self–absorption, and true love, 96
self–improvement to a loving be-
    ing, 109
self–reliance, and debt, 141–142
Serenity Prayer, 28
Shakespeare, William, teachings:
    wakefulness and dreaming,
    113; more things in heaven

and earth, 325
shame and violence, 189
slothfulness, and faith, 255
Smith, George A., on discerning of
    spirits, 177
Smith, Joseph, description of
    Zion, 145, 146; teachings:
    revelation, vi; personal revela-
    tion, vii; the comprehension
    of character, 35; the Holy
    Ghost on man's mind, 60;
    learning to become gods, 60;
    exaltation, 61; God will en-
    dow with intelligence, 70; the
    building up of Zion, 129, 134,
    135, 143, 144; the priesthood in
    Zion, 137; getting knowledge,
    179; the enticements of Satan,
    184, 185; false spirits, 186;
    evil spirits, 189; fundamental
    principles, 226; the mysteries,
    271; priesthood and the key of
    knowledge, 288; the revealing
    of sacred things, 292; dis-
    covering truth for ourselves,
    293, 294; perfection, 297;
    ministering angels, 299(fn);
    repentance, 311; measuring up,
    320, 321; the memory of his
    sins, 349
Smith, Joseph F., teachings: loving
    our enemies, 167, 168; fore-
    knowledge, 298(fn); sacrifice,
    319
Smith, Joseph Fielding, on women
    and priesthood authority, 287
Snow, Eliza R., on Lorenzo's
    rebirth, 218–220
Snow, Erastus, on evil influences,
    181, 182

Snow, Lorenzo, and his rebirth by
  fire, 218–220
sorrow and joy, 22, 23
Spencer, Nelda Mae, 328
Spirit of God, as creative light,
  37–40
spirit, as living water, 41(fn)
spiritual carelessness, 185(fn)
spiritual experience, ix
spiritual frontier of the mind, 60
spiritual ignorance, 187, 188
spiritual odyssey, 325
spiritual perception, 49–64
spiritual physics, 62–64
spiritual possibilities, 45
spiritual practice, as transformative, 101
spiritual realities, x
spiritualism, 335–337
string theory in physics, 38, 45
submission to the Lord, 24, 25
suffering, and negative thought,
  80–82
swallowed up in Jesus Christ, 197
Talmage, James E., teachings: godhood, 255; women and priesthood power in temples, 286
Tarrant, John, on knowledge in
  the journey, 325
Taylor, John, teachings: the plan
  of salvation, 13; the will of
  God, 26, 27; spark of Deity in
  man, 35; spirits and body, 53;
  divine attributes, 56; resolving
  conflict, 165, 166
temple endowments, and greater
  access to God, 289, 290
temple worship, 290
Thomas, Gordon K., on
  Wordsworth and happiness,

117; marriage to Catherine,
  343
Thomas, M. Catherine: her spiritual odyssey, 325
Thompson, Francis, on his flight
  from God, 239, 240
thought and its nature, 76
thoughts, and emotions, 76, 77
Tibetan Buddhism, on negative
  thought, 81; on softening our
  hearts, 98
Tolle, Eckhart, his personal transformation, 207, 208
teachings: dealing with hurt, 83, 84;
  negative energy, 180–184, 189
transformation in Christ, as a radical change of heart, 215
trials, and experiences, 5–6; and
  their purpose, 28, 29
truth, and its discernment, 45–64;
  and man's sustenance, 63, 64;
  and the light of Christ, xi, xii
unbelief, as resistance to truth, 245
veil, and natural man, 66–88
violence and shame, 189
Warner, C. Terry, teachings: being
  responsive to others, 160, 161;
  personal violence, 190; perfection, 308
weaknesses of man, 71
Widtsoe, John A., on the manifestation of the spirit, 51; on
  man's physical body, 53
wilderness mind, 65
wind, and the activity of spirit or
  breath, 3
women, and the powers of the
  priesthood, 285–288
Wordsworth, William, and his
  request for temple work

SCRIPTURE INDEX

Readers can contact the author
with their comments at
mcatherinethomas@yahoo.com